T0342046

Create Your Own Hedge Fund

Founded in 1807, John Wiley & Sons is the oldest independent publishing company in the United States. With offices in North America, Europe, Australia, and Asia, Wiley is globally committed to developing and marketing print and electronic products and services for our customers' professional and personal knowledge and understanding.

The Wiley Trading series features books by traders who have survived the market's ever-changing temperament and have prospered—some by reinventing systems, others by getting back to basics. Whether a novice trader, professional, or somewhere in between, these books will provide the advice and strategies needed to prosper today and well into the future.

For a list of available titles, visit our web site at www.WileyFinance.com.

Create Your Own Hedge Fund

Increase Profits and Reduce Risk with ETFs and Options

MARK D. WOLFINGER

WILEY

John Wiley & Sons, Inc.

Published by John Wiley & Sons, Inc., Hoboken, New Jersey.
Published simultaneously in Canada.

For general information on our other products and services, or technical support,
please contact our Customer Care Department within the United States at
800-762-2974, outside the United States at 317-572-3993 or fax 317-572-4002.

Wiley also publishes its books in a variety of electronic formats. Some content
that appears in print may not be available in electronic books. For more
information about Wiley products, visit our web site at www.wiley.com.

Library of Congress Cataloging-in-Publication Data:

Wolfinger, Mark D.
    Create your own hedge fund : increase profits and reduce risk with ETFs and
options / Mark Wolfinger.
        p.   cm. — (Wiley trading series)
    Includes bibliographical references and index.
    ISBN 0-471-65507-4 (cloth)
    1. Hedging (Finance)   2. Stock options.   3. Exchange traded funds.   I. Title
II. Series.
    HG6024.A3W65   2005
    332.64'524—dc22

                                                              2004016625

10   9   8   7   6   5   4   3   2   1

This book is dedicated in loving memory to my parents, Betty and Khiva Wolfinger. They would have loved to see their son become an author.

Contents

Acknowledgments

Many thanks to my family and friends who provided guidance, support, encouragement, and great information, particularly Lynn Seligman, Nancy Crossman, Gail Reichlin, and Camden McKinley. A special thank you to my life-partner, Penny Rotheiser, whose attention to detail proved invaluable.

And thank you to all the dedicated people at John Wiley & Sons who did their jobs well and provided encouragement and answers to my many questions. Their input made the completion of this project both more enjoyable and more efficient: Jeanne Glasser, for encouraging me to submit the book proposal in the first place; editor Kevin Commins; editorial director Pam van Giessen; editorial assistant Lara Murphy; editorial assistant Matt Kellen, who found the help I needed on every conceivable topic; marketing manager Felicia Reid; and production manager Alexia Meyers, who carefully transformed the raw manuscript into the finished product.

Thank you all.

Preface

Everyone wants to make money in the stock market, and each individual has reasons for owning stocks. Whatever your motivation—saving for retirement, saving to provide a college education for your children or a home for your family, even trying to earn more money so you can enjoy the good life—making money via investing is the goal of millions of people all over the world.

Although everyone agrees that making money is the goal, not everyone agrees on the best way to accomplish that goal. This book introduces you to a twenty-first-century style of investing that combines the best aspects of two important investment tools: exchange traded funds (ETFs) and stock options. You will learn to hedge, or reduce the risk of owning stock.

Most investors who make their own investment decisions overestimate their results and, if asked, would say their methods produce market-beating results year after year. They are not exactly failing to tell the truth, because most *believe* they can (and should) consistently outperform the market. And if they didn't do especially well this past year or two, well, that's okay, for they *know* their performance during the next few years will more than compensate for any recent underperformance.

The truth is that individual investors, on average, consistently underperform the market. That's sad because many people love making those investment decisions and being actively involved with trading. If you currently make all your own investment decisions, this book shows you an alternative method for handling your investments—a method that reduces overall risk at the same time it increases your chances of beating the market. And for those who enjoy being active traders, this methodology is fun. There are decisions and trades to make every month, although you can modify the method to trade less frequently (every three or even every six months), if that's your preference.

A great many investors have neither the time nor the inclination to make their own investment decisions. They feel more comfortable depending on others, and there are many professional money managers eager to take their money and make those investment decisions. These investors, who ordinarily do meticulous research before spending money on a vacation, a car, or even a home computer, and who seek every opportunity to determine which product provides the best performance or which received the best reviews from consumers, often invest money based on information gleaned from advertisements that gloat over recent good performance. They place their future financial security entirely into the hands of people they haven't bothered to research thoroughly—specifically, mutual fund managers. The fund managers who do achieve above-average results advertise those results to a public eager to invest. Unfortunately, evidence shows that recent track records bear little resemblance to future results. It's impossible to predict in advance who the successful fund managers will be this (or any) year. But, no matter, there are millions of investors eager to throw billions of dollars at those fund managers. The question is: Do those managers perform any better than individual investors? Are they able to outperform the market year after year? We'll take at look at the evidence, but the short answer is no. They perform no better than individual investors, yet they are not bashful about charging fees to manage investor money.

The recent scandals involving after-hours trading and allowing favored customers to buy and sell shares without incurring fees that individual investors would have to pay make it even more unlikely that mutual fund managers can provide individual investors with the service they deserve. Fortunately, there are viable alternatives, and you don't have to accept those poor results any longer.

There are several ways a public investor can earn better returns than are available by entrusting hard-earned savings to professional mutual fund managers. One simple way is to invest in index funds. At least these funds make no attempt to beat the market; they are content to match the performance of the averages. With fewer commissions and no research, this management style results in significantly lower annual expenses for the fund, and the savings are passed on to the investor. Average performance is better than underperformance, and paying smaller fees is better than higher fees.

But indexing, by itself, is not the final answer. There is more an investor can do to enhance investment returns. This book shows how to accomplish that goal.

You will learn to choose an investment advisor who is entirely trustworthy and capable of handling all your investment decisions. That advisor follows the teachings of modern portfolio theory (MPT). That advisor builds a well-diversified portfolio of stock market investments and manages those investments without charging a fee. That advisor uses methods that increase the probability of beating the market averages and does so with a reduced chance of incurring losses. That's right: Enhanced earnings and reduced risk. So where do you find such an advisor? That's easy: Look in the mirror. You can make your own investment decisions. You can be your own fund manager.

There is no magic formula involved, nor some high-risk hocus-pocus. There are no promises of getting rich in a hurry. The success of this investment methodology is based on the steady growth of capital that comes from doing well on a consistent basis. It is based on combining two readily available investment tools into one cohesive strategy. Exchange traded funds, the modern version of the traditional mutual fund, and stock options are the tools used to manage your investment portfolio.

You'll learn why ETFs are a more efficient investment vehicle than traditional mutual funds for most individual investors. They have tax advantages, charge lower fees, and essentially match the performance of the market averages. No more paying fees for underperformance!

Options are a misunderstood investment tool. Options were designed to reduce investment risk, but too many investment advisors tell their customers that options are dangerous and should be used only by speculators. We'll clear up that misconception, and you'll learn to use options to both reduce risk and enhance profits.

By combining these two tools into one investment methodology, you essentially create and run your own hedge fund. And the best part is that it's not complicated. You can readily learn to manage your investments yourself, but if you are a busy professional who believes there is not enough time to intelligently make your own investment decisions, you can turn the whole process over to a broker or financial planner you trust to follow your instructions.

Many investors reaped rich rewards during the strong stock market of the late 1990s, but a large percentage of those investors gave back all those profits (and then some) during the ensuing bear market at the beginning of the new millennium. Many are searching for the elusive holy grail of investing, namely finding a way to consistently outperform the market averages with limited risk. This book shows those investors such a path to financial security. Investors are no longer forced to rely on mutual fund managers because they don't feel there is any alternative. The methods taught here require some effort, but the rewards are worth it.

Investing is not a game. It's a project that must be taken seriously, as your future financial independence is at stake. It requires an understanding of the risks and rewards of investing. Successful individual investors who make their own decisions devote a great deal of time and effort to avoid making bad decisions. Some spend countless hours poring over annual reports and 10-k filings in an effort to find companies that have the potential to earn great profits in the future (fundamental analysis). Others spend time with charts and graphs, attempting to use price and volume data to predict future stock prices (technical analysis). If you follow the methods taught here, you can be spared those hours of research. Individuals, on average, are not able to find those great companies, and unless you have a proven track record of consistently outperforming the stock market averages, it's less risky to own a diversified portfolio, such as those represented by ETFs. Those investments can be hedged with options, reducing risk even further.

The methodology taught in this book does not guarantee profits. But it does present an investing strategy that increases your chances of being a successful investor. It increases the odds that your portfolio outperforms the market averages on a consistent basis, *and* it reduces your overall investment risk. Those are not just idle claims, and statistical evidence is included to support those claims. The path to investment success discussed in this book uses neither fundamental nor technical analysis. The recommended strategy is one that you, an individual investor, can readily adopt for yourself.

That investment method involves:

- *Asset allocation:* Determine the portion of your assets to be invested in the stock market and in other asset classes, such as bonds, cash equivalents, real estate, collectibles, and so forth. The methods discussed here are limited to working with the funds allocated to investing in the stock markets of the world.
- *Diversification:* Using the teachings of modern portfolio theory, you build a portfolio of stock market investments. Building an appropriate, diversified portfolio (diversification reduces risk) is much easier to accomplish than you might believe. You'll learn to use the modern version of the traditional mutual fund, the exchange traded fund, as the backbone of your portfolio.
- *Stock options:* We'll explode the myth that options are dangerous. This versatile investment tool can be used conservatively and intelligently to enhance the performance of your stock market portfolio. You'll learn to adopt an easy-to-understand options strategy that both enhances performance and reduces risk even further.

The journey begins with a brief discussion of MPT—what it is, why it's relevant to you, and how you can use its teachings to compile a portfolio that provides two substantial benefits: reduced risk *and* a better return on your investment. We'll take a look at the record and examine how well in-dividual investors and professional mutual fund managers have fared in their attempts to outperform the market. Then we'll move on to discuss how you can use modern mutual funds—but not traditional mutual funds—to achieve the goals of MPT. You'll learn why ETFs, or the twenty-first-century version of the traditional mutual fund, are superior to traditional funds and how you can use them to achieve your investment goals. Finally, you'll learn about the versatile investment tool: the stock option. After a primer for those unfamiliar with stock options, you'll see how to adopt either (or a combination) of two conservative options strategies to help you enhance your stock market success. We'll take time out to examine the his-torical evidence proving that these option strategies really do enhance in-vestment profits and simultaneously reduce risk.

Have you heard that options are dangerous and only for speculators? Options are not dangerous, and, in fact, you'll learn to use them to reduce risk. You'll see how to combine the best qualities of stock options with the benefits of investing in ETFs to achieve a portfolio with the potential to out-perform portfolios managed by professional money managers—and you won't have to pay professional money managers to achieve those results. Not only that, but your investment portfolio will be less volatile, reducing your stress level. You can expect to earn substantial profits when the mar-ket rallies, you'll love your profits when the markets are stagnant, and you'll lose less (and may even show a profit) when the markets decline.

You can easily learn to manage your own portfolio better and more ef-ficiently than professional money managers. Instead of paying someone else to provide for your future financial security, you get to own and oper-ate your own mutual fund—really a hedge fund.

If you are tired of paying excessive fees to others to (mis-)manage your money, it's time to make your own decisions. If you accept the fact (many do not) that it's difficult to beat the market averages, here's a method that greatly increases your chances to do so. If you love trading and want to be involved with the decision-making process, then this methodology is cus-tom made for you. And if you are a financial planner, here's a method you can use to enhance the profits of your clients.

Those who currently invest in index funds understand the folly of at-tempting to beat the market by buying individual stocks or mutual funds. They can do even better by adopting the strategies taught in this book.

Each of you may even come to cherish the time you spend working on your investments.

Get ready to update your investment methodology.

Create Your Own Hedge Fund

PART I

Outperforming the Market

CHAPTER 1

Modern Portfolio Theory

People invest money in the stock market with one primary goal in mind: to earn a satisfactory return on that investment. Some consider investing to be a full-time occupation with the goal of earning enough to provide for their day-to-day living expenses on a continuing basis. Some will be retiring soon and must plan to begin using their investment nest egg to meet expenses. Others have a much longer time horizon and are planning 30 or 40 years into the future.

With such a variety of time frames and purposes, there is no single investment strategy that suits all investors. There is no single "best" portfolio of investments to own.

INDIVIDUAL INVESTORS

Many individual investors decide for themselves which specific stocks to own. Whether the buying decision is based on sound research into the fundamentals, including a thorough reading of the various financial reports issued by the company, or whether price history charts are studied in an effort to perform a thorough technical analysis, or whether an investment decision is based on a tip received from a stockbroker, bartender, chat room, or a talking head on CNBC or *Wall Street Week*, investors seldom consider their entire portfolio when making a new purchase. The buying decision is often based on investors' belief (hope) that some information has been uncovered—information not yet known to other investors—that will soon make the price of the newly purchased stock soar.

Some investors make investment decisions alone, shunning the advice of others. Some rely on the camaraderie of an investment club. Some listen to the advice of professionals before making the final decisions themselves. Some blindly follow the advice of a stock market advisory newsletter while others do everything their stockbrokers suggest. Regardless of the source of an investment idea, most individual investors never think twice about whether the new investment is suitable or whether it helps them achieve their overall investment goals. In fact, many have no overall objectives in mind and simply make new purchases to produce a portfolio based on chaos. Some investors are happy with their results, while others are not. Modern portfolio theory (MPT) teaches us that this is a poor way to invest. With so many investors accumulating stocks and building a portfolio in this haphazard manner, it's important to know: Are individual investors generally successful? The answer to this question is postponed until Chapter 2.

Investing in Mutual Funds

Many millions of other investors don't want to take the time or make the effort to choose their own stocks. Instead, they rely on financial professionals to make investment decisions for them. Some of these investors follow the advice of a guru who sells stock market advice for a fee (e.g., newsletters and advisory services), while others accept the investment advice of financial planners or stockbrokers. But the vast majority of these investors buy shares of mutual funds.

Mutual funds serve a great purpose. They allow investors to quickly own a diversified portfolio of stocks without being required to buy shares in each of the individual companies. This is especially important for small investors who lack the funds to own a properly diversified portfolio of stocks. It has been known for a long time that proper diversification is a strategy that reduces the risk of investing in the stock market. It's one of the cornerstones of MPT.

Having decided to buy shares of mutual funds, investors must rely on the ability of fund managers to make intelligent investment decisions and earn a good return on investor capital. Some investors make a careful study of mutual funds before selecting which to buy. They study how well mutual funds have performed in the past; they check out Morningstar's[1] rating on the funds, or they accept the advice of a stockbroker.[2] Some investors go further and choose funds that invest in the type of stocks they want to own. For example, some funds only buy stocks of large companies; others specialize by investing in smaller, growing companies. Some funds buy stocks for income (dividends); others buy stock for long-term growth. Some funds specialize in the companies in one specific industry (sector funds); others are more diversified. Some buy stocks in American companies; others invest in businesses from around the world. There are many mutual funds in existence, each with its own investment strategy, and the public investor can choose any of them.

Some who buy shares of mutual funds invest their money, close their eyes, and, placing their trust in the fund's managers, hope for the best. Others take the opposite approach and constantly monitor the performance of their funds and hop from one fund to another, chasing those with the best recent performance.

Most of those who invest in mutual funds would be better served if they had an understanding of how to construct a safer and better-performing investment portfolio on their own. Our goal is to show you, the individual investor, how to do just that.

Some investors are sophisticated enough to know how to avoid paying a sales commission (load) when buying funds; others pay that load, not knowing there is any alternative. The bottom line for the vast majority of mutual fund investors is that once the decision to buy a fund is made, no further thought goes into the process. They leave it to the fund management team to produce superior returns on their money. Over the years, most investors have been satisfied with this methodology, especially since the trend of the American stock market has been bullish over the long term.[3] With so many Americans relying on mutual funds to meet their investment objectives, two important questions must be considered: Are mutual fund investors generally successful? Are they well served by the managers of those funds? Let's postpone a discussion of the answer until Chapter 5.

MODERN PORTFOLIO THEORY

Investors seldom, if ever, consider their entire portfolio as anything but a collection of individual investments, regardless of whether those investments are individual stocks, mutual funds, or any of numerous other assets, such as bank certificates of deposit, bonds, or coin collections. Few consider whether adding a new investment to a portfolio affects the overall risk parameters of the portfolio, or whether it helps to diversify their holdings. Usually asset allocation is totally ignored. This is not a good thing.

There exists a large body of knowledge that has collectively become known as modern portfolio theory. MPT tells us that investors can successfully (and easily) use a scientific approach to compile an investment portfolio. It's worthwhile to make a brief study of this collection of knowledge because it contains ideas you can easily adopt to make your own investing more efficient and more profitable. One of the great benefits of

MPT is that it shows how to increase the expected profits *and* lower overall risk at the same time

MPT is concerned with the methods used to compile an investment portfolio and with the performance of that portfolio. Investors can easily earn the risk-free rate of return by purchasing U.S. Treasury bills.[4] But to earn more, investors must accept the fact that a certain amount of risk must be accepted. It's generally understood in the investment world that the greater the risk of an investment, the greater the potential reward. This must be true, or else no one would ever knowingly accept greater risk. It's important to point out that the term "risk" is usually considered to represent the chances of losing money from an investment. According to MPT, risk is much more than that; it's also a measure of how much the return on an investment varies from the expected return. Thus, risk is a measure of the uncertainly of the future.

The work of Harry M. Markowitz changed the way investment managers think, when he demonstrated that including certain classes of assets in a portfolio influenced not only the profit potential of that portfolio, but also its volatility, or the rate at which the value of a portfolio fluctuates.[5] The major conclusion of MPT that concerns our discussion is how to construct an investment portfolio that aims for higher profits with reduced risk.

Markowitz did the original work in this field, and others have made significant contributions.[6] Among those are Professors Sharpe, Cootner and Fama.[7] A good discussion of MPT can be found in the text authored by Rudd and Clasing.[8] The theory is not some obscure topic of interest only to academics, but is widely used in today's investment universe. Markowitz and Sharpe shared the Nobel Prize in economics in 1990 for their contributions to this field.[9]

The early development of MPT relied heavily on statistics, and the pioneering work is highly technical. Nevertheless, the basics of MPT can be explained in simple terms (the more complex math remains available for those readers interested in such details[10]). The discussion here is limited to explaining what MPT is, why it's important for today's investor to understand its basic teachings, and how you can easily build a portfolio based on its precepts.

Here is a simple summary of how MPT describes the thought process behind investing:

> *An investment is made in a security, or portfolio of securities, in anticipation of receiving a monetary reward. The expected reward is the average reward that results from holding the specific investment(s). Some years the return on the investment exceeds the expected return, and some years the return on the investment is less.*

*The investment universe is filled with uncertainties, and, there-
fore, there is a certain degree of risk encountered when attempting to
collect the reward. The risk is a measure of the uncertainty of earning the expected return.*

*Thus (states the theory), an investor chooses among investment
possibilities based entirely on the two measures of risk and reward,
attempting to minimize the former and maximize the latter.*

ASSET ALLOCATION AND ITS ROLE
IN MODERN PORTFOLIO THEORY

What does MPT tell an investor about how to choose the components of a
portfolio? The first idea is to diversify one's holdings and to allocate part of
the investment capital among several asset classes. Reasonably enough,
this strategy is known as asset allocation. Not so many years ago, asset allocation meant owning a variety of stocks and bonds and some cash equivalents. The prudent man rule reinforced this type of thinking among
fiduciaries, or those responsible for investing other people's money.[11]
Today MPT goes further and focuses on the portfolio as a whole, and not on
its individual components. But proper diversification remains an essential
ingredient of MPT.

When following MPT to build a portfolio, it's not sufficient to compile
a portfolio simply by investing in different asset classes (e.g., stocks, bonds,
gold, and real estate). MPT teaches that it's important to find the *optimal* allocation of assets satisfying both the investor's risk tolerance and reward
(expected rate of return). It's important to own a variety of investments
that perform differently in the marketplace. In other words, there should be
minimal correlation in the performance of each individual investment with
each of the other investments. If it sounds difficult to build a portfolio one
stock at a time that satisfies these parameters, especially for an individual
public investor, be assured that it is indeed difficult. But don't fret, as there
is an easy method to accomplish this goal for the portion of your investment capital that you allocate to the stock market. That method is the basis
of this book. A well-qualified financial advisor ought to be able to help you
achieve the type of portfolio recommended by MPT for any assets you own
that are not stock market related.

Again, it's important to reiterate that our discussion focuses on only
that portion of your assets you have allocated to investing in the stock markets of the world. This book makes no recommendation on how you should
otherwise allocate your assets. MPT tells us that asset allocation should not
be ignored, as it represents the best method of reducing the overall risk of

your portfolio. Numerous books offer advice on how to allocate assets in accordance with MPT, and we'll leave that discussion to them.[12]

THE PRUDENT INVESTOR

The prudent man rule contains guidelines for those responsible for investing other people's money. The purpose of the rule is to offer protection to investors by providing those fiduciaries with investment guidelines. Over the years, the rule has changed with the times. At one point, it would have been considered lunacy to invest the savings of a public investor in the stock market. After World War II, as inflation became important in making financial decisions, it was considered extremely imprudent for a fiduciary *not* to invest in the market. Today it is not enough to merely invest in stocks, and the prudent man rule requires that fiduciaries invest at least part of an investor's funds via passive investing, using index funds. Passive investing is consistent with the teachings of MPT and represents an important part of our overall recommended investment strategy. It's the basis of further discussion in Chapter 2.

At one time, a fiduciary had the difficult responsibility of being certain that *each investment* was appropriate for an investor. Today, taking MPT into consideration, the prudent investor rule has been revised to "focus on the portfolio as a whole and the investment strategy on which it is based, rather than viewing a specific investment in isolation."[13] As a result, it's acceptable for fiduciaries to recommend shares that would be risky as stand-alone investments, as long as the entire portfolio is appropriate for the investor.

DIVERSIFICATION

Diversification is an essential element when following MPT. The easiest way for public investors to diversify has been to own shares of traditional mutual funds. Their very existence is one reason why so many Americans are currently stock market investors, as mutual funds make it easy for public investors to own a professionally managed diversified portfolio of stocks.[14] The wisdom of relying on these professional money managers is one of the subjects covered in MPT and this discussion is continued in Chapter 2.

CHAPTER 2

Can You Beat the Market? Should You Try?

The academics say, "No way." Professional money managers say, "We do it all the time." What's this argument about? It's a debate over whether anyone can build a portfolio of stocks that outperforms the market on a consistent basis. Academics claim the market's ups and downs are random and that it's not possible either to time the market[1] or predict which stocks are going to outperform the market in the future. Money managers claim the ability to do research and determine which stocks are undervalued and beat the market by buying those stocks. This is an ongoing disagreement with no end in sight.

Those who believe it's not possible to beat the market make this argument:

- Gross returns earned by investors as a group must equal the gross returns earned by the total stock market.
- Net returns—after advisory fees and other investment expenses—earned by investors as a group must fall short of the returns of the market by the amount of those costs.[2]

Those making this argument believe that simply hiring professional managers and paying fees for their services is enough to guarantee below-average returns over the long term. Their suggestion is to invest in index funds because those funds do not spend money on research and save money on commissions by owning and holding an investment portfolio. These funds charge much lower fees than traditional mutual funds, and those reduced fees enable index funds to come very close to matching the performance of the market (as measured by the index they are trying to mimic). This investment methodology is discussed further later in this chapter.

Those who believe in the efficient market theory believe that markets must be inefficient (information becomes available to different participants at different times) in order for any individuals to demonstrate the skills required to compile a portfolio of stocks that consistently generates above-average profits.[3] But, since they believe the market is efficient and all information that can possibly be known is already known, and that such information is already priced into the price of every stock, they believe no one has any special advantage and therefore no one can consistently outperform the market. Statistically there are always some who do outperform and others who underperform, but there is no way for an investor to know *in advance* who can generate above-average returns. Thus, efficient market theorists conclude, spending money in an attempt to outperform the market is a foolish endeavor.

Modern portfolio theory (MPT) agrees with the academics on this issue.

Most of the evidence tells us that markets are fairly efficient. As additional advances in information technology become available, the markets will become even more efficient. If that's true, then the question remains: With so much information available to everyone, and with sophisticated software available to analyze that information, is it possible for specific individuals to gain (and maintain) a sufficient advantage that allows them to build a portfolio that performs better than the portfolios of their peers? And if it can be done, is it reasonable for investors to spend time and effort in an attempt to find which funds to buy to benefit from that superior performance? In other words, can individual investors know which mutual funds are likely to do well in the future? Is past performance any indication of future results? Academia concludes that it cannot be done now, and in the future it will become even more unlikely that anyone can beat the market on a regular basis. The dispute goes on.

This author sides with the academic world and the teachings of MPT and believes that attempting to beat the market is an expensive, time-consuming, and fruitless endeavor for the vast majority of investors. As noted in the preface, most investors "feel" they can beat the market and attempt that feat year after year.

DO YOU STILL WANT TO CHOOSE YOUR OWN STOCKS WHEN INVESTING?

Do you believe that your stock-picking skills are excellent? Do you believe you have a trading system that allows you to do better than the market on a consistent basis? Do you believe technical analysis can tell you which stocks to buy and when? If you truthfully answered yes to any of the above, congratulations! You are already able to outperform the market and don't have to worry about diversification, risk reduction, or any part of modern portfolio theory. The lessons in this book are for everyone else, although you still can benefit by learning and adopting the options strategies taught in Part III and by learning to appreciate the advantages of diversification.

The question remains: Is there evidence on whether the average investor can beat the market by choosing individual stocks to buy and sell? Yes, there is and we'll take a look at the evidence later in this chapter.

WALL STREET SAYS YOU CAN BEAT THE MARKET

The professional brokers on Wall Street are in the business of trying to convince public investors that they easily can beat the market if they only would open a trading account with their brokerage house and follow their investment advice. But, to make money, individual investors must pick winning stocks, and, as you will see, the evidence tells us that the vast majority are unable to do it.

Managers of mutual funds take the same path in trying to convince investors to send them money. They often boast (via paid advertisements) of their recent market success. That advertising is effective, and investors rush to buy shares of mutual funds that recently have been able to beat the market.

RESEARCH SAYS YOU ARE UNLIKELY TO BEAT THE MARKET

Beating the market is a difficult task. With so many individual investors and so many professional money managers trying, the laws of probability tell us that some will be successful while others will not.

Some investors like to try to beat the market, especially if stock market investing is a hobby. By all means, enjoy yourself. But if your financial goal is to amass wealth over the years, and if your fun comes from success, then recognize that the odds are against those who try to beat the market on a regular basis. It's much easier (and more likely to be the winning strategy, according to modern portfolio theory) to own a suitable mix of ETFs. When

But I Can Beat the Market

If you still believe you have the ability to beat the market with your individual stock picks, don't stop reading. The strategy taught in this book works very well for investors who compile a portfolio of individual stocks, and gives you the information you need to enhance the return you earn on your investments—with the added bonus of doing so with reduced risk. Read on!

you modify your ETF strategy by adopting the methods taught in this book, your chances of enhancing your returns become even greater.[4]

If you still believe you can beat the market by selecting your own stocks, then you are certainly free to make the attempt. Just recognize the odds are not on your side. Owning a diversified portfolio of ETFs that meets the requirements of MPT can't be a bad thing. It *might* be possible to compile a portfolio by choosing individual stocks that gives you a slightly better than expected rate of return or a slightly lower level of risk, but there are two reasons not to attempt that feat: (1) It requires a great deal of research, and (2) it's not likely to make a significant difference. Professional money managers and individual investors have not been able to beat the market on a consistent basis,[5] and you will probably be better off spending your time deciding which EFTs are right for you.

If you are willing to consider the possibility that it's difficult, if not impossible, to outperform the market on a consistent basis, that doesn't mean you must sit back and do nothing. There are steps you can take to improve your performance. Asset allocation is the first step.

Once you have allocated a portion of your assets to the stock market, you can make additional modifications to standard investment methods that reduce your risk and raise your profit expectations. In this book, you will learn how to outperform the vast majority of investors who blindly buy mutual funds or who undertake the task of building their own portfolios one stock at a time.

WHAT IS INDEXING?

Let's begin our brief discussion on indexing with a definition. An index is a statistical representation of the performance of a hypothetical portfolio of stocks. That portfolio consists of each stock in the index, in its correct proportion.

When you choose the investment method of indexing, you are attempting to mimic the returns achieved by the market averages, rather than attempting to outperform those averages. Today many investors no longer feel it's appropriate to own shares of actively managed mutual funds— funds in which the managers frequently buy and sell stocks in an attempt to generate a higher return than competitive mutual funds. Indexers measure their performance against a benchmark, often the Standard & Poor's 500 index (considered by many to represent "the American stock market"[6]). More and more investors and fiduciaries are buying index funds and both the prudent man rule and MPT favor buying such funds. Public investors have come to accept owning investments that match the performance of the market averages, especially since those average returns were pretty spectacular during the bubble-building years of the late 1990s.[7]

BUILDING A PORTFOLIO TO MIMIC AN INDEX

An index fund is not hypothetical, but a real-world portfolio of stocks. The managers of the index fund attempt to mimic the performance of the index (and its hypothetical portfolio) as closely as possible. The best way to accomplish that task is to own the correct number of shares of each component of the index. For some indexes, that's a simple matter. For example, managing a fund that mimics the performance of the Dow Jones Industrial Average (DJIA) requires owning shares in only 30 different companies. Each stock is actively traded, and the shares are easy to buy or sell. Thus, when the managers of an index fund that mimics the performance of the DJIA receive cash from investors, it's a simple matter to invest those funds by buying the appropriate number of shares of each of the 30 stocks. Similarly, if there is an influx of redemptions (orders from shareholders to sell their holdings), the fund managers have no difficulty selling shares to raise cash to meet those redemptions.

However, some indexes consist of shares in a vast number of companies. For example, attempting to exactly replicate the performance of the Russell 3000 index or the Wilshire 5000 index is difficult. Each index contains thousands of stocks, and some are very thinly traded, meaning that only a relatively small number of shares trade every day. It is not efficient to trade those stocks frequently. When it becomes necessary to buy or sell a significant number of thinly traded shares, the fund managers easily could influence the price merely by attempting to buy or sell the shares.[8] Thus, it's a more efficient process to own a representative sampling of the stocks in such an index, rather that attempting to own each component. Fortunately, sampling is a viable strategy, and it's possible to compile a portfolio that produces investment results that are almost exactly the same as if the fund owned each of the stocks in the index.

If you ask why fund managers must buy or sell these thinly traded issues, consider what happens when the management team receives cash from investors. That cash must be invested (proportionately in each of the stocks that comprise the fund's portfolio) as soon as possible because holding a sizable cash position is not conducive to mimicking the market performance of an index. Holding uninvested cash runs the risk of underperforming in a rising market or outperforming in a declining market. Because matching the index is the managers' prime directive, they do not want to take the risk of timing the market. Neither beating nor underperforming the index is considered to be acceptable, but outperformance is always forgiven.

The managers constantly maintain a portfolio representative of the specific index they are trying to mimic and trade as infrequently as possible. This keeps expenses low. However, when a change in the composition of the index occurs (a new stock is added or an existing member of the index is removed, the portfolio must be adjusted accordingly.)[9]

When you buy shares of an index fund, you agree to accept a return on your investment that closely resembles the return of the overall market (or the market segment the fund is attempting to mimic). By saving management and execution fees, investors are ahead of the game.

Indexing is still a controversial topic and is likely to remain so for many years, but prudent investing favors indexing strategies. One recent book, *The Successful Investor Today*, gives an excellent summary (including additional references) that makes the case for accepting passive investing.[10] Other books on this topic also are available.[11]

The History of Indexing

The first index fund became available to public investors when Vanguard launched the First Index Investment Trust in August 1976. The fund's name has since been changed to Vanguard 500 Index Fund. The availability of such funds is important because MPT tells us that owning index funds is the best investment strategy for most public investors. Going even further, MPT teaches that each investor should own a suitable assortment of index funds, ensuring proper diversification. If you accept the argument that selecting individual stocks in an attempt to beat the market is not in your best interests, index funds represent an excellent investment vehicle, as they provide diversification accompanied by minimal management fees. For example, the Vanguard 500 Index Fund costs investors 18 cents per year, per $100 invested, compared with $1.25 per $100 investment for the average actively managed mutual fund.[12]

PASSIVE OR ACTIVE MANAGEMENT?

Portfolios can be managed passively or actively. The passive strategy, which is called indexing, involves building a portfolio that performs as closely as possible to the performance of a specific broad-based index, such as the S&P 500. Passive investing produces less stress for the investor, who no longer has to worry about the performance of the fund's management team. Of course, if the market undergoes a steep decline, the investor's portfolio loses value. For investors who want to be invested in the stock market, indexing is an excellent methodology, according to the teachings of MPT, as it provides a way to reduce risk through diversification. The passive portfolio manager exercises no judgment in building the portfolio, and no trading decisions are necessary. The most obvious benefit of this strategy is reduced expenses, as trading expenses are minimal and research expenses are eliminated. Indexing is becoming an increasingly popular investment choice.

The obvious disadvantage of passive investing is the inability to outperform the market. For some investors that's acceptable, as there is also the inability to underperform the market.

Managing traditional mutual funds is a hugely profitable business. Fund managers maintain those profit levels by charging their mutual funds (and thus, the fund's shareholders) much higher fees than they charge their institutional clients for identical services.[13] The managers of actively traded mutual funds are not going to sit quietly and give up their franchise to those who manage funds passively. These management companies spend huge sums on advertising, trying to convince the average public investor that investing with them is the smart thing to do. These managers always leave the impression they can beat the market averages in the future simply because they may have beaten them in the past.[14] The year's best-performing funds promote that performance, attempting to entice investors to place new money in their funds.

When running an actively managed fund, the managers not only choose which specific investments to own, but also use market timing strategies to determine *when* to invest in stocks and when to hold cash equivalents. By timing the market, managers add additional risk to the portfolio, as it becomes more likely the investment results of the fund will differ from that of the overall market.

MPT tells us that passive investing, including being fully invested *at all times* (not attempting to time the market), is beneficial and that the additional expense of paying higher fees to the managers of actively traded mutual funds is not justified. Of course, this conclusion of MPT is not universally accepted. Those who believe in technical analysis are the most adamant in their refusal to accept these premises. After all, if it were impossible to predict future prices by studying a stock's price history, then technical analysis would be a bogus science. This controversy is not likely to go away quietly. We'll take a look at some of the evidence and you can decide whether passive investing is suitable for you.

Do You Make Investment Decisions Alone?

Being in an investment club is fun. It's a great learning experience for people who are beginning their investment education. Members usually meet once per month, discuss various possible investments, and learn how to conduct research to analyze the investment worthiness of a company. The question remains: Do the portfolios compiled by these investment clubs outperform the market? Surveys of investment clubs tell us that these clubs are generally successful. But such surveys are flawed. In a study covering a six-year trading history of 166 randomly selected investment clubs (clients of one unnamed large discount brokerage firm), professors Brad Barber and Terrance Odean concluded that investment clubs "educate their members about financial markets, foster friendships and social ties, and entertain. Unfortunately, their investments do not beat the market."[15]

Many individual investors make their investment decisions on their own, without the comfort of being able to discuss those selections with other investment club members. Some seek advice from professionals, some rely on tips, and some even (I shudder at the thought) seek advice from Internet chat rooms. Do individual investors, regardless of whether they seek anyone else's advice, outperform the market on a consistent basis?

THE VERDICT, PART I. SHOULD YOU CHOOSE YOUR OWN STOCKS?

The evidence says no. Barber and Odean studied more than 2 million customer trades over a six-year period and found that individual investors significantly underperform the market.[16] They also found those who make the highest number of trades, running up the highest expenses, perform worse than those who trade less. This is an example of actively managed accounts performing worse than less actively managed accounts.

It may not be surprising that public investors who trade actively underperform their peers who trade less often, but can the situation possibly be the same for accounts managed by professional mutual fund managers? See the Verdict, Part II in Chapter 5.

ACCEPTING THE CONCEPT
OF PASSIVE INVESTING

If you, as an individual investor, cannot expect to beat the market on your own, what can you do? Must you accept below-average returns? Must you pay someone a fee in an attempt to earn better returns? Fortunately, there's an acceptable alternative. If you are willing to give up the dream of making an overnight killing in the market and to accept the fact that beating the market on a regular basis is an unlikely occurrence, then you can make the decision to accept returns that match the overall performance of the market. If you do that, you gain:

- Bottom line: You make more money. Average returns are better than below-average returns.
- Your trading costs are reduced, allowing you to make more money than those who invest in traditional mutual funds.
  - Passive investing involves fewer trades, lower commissions, and lower management fees.
  - By not selecting your own stocks, you trade less often, reducing costs.
  - You no longer have to spend time researching stocks to buy. No more analyzing balance sheets to determine financial soundness. No more studying historical stock price charts. No more depending on others for investment tips.
- The volatility of the value of your portfolio is reduced.
- Your tax situation improves, as passive funds seldom pay capital gains distributions.
- You suffer less stress, as you know in advance that the value of your portfolio increases or decreases in line with the market averages.

As mentioned earlier, owning index funds is becoming more and more popular, and the number of investors who choose to own shares of index funds is increasing. Even the current adaptation of the prudent man rule encourages this investment choice.

The managers of actively traded mutual funds are not going to disappear, and they are not going to stop trying to convince you to give them your money to manage. That's a good thing, both for you as an indexer and for the market. In order for investing in index funds (indexing) to work well, there must be those who do *not* adopt this strategy. If everyone owned only index funds, there would be virtually no trading. If neither investors nor professional money managers were attempting to beat the market, no one would be buying or selling stocks. Everyone would own the same or similar portfolios. Don't be concerned: Human nature being what it is guarantees that this will never happen. Be satisfied that if you choose indexing, you are making an investment choice that puts you ahead of the game. If indexing does not sound like something that appeals to you, be patient. In Part IV we'll use options to improve the performance of passive investing—an improvement that increases profitability and reduces risk.

Summary

The normal distribution of events, as represented by a bell curve, tells us that some investors and professional money managers will beat the market. But some also will fail in their attempt to beat the market. Since it's impossible to predict, in advance, just who the winners and losers will be, it's wise not to attempt to do so. It takes time, money, and energy to conduct the research necessary to try to beat the market yourself. It's foolish to hire others, incurring management fees on top of research and trading expenses, in an attempt to do so. Accepting an average return is a much more efficient method of investing. By saving the costs of those management and trade execution fees, investors are likely to be ahead of the game. Thus, indexing is not only expected to match the market, but, by saving all those extra costs, it is expected to do better than the professionals and beat them.

Frank Armstrong, an SEC registered investment advisor, put it this way: "Notice that we are not saying that you can never win, only that it is unlikely you can consistently win enough to overcome the costs of trying."[17]

CHOOSE INDEXING

MPT teaches that owning an assortment of index funds is the most efficient method for public investors to achieve a satisfactory return on an investment. Buying a mix of index funds may be rewarding, but it's not an exciting strategy. If you are the type of investor who wants to own a volatile portfolio with lots of "action," then indexing may not be suitable for your personality. But most people would be happy just to outperform the market year after year and would consider such an achievement as anything but dull. The strategy taught in this book enables you to actively participate in managing your portfolio by combining indexing with a hands-on options strategy. Investors who want only a small amount of hands-on decision-making can modify the strategy.

BEYOND INDEXING

The investment methodology outlined in this book goes way beyond traditional indexing. You are going to learn to go two steps further when building a suitable investment portfolio. Part II presents a discussion of the exchange traded fund (ETF), an improved version of the traditional mutual fund, and explains how to make them your major investment vehicle. Some ETFs are essentially index funds, and those are the ones to which we will pay the most attention. ETFs have many advantages over traditional mutual funds that make them a wiser choice for most investors.

In Part III, you'll learn about stock options and how to use them to enhance investment returns and reduce the risk of owning a diversified stock market portfolio. Part IV merges the strategies into one comprehensive, easy-to-adopt method of investing. You'll learn how to combine the strategy of covered call writing with the ownership of ETFs.

After you follow the recommended investment strategy, your portfolio will meet the requirements of MPT: reduced risk with the potential for better returns. Such an investment portfolio provides you with many of the benefits of investing in a hedge fund, but without having to pay the high fees.

But first, let's take a brief look at hedge funds.

CHAPTER 3

Hedge Funds

A hedge fund operates like a traditional mutual fund. The management team pools money raised from investors and puts that money to work in a wide variety of investment vehicles. But hedge fund managers are allowed a great deal of flexibility in choosing their investments and can use investment tools and techniques not available to managers of traditional funds. Their goal is to hedge, or reduce the risk of owning, their investments. For example, hedge funds are allowed to play both directions of the market by being long certain securities and short others simultaneously. Hedge funds use derivative products, such as options and futures, and have the ability to borrow money in an attempt to generate additional profits by using leverage. (Leverage means using borrowed money [buying on margin] to enhance returns without increasing the size of an investment.) Hedge funds also can participate in arbitrage opportunities. Arbitrage involves the simultaneous purchase of a security in one market and the sale of the same security, or a derivative product (an instrument whose value is dependent on the value of the first security), in another market. Due to occasional short-lived market inefficiencies, the arbitrageur occasionally can profit from price differentials between the two markets.

Traditional mutual funds have much stricter requirements and are not allowed to sell stocks short. Nor are they allowed to use leverage or derivatives. A few mutual funds can write covered call options (discussed in great detail in Part III), but most are prohibited from using any options strategy. By being forced to invest only on the long side of the market, traditional funds do well in rising markets and fare poorly when the stock market declines. The best they can do in declining markets is to hold cash instead of being fully invested. One of the great advantages of owning shares in a hedge fund is the opportunity to profit during both bull and bear markets.

Although hedging techniques cannot guarantee profits, they do reduce portfolio volatility and make it significantly more likely that investors earn a profit over the long term. That is why investors usually benefit when they add a hedge fund to a traditional investment portfolio. But most public investors don't understand the advantages of reducing the volatility in the value of their portfolios; instead they are concerned only with how much money they can make *right now*.

A great many public investors (and professional money managers) suffered huge losses during the recent bear market, making many afraid to invest and encouraging them to find investments that make money in both rising and falling markets. Hedge funds represent an investment choice to fill that niche.

FINDING A GOOD HEDGE FUND

Finding hedge fund managers who are skilled traders and who understand risk management is not an easy matter. Using leverage provides an opportunity to increase profits, but it also can result in increased losses if investment risks are not managed carefully. As with traditional funds, not all hedge fund managers are competent to manage an investor's money. But it's difficult for public investors to obtain the information necessary to judge the qualifications of hedge fund managers.

Unlike traditional mutual funds, hedge funds cannot advertise themselves to public investors. Legitimate funds managed by qualified management teams can advertise only to "qualified" investors, typically those who have $1 million or more to invest. Thus, public investors must learn about specific hedge funds from sources of unknown reliability.

INVESTING IN HEDGE FUNDS: THE BAD NEWS

Hedge funds charge very high fees to manage your money. It is customary to charge an annual management fee of 1 to 2 percent of the value of the investment, but that's not much more than traditional mutual funds charge. The real incentive for hedge fund managers is profit sharing—managers keep 20 percent of all profits. Because hedge funds originally were marketed only to very wealthy clients, and because these clients are willing to pay big fees for excellent results, the tradition of paying 20 percent of the profits continues. Investors get to keep 80 percent of the profits (before the 1 or 2 percent management fee) and incur 100 percent of all losses. Thus, making money is difficult for investors. Despite those high fees, many public investors are eager to enter the world of hedge funds.

Consider these facts: Operating a hedge fund can be very lucrative; many public investors are searching for hedge funds; hedge funds are unregulated and investment results do not have to be audited. These conditions made it very attractive for scam artists to enter the business of operating hedge funds. On top of this, the success of existing (legitimate) hedge funds during the bear market attracted investors who were losing large sums in traditional funds. Their ability to make money during bear markets enabled hedge funds to greatly outperform traditional mutual funds. News of their profitability spread, grabbing the attention of investors everywhere.

But hedge funds were not originally designed for the masses. Instead, an investor had to be "qualified" before being allowed to buy shares of hedge funds. These requirements barred the vast majority of public investors.

The rationale behind those restrictions is that hedge funds are considered too risky for most public investors. They are unregulated, given great latitude in the nature of their investments, and don't have to report their results—and if they do report results, often they are unaudited. Note that public investors were allowed to invest in the stock market and lose huge sums when the markets declined rapidly. Even the prudent man rule suggests that owning stocks is a conservative and intelligent thing to do. But investors were prohibited from buying shares of hedge funds because the government agency making the decisions thought these funds were too risky for the public. Imagine: Funds designed to reduce risk are considered too risky for the average investor!

Hedge Funds for the Masses

As stated, running a successful hedge fund is a very profitable proposition. Many new hedge funds were organized with the purpose of encouraging the public investor to enter the game. During the past three years, assets under management by hedge funds increased from $500 billion to $800 billion.[1] To make it easy to attract investors, initial investment requirements were as little as $5,000.

Deciding which hedge fund to invest in is even more difficult than choosing a traditional mutual fund. It's still impossible to know, in advance, who the skillful fund managers are and which funds are going to be successful. But beyond that, there often are no verifiable track records for the investor to consider. That makes choosing a hedge fund difficult. As if that's not enough, public investors have no idea of the background of the fund's managers.

In a recent article that is extremely critical of hedge funds, Neil Weinberg and Bernard Condon describe how many unqualified individuals were able to pass themselves off as qualified fund managers, open hedge funds, and raise capital from eager investors.[2] Although not able to advertise directly to investors, some were able to circumvent that rule by claiming huge profits. In turn, the tales of big profits sometimes were enough to gain a television interview for the hedge fund managers, during which they boasted of a great track record and told viewers how to obtain information on the fund. Notice that the managers were not advertising; they were merely describing their results to an interviewer.

Look at it from the perspective of hedge fund manager wannabes. If they can raise $50 million from the public, and if they earn a return of only 5 percent on the money, that's a profit of $2.5 million. Their 20 percent share of the profits comes to $500,000. That's enough money to attract many scam artists.

Unethical fund managers who are able to raise a great deal of money are in position to gamble with that money. If they take big risks in an attempt to earn large profits, they have nothing to lose. (They lacked integrity to begin.) If they go broke, it's not their money; if they hit it big and double the money, their share of the profits from a $50 million account is $10 million. These windfall possibilities, coupled with the fact that hedge funds are unregulated, was bound to attract some unscrupulous scam artists. Weinberg and Condon claim "it's amateur hour in the hedge fund business" because hedge funds are being operated not only by those well qualified to run such funds, but also by "shills, shysters, charlatans, and neophytes too crooked or too stupid to make any money." Sadly for public investors, the invested capital often disappeared quickly—either through trading losses or outright theft.

There are many excellent hedge funds available to the investor, but due diligence is required to find a legitimate fund with qualified managers. Good information often is difficult to obtain because legitimate funds are not allowed to advertise to those seeking information. Few take the time to attempt to verify the claims before investing after hearing (untruthful or exaggerated) claims of the fantastic results achieved by some hedge funds.

Fund of Funds

A breed of mutual fund is called a fund of funds. The managers of these funds invest money by buying shares of other funds—both traditional and hedge funds. Although this sounds like a good way to own a very well-diversified portfolio, consider the management fees. The investor who buys shares of a fund of funds must pay a management fee to those people who operate the fund of funds. Then the money is invested in other funds whose managers also charge a management fee. Finally, the hedge fund managers collect 20 percent of all profits. Too many fees!

If you ever consider buying shares of a hedge fund, be certain to read the prospectus carefully to determine the type of investments used by the management team and the level of risk involved. Remember, the greater the reward promised by the fund managers, the greater the risk required to earn that high reward. If possible, invest only in funds that produce an audit of their investment results.

DO IT YOURSELF

You can avoid the risk of hiring fund managers who are unqualified. You can eliminate the uncomfortable feeling of having money invested when you don't fully understand the investment methods used by those managing your money. If you follow the strategies outlined in this book, you won't have to worry about the integrity of the fund manager, because you will be managing your investments by yourself. There will be no worry about the managers taking more risk than you are willing to take, for you will be managing that risk yourself. In fact, if you adopt the methods described, your portfolio will be significantly less risky than the portfolio of a typical American investor—someone who buys a collection of stocks and seldom sells any of them (a buy-and-hold investor). Hedging is a way to reduce the risk of owning other investments, and the investment strategy described in this book reduces the risk of owning stock market investments.

If you learn to operate your own hedge fund, you are assured the fund manager is ethical. In addition, there are no fees to pay, and you keep all profits for yourself (except for taxes, of course). This book doesn't explain all of the many possible methods of hedging investments. Instead, we concentrate on two hedging methods that are easy for average investors to understand and implement. When you become satisfied with the results and feel comfortable, you can always expand your hedging education.

OR DO IT WITH HELP

If you like the ideas taught in this book and want to run your own hedge fund, but would like the reassurance of working with others, form an investment club. If you show this book to friends, family, and business associates, and if you suggest joining forces and adopting the strategies outlined here, you will be in position to discuss specific investment ideas with each other and rely on the pooled judgment of several people. That should help get you started, if you don't want to tackle this do-it-yourself strategy alone.

By pooling ideas and money, each club member contributes to the success of the club. These investment clubs represent a great educational opportunity. The NAIC (National Association of Investment Clubs) can help you get started with forming a club,[3] but be warned: The association is still using yesterday's investment methodology—namely buy and hold. The hedging strategy outlined in this book works well and is a sound basis for organizing a modern investment club.

A better choice for learning about investment clubs is bivio.[4] They offer an application enabling groups of investors to create and manage a club. Bivio is the only accounting service for investment clubs that supports options, and their software handles the club's bookkeeping chores.

In Part II we'll continue our journey with a discussion of exchange traded funds.

PART II

Exchange Traded Funds

CHAPTER 4

A Brief History of Mutual Funds and Exchange Traded Funds

E xchange traded funds (ETFs) are a recent innovation and the twenty-first-century version of the traditional mutual fund. They first appeared on the scene in 1993. Before learning more about this investment vehicle, let's take a brief look at the mutual fund industry and how it all began.

HISTORY

As noted earlier, public investors did not always invest their money in stocks. As recently as 100 years ago, no professional financial advisor would ever suggest that average investors place any savings in the stock market. But the world changed when the first official mutual fund, The Massachusetts Investors Trust (MIT), opened for business in March 1924. This fund is still in existence today. By establishing the minimum investment at $250, and a sales charge (load) of 5 percent, the fund managers made it easy for public investors to buy shares. MIT is an open-ended fund, meaning that new shares are issued to anyone who wants to buy them. The fund management team takes the newly invested cash and issues shares to the investor. The managers keep the cash in reserve or use it to make additional investments for the fund's portfolio. Investors can redeem shares by notifying the fund management of their desire to sell. New shares are issued, and existing shares are redeemed, at the true value of the fund, called the net asset value (NAV).

The existence of mutual funds such as MIT gave public investors an easy way to own a diversified portfolio of stocks and opened the gates of Wall Street to the masses. And eventually the masses became very interested. As of June 2004, the mutual fund industry managed more than $7.59 trillion of the public investor's assets, according to The Investment Company Institute (www.ici.org).

The first closed-end mutual fund arrived on the scene in 1927. Initially called investment trusts, closed-end funds do not issue additional shares. Instead, existing shares trade on an exchange where they can be bought or sold in a manner identical with stocks. The price of such shares is determined by supply and demand, not by the true value of the underlying fund (NAV). Most of the time these funds trade at a discount to their true NAV, but they have been known to trade at a premium.[1]

In April 1928, the no-load fund was born when the Norfolk Investment Corporation was established without a purchase fee (load). A month later the fund changed its name to the First Investment Counsel Corporation. Today it is part of the Scudder family of funds.

The market crash in 1929 and the depression that followed brought many changes to the investment industry. The Securities Act of 1933 required all funds to sell shares through a prospectus that points out the risks associated with such investments. Previously, salesmen were allowed to sell mutual funds without any government regulations. Three years later the Securities and Exchange Commission (SEC) was created, naming Joseph P. Kennedy (father of future president John F. Kennedy) as its first chairman.

In 1946 funds allowed investors to reinvest dividends without payment of the sales load for the first time. In 1951 the total number of mutual funds surpassed 100.

Money market funds appeared in 1971, giving investors an easy method of holding the equivalent of cash for those periods of time when they did not want to be invested in any of the mutual fund company's other offerings.

In 1976 Vanguard issued the first index fund, whose goal is to capture almost 100 percent of the market's annual return and is based on the belief of Vanguard's founder, John Bogle, that "beating the market is so difficult that people are better off trying to match the market."[2] They accomplish this goal by buying all the stocks in the Standard & Poor's 500 index and holding them forever. Today index funds are extremely popular, but the idea did not immediately catch the fancy of public investors, and the second index fund did not appear until 1984.

In 1993 the modern version of the mutual fund, the exchange traded fund, was brought to the market by State Street Global Advisors and the American Stock Exchange. Standard & Poor's Depository Receipts, nicknamed spiders, attempts to provide investors with the same return as the S&P 500 index.

As the technology bubble was expanding in the final years of the 1990s, the number of funds exploded. According to the Insurance Information Institute, there were more than 8,300 funds in existence at year-end 2001. Today some of those funds have disappeared, but the mutual fund industry remains huge and influential. How well it survives the competition provided by exchange traded funds and the scandals of the early 2000s is an open question.

For those interested in additional history of the mutual fund industry, Jason Zweig wrote an article commemorating the seventy-fifth anniversary of the mutual fund industry in 1999.[3]

HISTORY OF EXCHANGE TRADED FUNDS

It started in 1993 with spiders. Diamonds, qubes, webs, and vipers were added later. These newcomers to the investment world, with strange nicknames, have exploded in popularity, and a little more than one decade after their birth, this new class of securities has grown so rapidly that as of June 2004, investors had poured over $178 billion into them. At that time, there were at least 143 different ETFs, and the number is growing steadily. ETFs are not only American products; they exist overseas as well.

What makes these newcomers so popular? We'll take a look at how this modern version of the traditional mutual fund can be used by a great many (but not all) investors to obtain benefits not available from traditional funds. As you will see, ETFs provide an easy way to get around the high expenses and poor performance associated with the mutual fund industry.

ETFs can be considered as hybrid securities, part mutual fund and part stock. They're not exactly mutual funds, although they invest in a diversified basket of stocks, just as mutual funds do. They're not exactly stocks, but they trade on an exchange, just as stocks do. If these two attributes make you think they resemble closed-end mutual funds, that resemblance is superficial.

ETFs have advantages over traditional mutual funds that make them more attractive to both public and institutional investors. We'll discuss the advantages of ETFs in Chapter 6 after taking a look at traditional mutual funds and how well they serve the needs of today's public investor in Chapter 5. One major advantage of ETFs is that, unlike traditional mutual funds, many are optionable. This means investors can buy and sell put and call options on these ETFs. Optionability is important because you will learn how to incorporate a conservative strategy, called covered call writing, into your investment program to enhance the performance of your investment in the stock market. Part IV presents a detailed discussion of this topic.

CHAPTER 5

Traditional Mutual Funds

The mighty mutual fund industry has been in existence for more than 80 years and has pretty much had things its own way. But because some management companies have behaved questionably, the industry has been scrutinized intensely in recent times.

IS THE MUTUAL FUND INDUSTRY IN TROUBLE WITH THE PUBLIC?

Recent allegations that fund managers allowed some preferred customers to buy shares after trading hours rocked the public's confidence in the industry.[1] Additional charges of favoritism (allowing preferred customers to time the marker by frequently buying and redeeming shares) provided further trouble.[2]

Mutual fund mangers make a fortune.[3] As difficult as it may be to believe that they would jeopardize that income stream for the chance to earn a few extra dollars in fees, some clearly have done so.

The shareholders are the true owners of their mutual funds, and the management teams are charged with the responsibility of managing those funds with the best interests of the shareholders in mind. In fact, they are paid huge fees to do just that. However, it has become obvious that some managers operate the funds with their own bottom lines taking precedence over their responsibilities to their own shareholders. For example,

- Managers earn a yearly fee based on the amount of money under management, so it's to their advantage to attract new capital. But larger funds often have a difficult time trading huge quantities of stock, making managing the portfolio inefficient. That's unfair to the shareholder.
- Management teams do not offer the funds the same discounts offered to their institutional clients.
- Instead of absorbing marketing expenses, managers force shareholders to pay those expenses.
- Reports to the shareholders are supposed to provide accurate commentary on management team performance. A serious conflict of interest arises when managers gloss over their own shortcomings.[4]

Investors might overlook the shortcomings of their mutual funds if they produced superior profits. Thus, the question: Do mutual fund managers outperform the market?

THE FACTS ARE CLEAR: MUTUAL FUNDS UNDERPERFORM

The professionals on Wall Street are in the business of trying to convince public investors they can easily beat the market and that everyone either should open an account with their brokerage firm or give their mutual fund company money to manage. Do you remember those TV ads during the technology bubble of the late 1990s in which one brokerage firm tried to sell the idea that you could a) retire to your own Caribbean island or b) own your own helicopter and airplane if you would only invest with them? They may have been using tongue in cheek humor, but they were selling the idea—mainly to day traders—that the stock market was an easy path to riches. Indeed, many people quit their day jobs to become active day traders. In truth, it was a road to riches for the brokers, but not individual investors.

It's the same for the mutual fund industry. They try to convince public investors that they constantly produce excellent investment results, but the truth is professional money managers do not live up to expectations, and just like individual investors, they are unable to consistently beat the market. Details demonstrating how these professionals fail to perform better than the averages have been adequately covered elsewhere[5] and a summary of the findings is sufficient for our purposes. Using data from Morningstar and commenting on actively managed funds, Baer and Gensler conclude, "it is likely that fewer than 20 percent of all funds actually beat the market over a five-year period, and fewer than 10 percent over a ten-year period."[6]

A similar conclusion was reached by John Bogle, the father of the index mutual fund: "Over the past 25 years, only 32 percent of actively managed equity funds have outpaced this unmanaged index (S&P 500), and no one has ever suggested a methodology by which those few winners could have been selected in advance."[7]

It may not be surprising to find that public investors underperform the market. One might expect that as a group individuals can become too emotionally involved in their decisions and thus not make the best decisions when under pressure. By trading too often, costs increase and profits decline. Surely the expectation is that professionals can do better. After all, that's why they're paid those high salaries, isn't it?

You might ask, "How is it possible that the pros are no better than public investors?" Aren't we constantly being bombarded with advertisements boasting how one fund after another has an outstanding track record? Those funds advertising their performance provide data showing how well they have done over a specified period of time. Don't let those ads fool you. A normal distribution of results means there always are going to be some funds that earn bragging rights. Funds that have performed well in recent times take advantage of that fact and promote themselves to public investors as the solution to all their investment woes.

This leads to the obvious question: If a fund outperforms the market, does that mean its managers are making great investment decisions, and does it mean that you should invest your money in these funds and expect future results to resemble those of the recent past? Alas, when mutual fund managers tell us in their disclaimer that future results cannot be determined by past performance, they are telling the truth. A two-year study was made of 294 diversified mutual funds (funds investing in a wide variety of stocks, i.e. *not* sector funds) that placed advertisements in *Barron's* or *Money Magazine* boasting of their market beating recent performance.[8] The study found that recent past performance bears little relationship to future performance. In fact, on average, the performance of the funds that placed those ads was significantly lower than that of the market averages. The authors concluded the following:

- The funds performed well in the year before the ads appeared, averaging 1.8 percentage points better than the S&P 500.
- Comparing the inflow of capital to control groups, it was determined that the ads were effective, increasing capital inflows by 20 percent over expectations.

- The performance of these funds in the year following their boasting of results was quite poor, with the funds averaging (an almost unbeliev-able) 7.9 percentage points *worse* than the S&P 500 over the next year.
- When mutual funds tell consumers that past performance is no guar-antee of future performance, they are telling the truth.

WHAT ABOUT THE ADVICE OF MARKET GURUS?

There are a great many stock market advisory newsletters available for the public investor. Are they worth the price? Do the gurus who sell these newsletters have the ability to make money for their subscribers? Statisti-cal studies tell us that some must perform well and others must perform poorly. A statement by business tycoon Alfred Cowles III[9] provides the an-swer: "Market advice for a fee is a paradox. Anybody who really knew just wouldn't share his knowledge. Why should he? In five years he could be the richest man in the world. Why pass the word on?"[10]

THE VERDICT, PART II. SHOULD YOU HIRE PROFESSIONAL MONEY MANAGERS?

No. They are unable to deliver market-beating performance and they charge a fee to manage your money.

I believe the most serious problem with mutual funds is their under-performance. Much could be forgiven if the managers were able to provide outstanding investment results for their clients. Many investors don't bother to read the reports issued by management and don't follow the re-sults of their investments closely. They remain unaware that their funds un-derperform the market. Many pay scant attention when selecting mutual funds to buy in the first place. Jim Rogers, well-known author, investor, and global traveler, recently commented on this situation in an interview in *SFO Magazine*: "People send their life savings off to some investment manager they know nothing about. The idea of just blindly putting money into a mu-tual fund is madness."[11]

When they were making piles of money, especially during the soaring market of the 1990s, most investors never gave a thought to the perfor-mance of their funds, and it was easy for the managers to get away with underperformance.

Those few investors who were aware that funds earned less than the market averages probably didn't know what they could do about the situation. But when the market turned sour early in the new millennium, investors had to suffer the indignity of paying excessive management fees in addition to suffering real losses in the value of their holdings. Some investors might shrug their shoulders when learning of management improprieties, but when this behavior is coupled with poor performance, it's reasonable for public investors to seek other venues for their savings.

Investors are savvy enough to understand the ramifications of reports demonstrating the poor performance (and perhaps poor ethics) of mutual fund managers and realize that investing in mutual funds is not the no-brainer decision it once was considered to be. But most investors are unaware of the viable alternative to mutual funds. The mutual fund industry spends enormous amounts of money to see that the public remains unaware of the options. There is a sizable sales force, earning big commissions, selling those funds to the public, and it's not in their interests to educate investors. Thus, customers continue to plow billions of dollars into traditional mutual funds.

As of July 2003, more than 91 million Americans (53 percent of all households) owned shares of mutual funds, according to the Investment Company Institute. The vast majority of actively managed funds do not perform well enough to earn back their fees and loads. As a result,

- Investors pay fees to managers for underperformance.
- The mutual fund business thrives.
- Investors retain their ownership of mutual fund shares for lack of a better choice.

MUTUAL FUND FEES

Up to this point we have seen that mutual funds underperform the averages, charge a management fee for that underperformance, and advertise great results when they achieve them. Is there anything else the public ought to know about the mutual fund industry? Yes. Actively managed funds are expensive to operate. They make many transactions in their attempt to beat the market, driving up trading expenses, and the shareholders pay those expenses. They hire large research teams to back up their investment decisions, and again, the shareholders pick up the tab. Some funds charge a sales commission (load) to buy (and/or sometimes to sell) their shares. All in all, for a public investor, owning shares of a mutual fund is an expensive undertaking.

TABLE 5.1 How Mutual Fund Management Fees Consume Your Account

$10,000 Growing at 11.0 % per Year, but Reduced by Management Fees of 1.25% or 0.25% per Year

Years	No Fee	Fee 1.25%	$ Lost to Fees	Fee 0.25%	$ Lost to Fees
5	$ 16,851	$ 15,923	$ 928	$ 16,662	$ 189
10	$ 28,394	$ 25,354	$ 3,040	$ 27,761	$ 633
15	$ 47,846	$ 40,371	$ 7,475	$ 46,255	$ 1,591
20	$ 80,623	$ 64,282	$16,341	$ 77,068	$ 3,555
25	$135,855	$102,356	$33,499	$128,408	$ 7,446
30	$228,923	$162,981	$65,942	$213,950	$14,973

According to the Investment Company Institute, the average management fee for a fund was 1.25 percent per year in 2002.[12] Let's do a little arithmetic. Over the past 30 years, the S&P 500 index has grown at an annual compounded rate of approximately 11 percent. Assuming your fund exactly matched that average, and assuming it charged 1.25 percent per year to manage those funds, would that really have made a significant difference in the value of your account today? Yes, it would. Table 5.1 shows how much less you would have today for a variety of holding periods, assuming you began with an investment of $10,000.

Note that after 30 years, the account that paid annual fees of 1.25 percent is almost $66,000 lower than the equivalent account that paid no fees. And many funds charge even higher annual fees. For comparison, the table includes a hypothetical account paying an annual fee of only one-quarter of one percent. After 30 years, this account is only $15,000 lower than the account with no fees. If you manage your own portfolio, you can save all those fees. The methods taught in this book will enable you to manage your investments easily, and your chances of outperforming the market will be increased significantly.

If the information available concerning mutual fund management upsets you, it should. But take heart; a satisfactory alternative is available.

If yours is among those mutual fund-owning families, and if none of these reasons for withdrawing your money from mutual fund managers is enough for you, then this book should get you to reconsider. By using exchange traded funds to reduce investment expenses and stock options to hedge your investments, your chances of outperforming the market will be significantly increased.

CHAPTER 6

Exchange Traded Funds

I n an attempt to increase their revenues, the stock and options exchanges are always on the lookout for new financial products to introduce to the investing public. But finding an investment vehicle that attracts a strong following is not an easy task. Many such offerings fall by the wayside, and eventually the exchanges must delist them. One of the amazing new product success stories is the exchange traded fund (ETF). State Street Global Advisors and the American Stock Exchange (Amex) introduced the first ETF to an American audience in January 1993 when *Stan*dard & *P*oor's *d*epositary *r*eceipts (symbol SPDR) were listed for trading on the American Stock Exchange, and the rest is history. Today the Amex remains the leading exchange for ETFs.

Beginning with that single entry, ETFs have exploded in popularity. In the first decade of their existence (through year end 2002), ETFs attracted more than $102 billion of investor capital, according to the Investment Company Institute, and experts forecast continued rapid growth as more public and institutional investors become aware of the availability (and advantages) of investing in these products. By June 2004 the total invested in domestic ETFs increased to more than $178 billion. That's good news as ETFs provide an opportunity for investors everywhere to compile a portfolio that meets the demands of modern portfolio theory (MPT) regarding asset allocation, diversification, and passive investing.

Exchange traded funds have become so popular with the investing public that several constantly rank at the top of the most actively traded list. The most actively traded ETFs are QQQ (nicknamed qubes), SPDR (spiders), and DIA (diamonds); they mimic the performance of the Nasdaq 100, S&P 500, and the Dow Jones Industrial Average (DJIA) respectively.

I consider these ETFs to be the modern mutual fund, although they are not exactly like mutual funds. Each ETF is a collection of stocks that trades as a package, giving shareowners a proportionate investment in each of the stocks in the collection. In this respect, they are exactly like a traditional mutual fund. Technically, the first ETF, SPDR, is a type of investment vehicle called a unit investment trust (UIT). This novel investment vehicle rapidly gained acceptance in the marketplace and paved the way for acceptance of similar products. These unit trusts own a fixed portfolio of stocks. The roster of stocks in the portfolio is changed only when one company is dropped from the index and is replaced by another. In this respect, SPDR is similar to an index mutual fund. But, unlike an index fund, UITs must exactly replicate the index whose performance it is attempting to mimic, and sampling is not allowed. Sampling consists of compiling a portfolio that contains most, but not all, of the stocks in an index. (The goal of sampling is to achieve a very high correlation with the actual index using as few stocks as possible.) Details of the workings of UITs are presented later in this chapter.

ETFs are available to track many of the popular broad-based indexes, such as the Dow Jones Industrial (DIA) and Transportation (IYT) averages, the Nasdaq 100 (QQQ), or the Wilshire 5000 (VTI). In addition, holding company depositary receipts (HOLDRs) and sector spiders are two popular groups of ETFs that invest in specific sectors of the market. They are securities that represent an investment in companies in a specific industry, sector, or group. These, as well as other ETFs with slightly different characteristics, are described in greater detail below.

A SIMPLE ROAD TO A WELL-DIVERSIFIED PORTFOLIO

By buying shares of a broad-based ETF, investors essentially own the market. This accomplishes a major goal for investors: diversification. Of course, owning shares of a mutual fund accomplishes the same goal, so next let's compare ETFs with their cousins, traditional mutual funds. You will see why investing in ETFs is a viable alternative and how ETFs can be used as the centerpiece of your overall investment strategy. Following the precepts of MPT, our investment goals are to increase profit potential while reducing risk.

Owning ETFs is not without market risk. In that respect, ETFs are no different from traditional mutual funds. But the strategy recommended in this book is intended for investors who *want* to own stocks and who want to invest money in the stock markets of the world. If owning stocks is consistent with your investment philosophy, but if you prefer to do so with reduced risk, then you have come to the right place. If owning stocks is not for you, then this strategy is not for you. Except for the most risk-adverse investors, every asset allocation plan that follows the teachings of MPT recommends owning stocks as the heart of an investment plan.

HOW ETFs DIFFER FROM TRADITIONAL MUTUAL FUNDS

You buy shares of traditional open-ended mutual funds by sending money to the management company that operates the fund, or to a salesperson (usually your broker) acting on behalf of the fund. You pay the net asset value of the fund, as calculated from the day's closing prices.[1] If the fund carries a sales charge (load), then the purchase is made after the load is deducted.[2] If you buy a no-load fund, 100 percent of your investment is used to purchase shares. The fund's managers take your money (along with that of other investors) and decide to keep the money in cash, use it to pay shareholders who are redeeming shares, or use it to invest in the market.

Since the price of the shares is determined once per day, at the close of business, if your buy or sell order (or telephoned instruction) arrives during the trading day, you get that day's closing price (net asset value, or NAV). If it arrives after the close, you buy or sell your shares at the following day's NAV. This is a disadvantage if you want to buy or sell shares at the current market price. You must wait to the end of the day to learn the price at which you buy or sell shares.

It's much simpler to trade ETFs, as they trade on an exchange, just like stocks. They can be bought or sold any time the markets are open. Investors benefit by being able to choose when to place a trade, rather than being forced to accept the day's closing price as the entry or exit point.

Thus, advantage number one for ETFs is the ability to trade any time during market hours. As you will see, this is necessary because it allows you to make your ETF investment and immediately use options to hedge that investment.

Because the managers of traditional, actively managed mutual funds are constantly buying and selling shares in their attempt to beat the market, they often realize profits and losses. Profits are passed along to the shareholders in the form of capital gains distributions. Whether you accept those gains in cash or reinvest the gains to buy additional shares, you, the investor, are obligated to pay capital gains taxes on those distributions. You may receive such a capital gains distribution, and with it an income tax liability, even during periods when the fund's NAV is declining (the fund's shareholders are losing money).[3] As a shareholder, you have no say in whether you receive those capital gains. If you receive them, you must pay the taxes.

ETFs are much more tax efficient. Because ETFs seldom change the composition of stocks in the portfolio, they seldom have capital gains to distribute. That's a great benefit to you, the shareholder, as your tax liability is determined by when you buy and sell your shares. In other words, investors who trade ETFs can arrange the timing of their capital gains liability. That is advantage number two.

If you are a mutual fund shareholder interested in following your investments closely and want to know which stocks are contained in your portfolio, you are out of luck. Funds are required to publish their current holdings only two or four times per year. At other times, you cannot learn the makeup of the fund's portfolio.

ETFs, however, are transparent (advantage number three). Investors always know exactly which stocks are owned, since the list of stocks in the ETF portfolio is almost exactly the same as the components of the index. In fact, if the ETF is a UIT, the portfolio is exactly the same. Information describing the composition of the specific indexes is readily available online. (See, for example, www.amex.com.)

Mutual funds allow investors to invest money and buy more shares any time as long as a reasonable minimum investment (often $250) is made. Similarly, withdrawals are allowed at any time. In some cases, an additional fee (back-end load) is charged if shares are sold before a minimum holding period.

A fourth advantage in buying ETFs is that there is no minimum investment. In fact, except for HOLDRs, which require a minimum purchase of 100 shares, you can buy as little as one share. When buying shares of an ETF, the investor pays a brokerage commission, just as when buying stock. For the investor who has several thousand dollars (or more) to invest, the cost of commissions to purchase ETFs becomes insignificant (especially when using a deep-discount broker), when compared with the front-end sales load of traditional mutual funds. No-load funds are another matter, as they can be purchased with zero sales charge and no commission. However, these no-load funds cannot be combined with the options strategy discussed in the following chapters.

For small investors who make periodic investments (perhaps $50 or $100 every month), buying ETFs is not efficient, as the broker's commission may be higher than the sales load.[4]

As noted, managers of traditional mutual funds charge a management fee, regardless of performance. Individual managers may even earn a bonus if their performance is considered to be superior—but they pay no penalty for a very poor performance. Actively managed mutual funds generate huge expenses in the form of commissions and research costs. ETF managers seldom trade, thereby saving their shareholders those expenses. Lower management fees are advantage number five for ETFs.[5]

The discussion that follows assumes you are capable (alone or in consultation with a financial professional) of selecting a mix of ETFs that is suitable for you. For some investors, owning shares of one broad-based index ETF may be sufficient diversification. Other investors will be more comfortable with additional diversification. It's your decision. Chapter 13 presents examples of how to create a portfolio by buying shares of various ETFs.

DIVERSIFICATION CHOICES WHEN BUYING EXCHANGE TRADED FUNDS

Investors can choose to own shares of ETFs that own shares in various types of companies.

Different-Size Companies
• ETFs specializing in the shares of large, midsize, or small companies.

Businesses Located Worldwide
(Some foreign-based ETFs are not available for ownership by Americans.)[6]

• Single-country ETFs own shares of companies located in one specific country.
• Continent-specific ETFs invest in shares of companies located in Europe or Asia.

Specific Industries
• Both sector spiders and HOLDRs invest only in shares of companies doing business in a specific industry, such as semiconductor, retail, or biotechnology.

Specific Indexes
• ETFs track the performance of the following specific indexes from around the world:
  • Broad-based indexes, such as the Nasdaq 100 index, the S&P Mid-Cap 400 index, or the Russell 2000.

- Narrower indexes, such as the Dow Jones Industrial average or the Dow Jones Transportation average.
- Indexes based on foreign stocks that trade in the USA. Baskets of Listed Depository Receipts (BLDRs) own only ADRs (American Depositary Receipts—essentially foreign stocks that trade on American stock exchanges).
- Foreign indexes, such as the MSCI EAFE or the S&P 100 Global index.[7]
- Growth or value components of various indexes
  - Several broad-based indexes have been subdivided into "growth" and "value" sectors. That division is based on the price-to-book ratio of the individual stocks.[8]

DIFFERENT TYPES OF EXCHANGE TRADED FUNDS

From a technical point of view, there are three different legal structures for ETFs. They are:

1. Unit investment trusts
2. Open-ended mutual funds
3. Grantor trusts

Unit Investment Trusts

Investors who buy shares of a UIT are not buying shares of a mutual fund. As far as investors are concerned, the results of the investment are essentially identical with owning a fund, but for those interested in the details, this is the real-world situation (using QQQ as an example):

Unit investment trusts are investment companies that put together a collection of stocks and sell fractional interests to public investors. In this respect, they are identical with open-end mutual funds. One such unit investment trust, named the Nasdaq 100 Trust, Series 1, issues securities called Nasdaq 100 Index Tracking Stock. When you buy or sell QQQ shares, in reality you are trading the tracking stock that represents ownership in the portfolio of stocks held by the trust. That portfolio consists of the proper number of shares of each of the common stocks in the Nasdaq 100 index and is intended to mimic, before expenses, the price and yield performance of that index.

The Nasdaq 100 index does not represent an equal number of shares of each of the 100 companies, but instead is capitalization weighted.[9] (The companies with the greatest market value have the most weight in the index.) Thus, as stock prices change, their proportionate representation in the index undergoes subtle changes. To maintain the correspondence between the securities held by the trust and the stocks in the index, occasionally the securities are adjusted to conform to periodic changes in the relative weights of stocks in the index.

SPDR, the first ETF, is a UIT.

This type of trust is not allowed to sample the index it is attempting to mimic, but must own each of the entities of the index in its exact proportion. But even this requirement has an exception. No fund is allowed to invest more than 25 percent of its assets in the stock of any one company. If the weighting of any one company within an index is above this threshold, a fund statistically optimizes its holdings to reflect the weighting of the index while still adhering to the diversification rule.

UITs are not allowed to reinvest cash dividends. Instead, they deposit any income in a non–interest-bearing account and distribute those dividends (after first deducting the expenses of operating the ETF) periodically to shareholders. This is the major difference between UITs and open-ended mutual funds. For some UITs, the dividends are less than the fund's operating expenses, and no dividends are available to pay to shareholders.

Table 6.1 lists ETFs in this category.[10]

BLDRs Nasdaq sponsors BLDRs, the acronym for baskets of listed depositary receipts. Each BLDR represents ownership of shares of ADRs (American Depositary Receipts, equivalent to shares of foreign companies that trade in the United States) in one of the Bank of New York's ADR indexes. BLDRs operate as UITs.

Table 6.2 lists the four BLDRs.

PowerShares PowerShares are unique ETFs because they seek to replicate the performance (before expenses) of a *managed* group of stocks, specifically the Dynamic OTC Intellidex index and the Dynamic Market Intellidex index. These are different from all the other ETFs discussed so far because the group of stocks owned by the ETF is managed. Those management decisions are made on a quantitative, objective basis. That means

TABLE 6.1 Unit Investment Trusts ETFs

Unit Investment Trusts	Symbol
DIAMONDs	DIA
MidCap SPDRs	MDY
Nasdaq 100 Index Tracking Stock	QQQ
SPDRs	SPY

TABLE 6.2 BLDRs

Exchange Traded Fund	Symbol	Type
BLDRs Emerging Markets 50 ADR Index Fund	ADRE	International
BLDRs Developed Markets 100 ADR Index Fund	ADRD	International
BLDRs Asia 50 ADR Index Fund	ADRA	International, Regional
BLDRs Europe 100 ADR Index Fund	ADRU	International, Regional

Source: www.bldrsfunds.com

there are no investment managers imposing their biases on the stock selection process. There are no costly research departments. This management process is less costly than those of traditional mutual funds, and expenses are capped at 0.60 percent per year—less than traditional mutual funds but at the high end of ETF management fees.

These ETFs operate as UITs and represent one of the newer entries into the ETF marketplace.

Table 6.3 lists the two PowerShares ETFs. The American Stock Exchange recently announced that six new PowerShares have been approved, but a launch date has not been set. Table 6.3 lists these six new products as well.

Open-Ended Mutual Funds

Most ETFs operate as open-ended mutual funds.

iShares iShares are very similar to UITs, but they are not *exactly* the same. The differences are subtle and of no concern to most investors.

TABLE 6.3 PowerShares

Exchange Traded Fund	Symbol	Type
PowerShares Dynamic Market Portfolio	PWC	Broad based
PowerShares Dynamic OTC Portfolio	PWO	Broad based
PowerShares Dynamic Large Cap Growth Intellidex Index	ILH	Large caps
PowerShares Dynamic Large Cap Value Intellidex Index	ILW	Large caps
PowerShares Dynamic Mid Cap Growth Intellidex Index	ILJ	Mid caps
PowerShares Dynamic Mid Cap Value Intellidex Index	ILP	Mid caps
PowerShares Dynamic Small Cap Growth Intellidex Index	ILK	Small caps
PowerShares Dynamic Small Cap Value Intellidex Index	ILZ	Small caps

Source: PowerShares Capital Management

As of publication date, only PWC and PWO are traded.

iShares are open-ended mutual funds and reinvest dividends on a daily
basis. Thus, iShares are fully invested at all times, whereas UITs accumulate a cash position. This is not a significant difference and becomes important only when the market makes a strong move in either direction for
a sustained period. When such a sustained move does occur, the UIT lags
behind the iShares in a strongly rising market, but compensates by declining slightly less rapidly in a falling market.

Table 6.4A lists the broad-based iShares, and Table 6.4B lists the sector
iShares.[11]

TABLE 6.4A   Broad-Based iShares

Exchange Traded Fund	Symbol	Exchange Traded Fund	Symbol
iShares S&P MidCap 400	IJH	iShares Russell 3000	IWV
iShares S&P MidCap 400/		iShares Russell 3000 Value	IWW
BARRA Value	IJJ	iShares Russell 3000 Growth	IWZ
iShares S&P MidCap 400/		iShares Dow Jones US Total	
BARRA Growth	IJK	Market	IYY
iShares S&P SmallCap 600	IJR	iShares Morningstar Large	
iShares S&P SmallCap 600		Core Index	JKD
BARRA Value	IJS	iShares Morningstar Large	
iShares S&P SmallCap 600		Growth Index	JKE
BARRA Growth	IJT	iShares Morningstar Large	
iShares S&P Global 100		Value Index	JKF
Index Fund	IOO	iShares Morningstar Mid Core	
iShares S&P 1500 Index Fund	ISI	Index	JKG
iShares S&P 500 BARRA Value	IVE	iShares Morningstar Mid	
iShares S&P 500	IVV	Growth Index	JKH
iShares S&P 500 BARRA Growth	IVW	iShares Morningstar Mid Value	
iShares Russell 1000	IWB	Index	JKI
iShares Russell 1000 Value	IWD	iShares Morningstar Small	
iShares Russell 1000 Growth	IWF	Core Index	JKJ
iShares Russell 2000	IWM	iShares Morningstar Small	
iShares Russell 2000 Value	IWN	Growth Index	JKK
iShares Russell 2000 Growth	IWO	iShares Morningstar Small	
iShares Russell MidCap Growth		Value Index	JKL
Index Fund	IWP	iShares NYSE 100 Index Fund	NY
iShares Russell MidCap Index		iShares NYSE Composite	
Fund	IWR	Index Fund	NYC
iShares Russell MidCap Value		iShares S&P 100 Index Fund	OEF
Index Fund	IWS		

Source: Barclays Global Investors

TABLE 6.4B   Sector iShares

Exchange Traded Fund	Symbol	Exchange Traded Fund	Symbol
iShares Nasdaq Biotechnology	IBB	iShares Dow Jones US Consumer Cyclical	IYC
iShares Cohen & Steers Realty Majors	ICF	iShares Dow Jones US Energy	IYE
iShares Dow Jones US Utilities	IDU	iShares Dow Jones US Financial Sector	IYF
iShares Goldman Sachs Natural Resources	IGE	iShares Dow Jones US Financial Services	IYG
iShares Goldman Sachs Technology	IGM	iShares Dow Jones US Healthcare	IYH
iShares Goldman Sachs Networking	IGN	iShares Dow Jones US Industrial	IYJ
iShares Goldman Sachs Software	IGV	iShares Dow Jones US Consumer Non-Cyclical	IYK
iShares Goldman Sachs Semiconductor	IGW	iShares Dow Jones US Basic Materials	IYM
iShares S&P Global Energy Sector	IXC	iShares Dow Jones US Real Estate	IYR
iShares S&P Global Financial Sector	IXG	iShares Dow Jones Transportation Average Index Fund	IYT
iShares S&P Global Healthcare Sector	IXJ	iShares Dow Jones US Technology	IYW
iShares S&P Global Information Technology Sector	IXN	iShares Dow Jones US Telecommunications	IYZ
iShares S&P Global Telecommunications Sector	IXP		

Source: Barclays Global Investors

International ETFs   All foreign-country ETFs operate as iShares (open-ended mutual funds). These ETFs are mostly based on stocks of one foreign country, but a few represent broad-based indexes. Table 6.5 presents the list of international ETFs.

VIPERs   Vanguard index participation receipts (VIPERs) are ETF versions of different Vanguard index funds and are structured as open-ended funds. Table 6.6 lists the VIPERs.

Sector SPDRS   ETFs are available to track many of the popular broad-based indexes. For those investors who prefer to concentrate their holdings in a much narrower group of companies, a group of ETFs is available that tracks the performance of stocks in each of several specific industries.

A group of ETFs that owns shares in only one specific sector of the market is known as sector SPDRs. These ETFs operate as open-ended mutual funds.

TABLE 6.5 International ETFs

Exchange Traded Fund	Symbol	Exchange Traded Fund	Symbol
iShares MSCI-Emerging Markets	EEM	iShares MSCI-Pacific Ex-Japan	EPP
iShares MSCI-Australia	EWA	iShares MSCI-Singapore	EWS
iShares MSCI-Austria	EWO	iShares MSCI-South Africa	EZA
iShares MSCI-Belgium	EWK	iShares MSCI-South Korea	EWY
iShares MSCI-Brazil	EWZ	iShares MSCI-Spain	EWP
iShares MSCI-Canada	EWC	iShares MSCI-Sweden	EWD
iShares MSCI-EAFE	EFA	iShares MSCI-Switzerland	EWL
iShares MSCI-EMU	EZU	iShares MSCI-Taiwan	EWT
iShares MSCI-France	EWQ	iShares MSCI-U.K.	EWU
iShares MSCI-Germany	EWG	iShares S&P Europe 350	IEV
iShares MSCI-Hong Kong	EWH	iShares S&P Latin America 40	ILF
iShares MSCI-Italy	EWI	iShares S&P/TOPIX 150	ITF
iShares MSCI-Japan	EWJ	Fresco DJ Stoxx 50 Index	FEU
iShares MSCI-Malaysia	EWM	Fresco DT Stoxx 50 Euro Index	FEZ
iShares MSCI-Mexico	EWW	streetTracks DJ Global Titans	
iShares MSCI-Netherlands	EWN	Index Fund	DGT

Source: American Stock Exchange

TABLE 6.6 VIPERs

VIPER	Symbol
Vanguard Materials VIPERs	VAW
Vanguard Small-Cap VIPERs	VB
Vanguard Small-Cap Growth VIPERs	VBK
Vanguard Small-Cap Value VIPERs	VBR
Vanguard Consumer Discretionary VIPERs	VCR
Vanguard Consumer Staples VIPERs	VDC
Vanguard Financial VIPERs	VFH
Vanguard Information Technology VIPERs	VGT
Vanguard Health Care VIPERs	VHT
Vanguard Mid-Cap VIPERs	VO
Vanguard Utilities VIPERs	VPU
Vanguard Total Stock Market VIPERs	VTI
Vanguard Value VIPERs	VTV
Vanguard Growth VIPERs	VUG
Vanguard Large-Cap VIPERs	VV
Vanguard Extended Market VIPERs	VXF

Source: American Stock Exchange

TABLE 6.7 Sector SPDRs

Exchange Traded Fund	Symbol
streetTRACKS Morgan Stanley Technology Index Fund	MTK
streetTRACKS Wilshire REIT Index Fund	RWR
Select Sector SPDR-Materials	XLB
Select Sector SPDR-Energy	XLE
Select Sector SPDR-Financial	XLF
Select Sector SPDR-Industrial	XLI
Select Sector SPDR-Technology	XLK
Select Sector SPDR-Consumer Staples	XLP
Select Sector SPDR-Utilities	XLU
Select Sector SPDR-Health Care	XLV
Select Sector SPDR-Consumer Discretionary	XLY

Source: American Stock Exchange

Table 6.7 lists the sector SPDRs.

Grantor Trusts

Grantor trusts are the least common type of ETF and are represented by HOLDRs.

HOLDRs A group of ETFs collectively known as HOLDRs—an acronym standing for holding company depositary receipts (pronounced "holders")—represent ownership in the common stock, or ADRs of specified companies in a particular industry, sector, or group.

HOLDRs are trust-issued receipts (also known as grantor trusts). There are two big differences between grantor trusts and the other types of ETFs. The first is that grantor trusts represent the investor's undivided beneficial ownership in the underlying securities, and the trust maintains the underlying shares on behalf of the investor. Thus, any corporate action undertaken by an underlying security, such as a spin-off or merger, is treated as if the investor owned the underlying shares directly. Shareholders also retain voting rights on the underlying stocks.

The second big difference is that HOLDRs represent a true buy-and-hold philosophy because they are never rebalanced. Thus, over time, HOLDRs can become a nuisance to own if it becomes overweighed in one specific stock (losing the advantages of diversification) or contains minute quantities of shares resulting from spin-offs. This is not a reason to avoid

TABLE 6.8 HOLDRs

Exchange Traded Fund	Symbol	Exchange Traded Fund	Symbol
Biotech HOLDRs	BBH	Pharmaceutical HOLDRs	PPH
Broadband HOLDRs	BDH	Regional Bank HOLDRs	RKH
B2B Internet HOLDRs	BHH	Retail HOLDRs	RTH
Europe 2001 HOLDRs	EKH	Semiconductor HOLDRs	SMH
Internet HOLDRs	HHH	Software HOLDRs	SWH
Internet Architecture HOLDRs	IAH	Telebras HOLDRs	TBH
Internet Infrastructure HOLDRs	IIH	Telecom HOLDRs	TTH
Market 2000+ HOLDRs	MKH	Utilities HOLDRs	UTH
Oil Service HOLDRs	OIH	Wireless HOLDRs	WMH

Source: American Stock Exchange

HOLDRs, but it makes holding them less convenient for investors who want to know exactly what they own. To avoid the problems associated with owning HOLDRs, an investor can choose to own shares of a sector SPDR (if the appropriate one exists).

Merrill Lynch issued the first of the HOLDRs in 1998.[12]

Table 6.8 lists all HOLDRs.

Miscellaneous ETFs

A few ETFs that operate as open-ended mutual funds but do not fit into any particular category are listed in Table 6.9 as miscellaneous ETFs.

TABLE 6.9 Miscellaneous ETFs

Exchange Traded Fund	Symbol
StreetTracks Global Titans Index Fund	DGT
StreetTracks US Small Cap Growth Index Fund	DSG
StreetTracks US Small Cap Value Index Fund	DSV
StreetTracks US Large Cap Growth Index Fund	ELG
StreetTracks US Large Cap Value Index Fund	ELV
Fidelity Nasdaq Composite Fund	ONEQ
Rydex S&P 500 Equal Weight Index Fund	RSP

Source: American Stock Exchange

Nonequity ETFs

So far we have covered only these ETFs that invest in stocks. As mentioned earlier, this book is concerned only with the portion of your investments allocated to equities, but for the sake of completeness, let's take a brief look at other types of ETFs available to the investing public.

Closed-End ETFs

A closed-end ETF issues a fixed number of shares when it undergoes an initial public offering (IPO). Investors who buy or sell the shares do so directly on a stock exchange (just like stocks), not from the issuer of the fund. The market price of a closed-end ETF typically resembles the net asset value of the fund, but it also may trade at a premium or a discount to that value, based on supply and demand. No new shares are issued.

Closed-end ETFs differ from other ETFs because they can use leverage to enhance returns. They accomplish this by borrowing capital or by issuing preferred shares.

Currently more than 500 closed-end ETFs trade on the stock exchanges. One good source of information about these funds is ETF Connect, run by Nuveen Investments (see www.etfconnect.com). These funds are primarily fixed income ETFs and invest in debt instruments (bonds). A hybrid ETF—the Nuveen Diversified Dividend and Income Fund (symbol JDD)—began trading in September 2003. It invests in shares of dividend-paying equities, real estate investment trusts (REITs), and two types of debt instruments.

The modern mutual fund, or ETF, is going to be claiming an ever-increasing share of the investment assets of both public and institutional investors. Originality and imagination are constantly in play, and investors undoubtedly will be able to select from funds based on premises not yet imagined. One day there may even be an ETF that invests only in stocks that have covered call options written on them.

SUMMARY

Historically, there have been two major advantages to owning traditional mutual funds: (1) professional management; and (2) the ease of owning a well-diversified portfolio of stocks. By owning ETFs, investors gain the advantages outlined in this chapter without the disadvantages of owning traditional funds.

Traditional mutual funds greatly outnumber ETFs, and spend huge amounts on advertising. Many salespeople push traditional funds. Still, the educated investor (you, the reader) can ignore all the sales pressure and make the intelligent choice of investing in ETFs. There is a sufficient variety of ETFs to meet the needs of almost any investor who wants to own a diversified portfolio of stocks.

Let's take a break from ETFs and learn about stock options and how to use them to achieve enhanced profit potential and reduced risk. Then we'll combine our knowledge of ETFs and options to define a risk-reducing, income-enhancing strategy suitable for the vast majority of those who invest in the stock market.

PART III

Options

CHAPTER 7

What Is an Option and How Does an Option Work?

I f you are unfamiliar with options, you will not be left behind. We'll begin our discussion with the most basic concepts of options, including a discussion of what an option is and how an option works. You'll see that you are already familiar with the concept of options and use them in your everyday lives—even if you are not currently aware that you are doing so. After the options tutorial, you will learn two practical option strategies you can use to enhance profits and reduce risk.

To adopt the overall investment methodology emphasized in this book, it's important to have a good understanding of how options work because this versatile investment tool plays a crucial role in the investment process. The teachings of modern portfolio theory are compatible with using options in the prescribed manner, because options are an investment tool that further increases anticipated returns while reducing both portfolio volatility and risk. The story of options offered here is not meant to be complete. Instead the goal is to provide enough information for you to understand how options work and how you can use them intelligently to achieve your investment goals. Many texts devoted to options are available for readers who want a more complete options education.[1]

We'll begin by taking a brief look at what options are and how they work.

Readers who are confident they understand how to use options may prefer to skip ahead to Chapter 10.

TERMINOLOGY

Participants in the options universe use a language of their own, and it's important to understand some of the lingo. As the most important terms are introduced, each is italicized. These terms are also included in the glossary.

WHAT IS AN OPTION?

An *option* is a contract describing the terms of an agreement between two parties: the buyer of the option: contract and the seller. The price paid by the buyer to the seller is known as the *premium*.

There are two types of options: puts and calls. A *call* option gives its owner the right to <u>buy</u>, and a *put* option gives its owner the right to <u>sell</u>

- a specified item, called the *underlying* asset. For our purposes, the asset is 100 shares of a specified stock (or ETF).
- at a specified price, called the *strike price*.
- for a specified period of time. An option has an *expiration* date.

Thus:

- A call option gives its owner the right to buy 100 shares of the underlying stock at the strike price any time before the option expires.
- A put option gives its owner the right to sell 100 shares of the underlying stock at the strike price any time before the option expires.

That's all there is to an option. Options may be used in either simple or complex strategies, but the concept of an option is not complicated.

You probably have heard about someone taking an option to buy a piece of property. All that means is that the option holder has paid some money and has the exclusive right, for a limited amount of time, to buy the property for an agreed-on price. The property owner cannot sell to anyone else, but must wait until the option holder makes the decision to buy or not to buy. Once the option expires, the property owner is free to sell to anyone. Despite stories to the contrary, options are easy to understand.

HOW DOES AN OPTION WORK?

In return for paying the premium, the option owner gains certain *rights*. In return for receiving the premium, the seller accepts certain *obligations*.

Rights of an Option Owner

The buyer of the option has the right to *exercise* the option any time, as long as it is before the option expires. When exercising, the option owner is doing what the contract allows. The call exerciser buys 100 shares of the underlying stock at the strike price. The put exerciser sells 100 shares of the underlying stock at the strike price.

Obligations of an Option Writer

The seller (writer) of a call option accepts the obligation to sell the underlying stock at the strike price—but only if the option owner chooses to exercise before the option expires.

The seller of a put option accepts the obligation to buy the underlying stock at the strike price—but only if the option owner elects to exercise before the option expires.

How do you learn that the option owner has exercised the option if you are the option writer? Your broker informs you. For details of how this works, see the boxed text.

Exercise/Assignment Process

The Options Clearing Corporation (OCC) maintains a listing of every account that owns, or has sold, each option that trades on any of the (currently six) options exchanges in this country. When an investor exercises an option, the OCC first verifies that this person really owns the option and has the right to exercise it. Then it randomly selects one account (from among the many) that currently has a short position in that specific option and assigns that account an *exercise notice*. That notice (called an *assignment*) informs the account holder that the option owner has exercised the option and that the account holder is obligated to honor the conditions of the option contract. No action is required on the part of the person who has been assigned an exercise notice, as the transaction is automatic. For example, the call writer's broker credits the account with cash (100 times the strike price) and 100 shares of stock are removed from the account, just as if the account holder sold the stock in the usual manner. If the account holder does not own the shares, then the stock is *sold short*.[2]

Similarly, when a put writer is assigned an exercise notice, 100 shares of stock are deposited into the put writer's account and the cash to pay for those 100 shares of stock is removed.

Note: Because the option owner has the right to exercise any time before the option expires, the option writer never knows if, or when, the option owner is going to exercise those rights. That choice remains at the sole discretion of the option owner. Thus, don't be surprised if occasionally you are assigned an exercise notice before expiration. Most of the time, though, the decision to exercise is made at the last possible moment, when the stock market closes on *expiration day* (the third Friday of the expiration month[3]). When that happens, the person assigned an exercise notice learns about the assignment before the market opens for trading on the following Monday morning. (If you have an online brokerage account, you probably can learn about the assignment on Sunday.)

Technically, options expire on the Saturday morning following the third Friday of the expiration month. But the deadline for deciding whether to exercise an option is shortly after the market closes on the third Friday. It is customary to refer to the third Friday as expiration day for the options. Adopting that custom in this book, we'll refer to expiration day as the third Friday of the month.

Again, that's all there is to it. Options are neither complicated nor difficult to understand. In fact, you probably have used options many times.

OPTIONS ARE PART OF YOUR EVERYDAY ROUTINE

The rain check you receive from a grocery (or other retail) store is a call option. The discount coupons you clip from the daily newspapers are call options. The insurance policy you own on your home, car, or life are put options. Let's see why.

When you attempt to buy an advertised special at a retail store, sometimes the store is sold out and you are unable to buy the item. When that happens, it is customary for the store to issue a rain check to you. That rain check gives you the right to return to the store to buy a specific item (the underlying asset) at a special sale price (the strike price). The rain check is good for a limited period of time—until the expiration date. Thus you have the right—but not the obligation—to return to the store to buy the sale item at the sale price for a limited amount of time. You don't have to use the rain check; it's your choice. The rain check grants its owner the identical rights as the owner of a call option, and, thus, your rain check is a call option. You can simply throw the rain check in the trash. Alternatively, you can exercise your rights to buy the sale item at the sale price. When you notify the sales clerk at the retail store that you want to buy the item, you are doing two things: (1) you are exercising your rights as the option owner, and (2) you are assigning the store owner an exercise notice. That's exactly the way a stock option works. When you own a stock option, you have the right to buy 100 shares at the strike price, but you are under no obligation to do so.

A discount coupon works in the same way. It allows you to buy (for example) a one-topping pizza for $3 off the regular price for a limited amount of time. Again, it's your choice. You can exercise your option to buy the pizza at the discounted price, or you can discard it.

An insurance policy is similar to a put option because it gives you the right to sell (for example) your destroyed car or stolen necklace to the insurance company at the strike price (the amount for which it is insured). In return for accepting the premium you paid, the insurance company accepts the obligation to buy the specified item. Of course, there are conditions. You cannot simply force the insurance company to buy your car or necklace—the items must be either lost or damaged. Thus, these insurance policies are not as flexible as stock options. When you own a stock option, you can exercise your rights at any time for any reason.

Stock options can be your friends. They can be used as part of a conservative investment plan that allows you to enhance the performance of your stock market portfolio and reduce risk at the same time. Unfortunately, options also can be used for risky propositions. Far too many options novices learn to use options only as tools for speculation. That's why so many people have negative feelings when they hear the word "options." They hear about someone who lost a pile of money trading options and immediately conclude that options are only for gamblers. No one ever explains that the poor choice of an options strategy caused the loss. The blame is always placed on options themselves. One purpose of this book is to dispel the notion that options are dangerous investment tools.

We'll take a closer look at specific, conservative strategies that show you how to use options in Chapters 10 and 11.

CHAPTER 8

More Options Basics

When the Chicago Board Options Exchange (CBOE) first listed call options on individual stocks in April 1973, it revolutionized the way options were traded. Previously, trading in puts and calls was haphazard, with brokers and dealers advertising specific options for sale in the *Wall Street Journal*. These options had random exercise dates and strike prices. Investors who bought one of those options had almost no hope of finding a buyer, if they wanted to sell the option before expiration. The listing of options at the CBOE changed everything.

With the advent of trading on an exchange, options became standardized (see boxed text), and customers were able to buy and sell options as easily as stock. Trading options on an exchange began with the listing of call options on 16 stocks at the Chicago Board Options Exchange. Today there are six options exchanges in the United States and others around the world.[1] Options are available on thousands of different stocks and a multitude of indexes.

Standardization of Options

When options began trading on an exchange in 1973, they were offered with specific and predictable strike prices and expiration dates. Expiration for all listed equity options was established as the Saturday morning following the third Friday of the month, and the last day of trading for each option is the third Friday.

Strike prices for each stock originally were offered at three-month intervals. For example, IBM's options offered expirations in the nearest three of the months of a quarterly cycle: January, April, July, or October. To offer a variety of expiration dates to options traders, other stocks had options expiring on the February cycle (February, May, August, November). Later, stocks were listed with options expiring in the last remaining quarterly cycle: March, June, September, and December.

Even later it was recognized that investors prefer to trade options with shorter lifetimes. Today each underlying stock offers options with at least *four* different expirations: the nearest two months, plus two additional months from the stock's original quarterly expiration cycle. (Some of the more actively traded stocks also list *LEAPS*, or *long-term equity anticipation series*. These are longer-term options, expiring in January, up to three years in the future.)

Example: Assume it is early August 2005.

IBM options expire in August, September, and October 2005, and January 2006.

- August and September are the next two months
- October and January are the next two months of the quarterly cycle

IBM LEAPS expire in January 2007 and January 2008.

When there are only eight months remaining in the lifetime of the January 2007 LEAPS option, it becomes a "regular" IBM option, and a new LEAPS option, expiring in January 2009 is listed.

Strike prices are offered according to a fixed, but flexible, schedule:

- Options are offered with strike prices every $2\frac{1}{2}$ points from 5 through 25. Some less volatile stocks extend this range to $32\frac{1}{2}$.
- Stocks priced from 30 through 200 have strike prices every 5 points.
- When the stock price is above 200, strike prices are 10 points apart.
- A pilot program was initiated recently offering strike prices every 1 point for some stocks priced under $20 per share.[2]

FORMAT USED TO DESCRIBE AN OPTION

When a customer places an order to buy or sell an option, there must be a uniform method of describing that option so everyone involved in the transaction understands which specific option is being traded. Fortunately that's easy to accomplish. To describe an option accurately, four pieces of information are required:

1. Underlying stock symbol
2. Strike price
3. Type of option (put or call)
4. Expiration date

Options trade on a number of exchanges around the world, and each uses the same format to describe an option.

Format Example 1:   GE Jun 35 call

This option represents an option to buy (call option) 100 shares of GE (underlying stock) at $35 per share (strike price) any time before the option expires on the third Friday of June.

Each GE Jun 35 call option is identical to every other GE Jun 35 call option. That means the options are *fungible*. Thus, if you sell an option and want to repurchase it at a later date, it is not necessary to find the person to whom you sold the option originally. You can close your position simply by buying any GE Jun 35 call from anyone, for all such options are the same.

Format Example 2:   IBM Oct 95 put

This represents an option to sell (put) 100 shares of IBM at $95 per share any time before the option expires on the third Friday of October.

ADDITIONAL OPTIONS TERMINOLOGY

It's necessary to introduce a few new terms. *In the money* (ITM), *at the money* (ATM), and *out of the money* (OTM) are terms used to compare the strike price of an option with the price of the underlying stock. The terms themselves give clues to their meanings.

In-the-Money Options

A call option is in the money when the stock price is higher than the strike price of the option. When this occurs, the option owner has the right to buy stock (by exercising the option) at a discount to the real-world price. In other words, the option allows the call owner to purchase a bargain. The term used to describe this situation is in the money.

A put option is in the money when the stock price is lower than the strike price of the option. When this occurs, the owner of the put option has the right to sell stock at a high, or premium, price.

When an option is in the money, it has an *intrinsic value*. The intrinsic value equals the amount by which an option is in the money.

Examples

WXY is $34 per share.

- WXY Jul 30 call is in the money. It has an intrinsic value of 4 points, or $400.
- WXY Nov 35 put is in the money, with an intrinsic value of $100.

Options Deep and Far

There is no exact definition for the term "far out of the money," but it is used when the option is more than one strike price out of the money *and* unlikely to be in the money before expiration.

Example: A stock that is not very volatile is currently $42 per share. Call options with a strike price of 50 (and above) are considered to be far out of the money. Similarly, put options with strike prices of 35 and lower are also considered to be far out of the money. Since this stock is not very volatile, there is little chance it can move sufficiently for the option to go in the money before it expires.

However, if this $42 stock is very volatile and frequently undergoes large price changes, even a call option with a strike price of 60 may not be thought of as being far out of the money. There is a reasonable chance the stock could trade above the strike price if there are at least a few weeks remaining before expiration.

The opposite of a far-out-of-the-money option is a *deep-in-the-money* option. Again, there is no exact definition, but the term is used for an option that is more than one strike price in the money *and* unlikely to be out of the money when expiration day arrives.

XYZ is $32.75.

- The XYZ Oct 30 call is in the money. It has an intrinsic value of $275.
- The XYZ Jan 50 put is in the money, (it is deep in the money; see Options Deep and Far box) with an intrinsic value of $1,725.

When expiration day arrives, an in-the-money option has value and is either sold or exercised.

At-the-Money Options

An option is at the money when the strike price of the option is the same as the stock price. At-the-money options have no intrinsic value. Sometimes the definition is loosened to include options that are almost at the money. For example, an option with a strike price of 35 often is referred to as being at the money when the stock is trading at $35.05.

When expiration day arrives, at-the-money options are usually allowed to *expire worthless*. However, because the option owner may have a good reason to do so, the option is sometimes exercised.[3]

Out-of-the-Money Options

A call option is out of the money when the strike price of the option is higher than the stock price. A put option is out of the money when the strike price of the option is lower than the stock price.

An out-of-the-money option has no intrinsic value.

Examples

ABCD is $8.75.

- The Mar 10 call is out of the money.
- The Feb 7½ put is out of the money.

MNOP is currently $41 per share.

- The June 60 put is out of the money. In fact, it is far out of the money. (See Options Deep and Far box.)
- The Aug 40 put is out of the money

When expiration day arrives, an out-of-the-money option has no value and is allowed to expire worthless.

Investors who buy out-of-the-money options hope the underlying stock moves in the appropriate direction (higher for calls and lower for puts) and the option becomes in the money. For example, if JKL is trading at $43 per share, the JKL Dec 45 call is out of the money. However, if the stock price rises above 45, the call becomes in the money.

When using these terms (in, at, or out of the money), the expiration month is immaterial, as the only consideration is the comparison of the strike price with the stock price.

INTRINSIC VALUE AND TIME VALUE

The option premium (price) is composed of two parts: *intrinsic value* and *time value.*

The intrinsic value of an option is the amount by which the option is in the money. Another way to look at the intrinsic value of an option is to say it is equal to the cash you can collect (ignoring trading expenses) by exercising the option and immediately selling (if the option is a call) or buying (if the option is a put) the underlying stock in the open market.

The easiest way to understand the time value of an option is to say that it represents the rest of the value of an option. That is, time value is the portion of the option price that is *not* intrinsic value. If an option has no intrinsic value, then the entire price of an option is its time value. *The time value of the option equals the amount of profit you can earn when writing that option.*

Examples

XYZ is $42 per share.

The XYZ Oct 40 call is trading at $3.40.

- The Oct 40 call has an intrinsic value of $2 per share, or $200.
- Thus, the time value of the option is $1.40, or $140.

The XYZ Jan 45 put is trading at $3.80.

- The intrinsic value is $300
- Thus, the time value is $80

The time value of an option represents the opportunity value, and it's the amount buyers are willing to pay to acquire the rights that go with owning an option. The option buyer is hoping the option will increase in value as a result of a change in the price of the underlying stock. If that happens, the option buyer can earn a profit. The opportunity to collect that future profit is the driving force behind an investor's decision to buy an option. We'll discuss why investors buy options in Chapter 9.

The opportunity value for the buyer also represents the option seller's potential profit.

The important factors that contribute to time value are:

- *Time.* The more time in the life of an option, the more the option is worth, as there is more opportunity for the underlying stock to move in the "correct" direction.
- *Volatility.* The underlying stock changes price on a daily basis. More volatile stocks undergo larger price changes, increasing the profit possibilities for the option owner. Thus, the more volatile a stock,
  - the more buyers are willing to pay for its options.
  - the more sellers demand to sell its options.
  - the more its options are worth.

CHOOSING AN OPTION TO TRADE

Chapter 9 discusses buying or selling options. Here let's take a look at which specific options are available for trading. If you are interested in trading the options on a specific stock (note that options are not available for every stock), you always have a choice. The selection of available options is not random. Instead, a protocol determines which strike prices and which expirations are listed for trading for each underlying stock.

Strike Prices

On the Monday following an options expiration, in addition to the options already trading, new options are listed. A minimum of two strike prices is made available for each stock (more volatile stocks offer a wider selection of strike prices)—one above and one below the current stock price. Thus, customers always can always buy or sell an in-the-money call or put and an out-of-the-money call or put. If the stock price is near a strike price, then three new strike prices are added—one above, one below, and one near the stock price.

As time passes and the price of the stock changes, new strike prices are added. When the stock price reaches an existing strike price, the next strike price is listed for trading (usually the next day).

Example

LMN has options with strike prices of 35, 40, and 45. If the stock trades as high as 45, the 50 calls and 50 puts are listed the following day. If the stock trades as low as 35, then the 30 calls and 30 puts are listed the following day.

Expiration Months

On the Monday following expiration, one new expiration month is added to replace the recently expired options, such that there are always options with at least four different expiration months available for trading for each underlying stock. Most of the more actively traded stocks also have LEAPS.

When the price of the underlying stock changes sufficiently to cause new options to be listed for trading, those options are listed for each month (LEAPS are sometimes excluded), with one exception: The nearest expiration month is not included, unless there are at least 30 days remaining before expiration.[4]

VALUE OF TIME IN THE PRICE OF AN OPTION

Now that you understand there is a choice of options from which you can choose, let's take a look at a typical out-of-the-money call option. Assume it's the first week of June and DEF is $19 per share. A bullish investor is considering buying a call option with a strike price of 20 and finds four choices:

1. DEF Jun 20 call can be bought for $0.20 (20 cents per share, $20 per contract).
2. DEF Jul 20 call can be bought for $0.50.
3. DEF Sep 20 call can be bought for $0.95.
4. DEF Dec 20 call can be bought for $1.25.

If you are new to the world of options, you may wonder why these options are priced differently. After all, each gives its owner the right to buy 100 shares of DEF at $20 per share. This difference is the amount of time remaining before the option expires. The more time remaining, the more an option is worth. That makes sense because additional time gives the underlying stock a greater opportunity to make a move favorable to the option owner (who then can sell the option for a profit). The option buyer is willing to pay extra for that additional time. Of course, more time also gives the stock an opportunity to make a move unfavorable to the option owner. But to the option buyer, only a favorable move is of importance.[5]

The same principle applies to all options, whether they are out of the money, at the money, or in the money. The more time remaining until expiration, the more an option is worth. (See box on next page.)

When Time Is Not Money

There are some exceptions to the rule that more time increases the value of an option, but for our purposes they can be ignored. For the purist who wants to know the exceptions, here are two:

1. When a stock pays a large enough dividend, it is often advantageous for the call owner to exercise a deep-in-the-money call option the day *before* the stock goes ex dividend. (Without the dividend. To receive the dividend you must own shares before the date.) By doing so, the call owner becomes the stockowner and is entitled to receive the dividend. If the dividend is high enough (we'll omit the other factors to consider to keep the discussion simple), options with a month or two remaining before expiration sometimes are exercised for the dividend. Thus, each option (with the same strike price) that is subject to being exercised for the dividend trades at the same price, and the extra time remaining in the lifetime of the option loses its value.

   After the ex-dividend date, time value is reattached to options that have a more distant expiration date (as there is no longer any reason to exercise the option early), and the customary situation (more time equals a higher option price) returns.

2. If a put option is deep in the money, it is often a good strategy to exercise it, even if there is time remaining before expiration. A put owner who also owns stock often pays interest on the cash used to buy stock. By exercising the put, the stock can be sold, eliminating the payment of interest. This exercise of deep-in-the-money put options is common when interest rates are high (and borrowing cash is expensive). When it is mathematically attractive to exercise these puts, they trade at their intrinsic values and lose any remaining time premium.

In the next chapter we'll look at why investors buy or sell options.

CHAPTER 9

Why Investors Buy and Sell Options

The term "option" is derived from the Greek word for choice. That's appropriate, because an option owner has choices to make. Before examining those choices and how one goes about making the appropriate decision, let's consider why investors buy options in the first place and what they hope to achieve. Then we'll look at why some investors prefer to sell options and what motivates them.

Options are very versatile investment tools and provide benefits to both buyers and sellers. In this and the next two chapters, you'll gain an understanding of why the options markets exist and why options play such an important role in today's investment world.

Consider a stock (WXY) currently trading at $34 per share. If you want to own the stock and are willing to pay that price, you can buy the shares. But instead of buying stock, you can buy a call option, granting you the right to buy the stock. For example, you could buy a call option giving you the right to buy 100 shares at $35 per share any time during the next three months.

If you never thought about options before, you might wonder why anyone would be willing to pay cash for the right to buy 100 shares of stock at $35 at some time in the future when the stock can be bought today at a lower price ($34). You might conclude that it's far better to buy stock now rather than pay someone a cash premium for the "privilege" of paying a higher price for that same stock in the future. To understand why it's reasonable for both buyers and sellers of options to exist, let's take a closer look.

WHY WOULD ANYONE BUY A CALL OPTION?

Let's look at an example of how a real option is valued in the marketplace. Assume:

- It's the middle of January, and April expiration is 13 weeks in the future.
- WXY stock is currently trading at $34 per share.
- WXY April 35 call is trading at $2.
  - The option premium is $2 (per share, or $200 per option contract).

An Investor Wants to Own a Long Position in WXY

Let's assume you're a traditional investor who wants to own 100 shares of WXY. The usual method is to purchase 100 shares of stock at a cost of $3,400. If the stock price goes higher, you make money. If it goes lower, you lose money. Let's assume you buy your 100 shares of stock and it's now 3 months later.

Investment Results for the Stockholder

If the stock increases in value to $40 per share, you have a profit of $600. That's a return of 17.6 percent on your $3,400 investment. If the stock does even better and runs to $50, your profit is $1,600 (47.0 percent).

If the stock is unchanged and is still trading near $34 per share, you have neither profit nor loss.

If you are unlucky and the stock drops to $30, your loss is $400, or 11.8 percent of your investment. If the bottom falls out from under this stock and it drops to $20, your loss is $1,400, or 41.2 percent of your investment.

These results are straightforward. When you own an asset, you either make or lose money depending on how that asset is valued at some time in the future.

Results When Owning Options

Options offer an investment alternative. Instead of buying stock, you can gain control of those same 100 shares by buying a call option. The reason you have "control" of those 100 shares is that you, the owner of a call option, can exercise your option to buy those 100 shares any time you choose (as long as it's before the option expires). That places you, the option owner, in position to profit if the stock increases in value.

Using the same example as above, let's look at the results when you buy one WXY Apr 35 call, at a cost of $200. This option gives you the right (expiring in 13 weeks) to buy 100 shares of WXY at $35 per share. *Note:* Much less cash is required ($200 vs. $3,400). This is one of the major attractions for those who buy options. Sometimes investors do not have enough cash to buy 100 shares and can gain control of the shares with a much smaller amount of money. (This is an example of using leverage—less money is invested to control the same amount of stock.)

Let's examine the five results discussed above from the perspective of the option owner. Assume three months pass. It's expiration day, or the third Friday of April.

If the stock rises to $40, the Apr 35 call is worth $500 (see box below).

Since you paid $200 for the option, your profit is $300, or a 150 percent return on your investment. This illustrates the second reason why investors buy options: It's possible to earn a large percentage return on a small investment.

If the stock rallies all the way to $50, the option is worth $1,500 (i.e., it's in the money by 15 points and has an intrinsic value of $1,500). That's a profit of $1,300, or 650 percent, on your $200 investment.

If the stock remains unchanged at $34, then the option is worthless (see box on next page), and you lose your entire investment of $200. This is one of the major disadvantages of buying an option. If the stock does not move as you hoped, you can lose your entire investment.

If the stock drops to $30 or $20 (the sample prices used when discussing owning stock), the option is also worthless. Any time the option is out of the money when expiration arrives, the option has no value. The option buyer loses 100 percent of the amount invested. Note that the option owner never loses more than the cost of the option. That's the third reason why investors buy options: Losses are limited to the amount paid for the option.

The Valuable Option

Why is the option worth $500? If you own this option, you have the right to exercise it, buy 100 shares at $35, and immediately sell those shares in the market at $40, collecting $500 in the process. The option is worth $500 because anyone who owns the call option can do the same.

The option is in the money by $500, has an intrinsic value of $500, and is worth $500.

The Worthless Option

Why does the option have no value when the stock is $34? Weren't investors willing to pay $200 for this option when the stock was the same price 13 weeks ago?

Yes, they were. And this illustrates a crucial point in understanding options. Options have an expiration date, and the amount of time remaining before that expiration date arrives is critical in determining the value of an option. Before an option expires, there is an opportunity for the underlying stock to make a move favorable to the option owner. More time translates into more opportunity. More opportunity translates into additional value for the option. As time passes and expiration day nears, the value of an option decreases. Thus, an option is a *wasting asset*. When the market closes on expiration day, there is no time remaining, and out-of-the-money options become worthless and in-the-money options are worth no more than their intrinsic values.

The option owner must make a decision before the stock market closes for business on expiration Friday. One of the choices the call owner can make is to exercise the right to buy stock at the strike price. But no one does this when stock can be bought at a lower price. In our example, you have the right to buy stock at $35 per share today when the current price is $34. Thus, the option has no value. It is going to expire worthless.

Comparing Stock Ownership with Call Ownership

Table 9.1 compares these results.

There are several important points to consider when comparing the results.

When the Stock Increases in Value

- The stock owner makes a *larger profit* (when measured in dollars) than the option owner because no premium ($200 in this example) is paid to own the stock.
- The option owner has the potential to make a much *higher rate of return* on an investment. Compare the 150 percent return with the 17.6 percent return when the stock increases to $40.

When the Stock is Unchanged

- The stock owner breaks even.
- The owner of the option loses the entire investment.[1]

When the Stock Declines in Price

- The stock owner can lose a substantial sum (the entire investment if the company goes bankrupt).

- The option owner's loss is limited to the relatively small amount paid for the option, even though that represents the entire investment.

TABLE 9.1 Comparing Ownership: 100 Shares of Stock @ 34 vs. One Call Option (Strike Price, 35) 13 on Expiration Day

Ending Stock Price	Stock Owner		Call Owner	
	P/L	% P/L	P/L	% P/L
50	$1,600	47.06%	$1,300	650.00%
40	$600	17.65%	$300	150.00%
34	$0	0.00%	($200)	-100.00%
30	($400)	-11.76%	($200)	-100.00%
20	($1,400)	-41.18%	($200)	-100.00%

Is It Better to Buy Stock or an Option?

Because you never know the result of an investment in advance, it's necessary to understand why some investors prefer to buy options and others prefer to buy stock. Some results favor the stockholder and some favor the option owner. Thus, two reasonable questions are:

1. Who should consider buying call options instead of stock?
2. Is option buying a sound investment strategy?

This author does not recommend the strategy of buying options. The evidence presented so far may make buying options seem to be an attractive strategy, and there are good reasons for certain investors to buy options, but it is difficult to make money consistently with an options-buying strategy.

Rationale for Buying Options

- Loss is limited to the cost of the option.
- Less money is required for an initial investment, compared with buying stock.
- An option buyer has the opportunity to earn a large profit from a small investment (*leverage*).
- Some investment gurus advise their clients to buy options.

Despite these advantages of owning options, the odds of success are stacked against option buyers. Before discussing why this writer strongly recommends writing, or selling, options, instead of buying them, let's consider why it's so difficult to make consistent money when buying options.

At first glance, buying options may appear to be an attractive investment alternative. You like a stock and expect it to move higher, so you buy a call option. For a relatively small amount of money, you gain control of 100 shares of the stock you want to own. If the stock moves higher, as you hope it will, there is the opportunity to earn a big profit. Who wouldn't like that scenario? Well, you *shouldn't* like it. It's a very unlikely outcome, unless you are a very skilled stock picker. If you have the ability to know which stocks are about to undergo a significant price movement before that movement occurs, then you are in position to conquer the investment world with no further help from anyone. Because very few people have these abilities, buying options is not as attractive as it first appears.

Rationale for Not Buying Options   Although some advisors suggest buying options, they fail to mention that to profit from an option-buying strategy, you must not only correctly predict the direction in which the stock will move (up for call buyers and down for put buyers), but the move must occur quickly, as the option is a wasting asset with a limited lifetime. As if that's not enough, the movement must be sufficiently large to overcome the cost of the option. Three examples follow showing how buying an option results in a loss, even though the stock moves as predicted. These situations are common and represent a very unpleasant surprise to the option-buying novice.

Assume it is mid-February and PQR is trading at $45.

Example 1: Bullish investor 1 pays $100 for an out-of-the-money option, the PQR Jun 50 call. The investor is successful in predicting the stock will go higher, as PQR slowly rallies to $49 over the next four months. However, the investor loses the entire investment when the option is out of the money when expiration arrives.[2]

The stock has moved higher, as the call buyer hoped. The stock even moved higher within the allotted time frame. But the price increase was not sufficient and the entire cost of the option is lost.

Example 2: Bullish investor 2 buys an at-the-money option, the PQR May 45 call for $320. The stock slowly rises to $48 over the next three months, and the option is worth $300 at expiration. In this scenario, the investor correctly predicts the price increase and the time frame in which it occurs. But the stock rise is not sufficient to overcome the option premium, and the investor has a small loss.

Example 3: The stock fails to rally before the option expires. Both investors 1 and 2 lose their entire investment. Unfortunately, one week after the options expire, the company announces that earnings are going to be better than expected, and the stock rallies to $52. But it's too late to help either of these investors, who have only a loss to show for their efforts, despite the fact that they correctly predicted the stock price increase. In the options universe, timing is everything.

It may appear that these examples were constructed (as indeed they were) to produce inferior results for the option buyer, but these situations are common. When you buy options, the probabilities of making a profit are stacked against you. To show a profit, you must pick the correct direction for the stock to move and must have the predicted change occur before the option expires. In addition, the amount of the move must be sufficient to overcome the cost of the option. That's a huge hurdle.

It's common for options either to expire worthless or to be worth less than their original cost. So, why do so many investors buy options? The lure for the options buyer is that an occasional large profit can more than offset several losses. Option buying is a very difficult strategy and can be used successfully only by those who have the skill to select both the direction in which stocks are going to move and the timing of that move. Despite boasts to the contrary, only a very small number of investors or traders are able to accomplish this feat. For these reasons, the investment strategy recommended in this book does not include buying options.

Fortunately, there are always going to be investors who buy options. The possibility of earning large profits from a small investment is too enticing and remains attractive to many speculators. An entire industry of newsletter writers recommend options buying as the path to stock market success to their subscribers. That's good news for you. It's not our purpose to dissuade investors from buying options. After all, if we're going to be adopting a strategy of selling options, it's necessary to have investors who want to buy them.

Before moving on to learning why this author recommends writing (selling) options, let's consider the choices available to the option owner.

WHAT OPTION OWNERS CAN DO WITH OPTIONS

Option owners have three choices:

1. Sell the option.
2. Exercise the option.
3. Allow the option to expire worthless.

When an option is in the money on expiration day, it has an intrinsic value and should be sold. Of course, option owners have the right to exercise the option, but they should do so only if they want to own a position (long for calls, short for puts) in the underlying security. Most of the time it is far easier and more economical (lower commission costs) to sell the option. Option owners should receive approximately the intrinsic value when selling on expiration Friday.

When expiration day arrives, if an option is out of the money, it has no intrinsic value and is worthless. There will be no bids for the option, and the only choice is to allow it to expire worthless.

But it's not necessary to hold the option until expiration day. In fact, it is undesirable to do so. If you ever buy an option, you become the owner of a wasting asset. Your goal should be to sell it as quickly as possible. Once the stock makes its move in the direction you predict, or if you decide that you were wrong and the stock is not going to make that move, it's time to sell the option. One mistake inexperienced options traders make is to buy an option, hope for the best, and never sell it. Sometimes it's a good idea to accept a small loss and sell the option before it becomes worthless.

Next we'll see why some investors sell options, then we'll take a detailed look at two conservative strategies involving the sale of options.

WHY WOULD ANYONE SELL AN OPTION?

As mentioned earlier, I am a strong proponent of option-writing strategies that reduce risk. Note that the term "write" and "sell" are used interchangeably.

Let's begin by adding two new words to your options vocabulary: covered and uncovered.

COVERED VS. UNCOVERED

When you write a call option, you are accepting an obligation to sell the underlying stock at some time in the future. If you are able to fulfill that obligation by selling stock you already own, then you are *covered*. If you don't own any stock, or if you own an insufficient quantity to completely fulfill that obligation, then you are *uncovered* or *naked*.

If you are initiating a new position and buy stock at the same time you write call options (a *buy-write transaction*), you are covered.

When you write a put option, you are accepting an obligation and may later be forced to buy shares of the underlying stock. If you are able to fulfill that obligation because you already have a short position in the stock, then you are covered.[3] If you do not have a short position, or if the short position is not large enough to completely fulfill that obligation, then you are uncovered. As with calls, if you write the put options at the same time you sell the stock short, then you are covered.

> **Example:** You write 2 TUV Oct 45 calls. If you own at least 200 shares of TUV, you are covered. If you own fewer than 200 shares (including owning no shares), then the position is uncovered.

> **Example:** You write 4 Feb 60 MNO puts. If you are short at least 400 shares of MNO, you are covered. Otherwise you are uncovered.

Writing covered calls is a bullish option strategy used by many investors. Writing covered put options is a bearish investment strategy and is a far less popular strategy. Although we will not be discussing this strategy in detail in this book, if you understand the principles behind the bullish strategy of writing covered call options, you will be able to translate that knowledge into the ability to write covered put options, if and when you choose to be short the stock market. But be aware that writing covered puts is riskier (for reasons discussed later in this chapter) than writing covered calls, and many brokerage firms do not allow their customers to adopt this strategy.

WHAT DO YOU HAVE TO GAIN BY SELLING AN OPTION?

When you write a covered call option, or an uncovered put option (these recommended strategies are discussed in great detail in the next two chapters), your potential profit is limited. In exchange for accepting a limit on your possible profit:

- You have more winning positions.
- You have fewer losing positions, and losses (if any) are reduced.
- The overall fluctuation in the value of your investment portfolio is less.

If you are able to accept limited profits and recognize that you no longer will be able to make a killing on any single investment, the odds are that your overall performance is going to improve. Chapter 12 presents evidence to support that statement.

INVESTMENT OBJECTIVES

Option writers have different investment objectives, depending on the specific option strategy chosen.

Naked call writing is a bearish strategy adopted by investors who expect time to pass, the stock to remain below the strike price, and the option to expire worthless, enabling them to keep the entire proceeds from the sale of the option as their profit. This high-risk strategy (potential losses are unlimited) is too risky for our purposes and is not discussed further.[4]

Naked put writing is a bullish strategy adopted by investors who have one of two objectives in mind:

1. Collect the option premium. If the stock is above the strike price when expiration day arrives, the option expires worthless and writers keep the entire premium as the profit.
2. Buy shares of a stock they want to own at a discount (to the current price). If the stock is below the strike price when expiration arrives, put writers are assigned an exercise notice and buy stock at the strike price.

Some investment professionals consider naked put writing to be as risky as selling naked calls, but they are mistaken.[5] In fact, as you will see, this strategy is significantly less risky than owning individual stocks—and almost everyone considers owning stocks to be a prudent investment.

Chapter 11 covers the strategy of writing uncovered put options in detail.

Covered call writing (discussed in detail in Chapter 10) is a strategy adopted by investors who have three investment objectives:

1. Increase the likelihood of earning a profit.
2. Reduce the frequency and size of any investment loss.
3. Reduce the volatility of their investment portfolio.

A fourth, often underestimated, benefit is the psychological boost investors experience when earning good profits in a stagnant stock market.

Covered put writing is adopted by bearish investors with goals similar to those who use naked call writing. This high-risk strategy is essentially identical to selling naked call options and is too risky for our purposes.

Option writing is part of an investment philosophy that accepts *hedging* as a method of reducing *both* the profit and loss potential of an investment. (Hedging reduces the risk of owning an investment by taking on a position that partially offsets its risks and rewards.) In return, investors earn a profit more often and experience losses less often. It's a trade-off that increases the chances that investors can outperform the market. Of course, if your stock selection skills are outstanding and you always earn a better return than the market benchmark (e.g., the S&P 500 index), then you don't have to hedge your portfolio.

The best way to illustrate the advantages and risks of writing options is by examining some examples. We'll do just that in the next two chapters.

CHAPTER 10

Option Strategies You Can Use to Make Money

Covered Call Writing

It's time to move beyond the basics and discuss how you can use options in the real world. Because our goal is to adopt a strategy based on the teachings of modern portfolio theory (MPT), we want to find a strategy that reduces the risk and increases the rewards of holding a well-diversified portfolio of stocks. We'll concentrate on two options strategies that can help you achieve those goals. The first of these strategies is covered call writing. The second is uncovered put writing (see Chapter 11).

Options are versatile investment tools that can be used in many ways, ranging from very conservative to wildly speculative. Our discussion focuses on two of the more conservative options strategies available to the investor who wants to put money to work in the stock markets of the world. After a thorough discussion of these strategies, we'll see how to use them as a significant part of your overall investment technique (Part IV).

Let's begin by examining covered call writing and the reasons why investors would consider adopting this strategy.

COVERED CALL WRITING: THE STRATEGY IN A NUTSHELL

Covered call writing is an investment strategy in which you (the option seller) enter into an agreement with another party (the option buyer). You agree to allow the other party to buy 100 shares of your stock at an agreed-on price, called the strike price. That agreement is effective for a limited period of time. You have no say in whether (or when) that other person chooses to buy your stock, as that decision rests entirely with the option owner. Because the maximum price you can receive when selling your stock is limited to the strike price, you give up the chance to earn a bonanza on your stock. Some investors, holding onto the dream of owning the next stock that performs like Microsoft, Intel, or Wal-Mart, choose not to write covered calls. If that's your dream, this strategy is not suitable for you. If, however, you are interested in increasing your stock market performance year after year, and if you believe that steady growth over time is the path to building wealth, this strategy is made to order for you.

The person who buys the call option has a different strategy in mind. Rather than attempting to build wealth over the years, that investor is making a short-term wager on the price of your stock. The investor is hoping the stock price soon moves much higher than the strike price. If that happens, the owner of the call option can sell the option and earn a profit.

It's important to remember that no strategy produces the optimum result every time. Your goal with covered call writing is to increase your profits from investing in the stock market. And you want those increased profits year after year. Don't be concerned with making the maximum profit from each and every trade. When you own individual stocks, it's highly unlikely that you would sell at the high, and selling at the high price is the only way to achieve the maximum possible profit.

Thus, if the stock price does move significantly higher than the price at which you agreed to sell it, that's okay. When that happens, you earn the maximum profit this strategy allows. Writing covered call options enhances the returns you can expect to earn on a consistent basis, but it cannot produce the best possible result every time. After all, if you want to continue to sell options, there must be investors to buy them. There would be no such investors if they didn't make money at least part of the time.

Usually, you will be very pleased with the results produced by this strategy.

- You make money when the stock market is going nowhere and everyone else is breaking even.
- You may make money when the markets decline, but even if you don't show a profit in a declining market, your losses are reduced when you adopt a covered call writing strategy.
- You make money in rising markets. Often you make more than investors who do not use your new strategy, but sometimes they make more than you.

When expiration day (the last day the agreement is valid) arrives, if the stock price is above the strike price, then the option owner elects to buy your stock at the agreed-on price, and you are obligated to sell. If the stock price is not higher than the strike price, then the option owner elects not to buy your stock, the option expires worthless, and your obligation to sell your stock at the strike price ends.

If you are giving up the opportunity to make a huge profit on your stocks by writing covered calls, you must receive something of value in exchange. In return for limiting your potential profit, you are paid a cash premium. You receive this money up front, and it's yours to keep, regardless of whether the other party ever buys your stock.

Those who are considering adopting covered call writing generally have certain questions. For example:

- Isn't it foolish to accept the option premium in exchange for forfeiting all potential profit beyond the strike price?
- Wouldn't I be better off trying to find stocks to buy that can provide an exceptional return on my investment? Isn't the purpose of investing in the stock market to find stocks that double in price again and again?
- If my goal is to accumulate wealth over the years, don't I have to own some stocks that provide outstanding returns?

For most investors, the answer to each of these questions is *no*.

- Over the years, you earn more money on average, by repeatedly collecting option premiums than by owning stocks that increase in value.
- As discussed in Part I, it's very difficult for individual investors to find stocks that provide spectacular returns. Attempting to do so is a wasted effort for the vast majority of investors.
- A person whose goal is to achieve the steady growth that comes with outperforming the market on a consistent basis is much more likely to be successful than one who attempts to hit the jackpot on a single investment.

In summary, investors who own a well-diversified portfolio of stocks can make more money by adopting covered call writing.

COVERED CALL WRITING IN ACTION

The easiest way to understand the advantages of adopting covered call writing as your primary investment strategy is to closely examine some examples. At the same time, we'll take a look at how you can vary the methodology to suit your needs.

No investment in the stock market is without risk, as bear markets are a fact of life. But covered call writing is a strategy that significantly increases your chances of outperforming the market and earning better returns than are available from U.S. Treasury bills (risk-free rate of return). When choosing your investments, you still must choose among:

- Conservatively aiming for smaller potential profits. This goal has a high probability of success and comes with extra protection against loss in case the market declines.
- Aggressively shooting for higher profits. This goal requires that you accept less protection against loss and a lower probability of earning as much profit as you hope. One tenet of investing is that higher rewards require accepting higher risk.
- Choosing a strategy that falls between the extremes. This is likely to be successful for most investors. Higher profits and reduced risk are available as a package.

The following examples illustrate factors that go into making your choice.

More conservative strategies are appropriate if you are nearing retirement or if you will need some of your capital in a few years (e.g., to pay for college for the kids or to buy a new home). If you believe the market is entering into a bearish phase (remember—MPT tells us not to make such predictions), you may find a more conservative strategy to be appropriate.

Aggressive methods may be suitable for both very bullish investors and younger investors (who have many years to recover if they incur losses trying for those big profits). These investors probably already own an aggressive portfolio of stocks, so adopting covered call writing reduces their risk while maintaining the opportunity for very significant profits.

As a writer of covered call options, you make investment decisions frequently (perhaps monthly), and it's a good idea to maintain a consistent style, but it's not necessary to adopt the identical strategy every time you write new options. The ability to modify the strategy prevents this method from becoming tedious (not that making more money can ever be tedious), and it also allows you to adjust your strategy according to your investment objectives at any given time.

Comparing Results

When discussing the earnings potential of covered call writing, it's necessary to compare the results with an investment method that does not utilize this strategy. For the purposes of our discussion, there are two assumptions:

1. The covered call writer holds the position until the option expires.
2. The investor who is not a covered call writer also holds the stock position through the options expiration date.

It's a simple matter to compare how writing the call option affects the return on your investment. The details are illustrated in the following examples.

When using covered call writing, there are two possible outcomes when expiration day arrives: either the option you write expires worthless (the option owner chooses *not* to buy your stock), or the option owner exercises the option and you sell your stock.

Most, but not all, of the time you achieve a better investment result by writing the option. If it expires worthless, you are better off by the entire amount you collected from the option sale. The only time this strategy fails to provide a better result (compared with simply holding the stock) occurs when the stock increases in price beyond the upside break-even point (see box on next page).

STRATEGY 1: WRITING OUT-OF-THE-MONEY CALLS

Writing out-of-the-money calls is the most bullish (and aggressive) covered call writing strategy. The investor who adopts this method has two main investment goals:

1. Profit from a rising market.
2. Earn money by collecting the option premium.

When should you consider writing out-of-the-money call options?

- When protecting your investment against a market decline is less important than giving yourself a chance to earn higher profits.
- When you are very bullish and willing to accept less option premium in return for the chance to sell your stock at a higher price.

Deciding you are bullish and attempting to profit from higher market prices goes against the teaching of MPT. But it's your money, and you have every right to use covered call writing in this manner.

Break-Even Points

Example

You own 200 shares of FGH (currently $47) and write 2 Nov 50 calls at $3.

The *upside break-even point* is the stock price at which you make the same profit regardless of whether you write a covered call option or simply own stock. That point equals the sum of the strike price plus the option premium. In this example, the upside break-even point is $53 (strike price = 50; premium = 3).

Here's why: When FGH is $53 per share, an investor who owns 100 shares has an investment worth $5,300. If the stock moves higher, that investor makes money.

To the covered call writer who owns 100 shares, the position cannot be worth more than $5,300. The investor already received $300 from the option sale and can receive no more than an additional $5,000 when assigned an exercise notice. That sum, $5,300, represents the covered call writer's maximum value for the position. If the stock moves higher, the writer makes no additional profit. Thus, in this example, $53 is the upside break-even point. Above that price, the covered call writer earns less than the investor who does not write call options.

Note: The *only* situation in which the call writer does not make more money than the investor who adopts a buy-and-hold strategy occurs when the stock moves higher than the upside break-even point.

The *downside break-even point* is the stock price at which you no longer earn any profit from the position. At lower prices, you have a loss. That point occurs at a price equal to the current stock price at the time the option is written, less the option premium received.

Here's why: Your cost to buy stock is reduced by the option premium you received. You incur a loss only if the stock goes below your reduced cost.

For this example, the downside break-even point is $44 (current price = 47; premium = 3).

Note: The upside break-even point compares your result with that of the buy-and-hold investor. The downside break-even point has nothing to do with the buy-and-hold investor, as the covered call writer *always* does better than the buy-and-hold investor when the stock declines in price.

Example

You own (or buy) 500 shares of BCD, currently priced at $32.50.

You write 5 BCD Sep 35 calls (expiring in one month) and receive $90 for each.

Downside break-even point: $31.60 (32.50 – 90)

Upside break-even point: $35.90 (35.00 + 90)

Maximum profit (per 100 shares): $340 ($90 from option; $250 from stock increase)

What Happens Next?

After you sell the options:

1. You receive the proceeds from selling five options, or $450, less commission.[1] The cash goes into your account, is yours to keep, and begins to earn interest.
2. You still own the stock. If it pays a dividend, you receive it.[2]
3. That's it. The only change you notice in your brokerage statement is that you now have a short position of five call options.

Expiration Possibilities

Although it's possible to be assigned an exercise notice prior to expiration, it's unlikely. Assume one month passes and that it's now after the market closes on expiration Friday (third Friday of September). Let's look at the possible results for this investment.

Scenario 1   BCD is below $35 (the strike price). The call option is out of the money. Whoever owns the option will not elect to pay $35 per share for your stock. Anyone wanting to own stock could have purchased it (before the market closed) at a lower price. The options you sold are going to expire worthless. You are no longer under any obligation to sell your stock. When the market opens next Monday (or any time thereafter), if you choose to do so, you can write another five call options against your 500 shares.

This is a satisfactory result. By writing the options, you earned $450 that you would not have earned otherwise.

Scenario 2   BCD stock closes at $35, and the option is at the money. You don't know whether the person who owns the calls will choose to buy your stock. You must wait until next Monday morning to find out if you have been assigned on your call options. Some brokers are not efficient when it comes to giving you this important information, so be certain to call your broker next Monday, before the market opens.[3]

This is a satisfactory result. You keep the $450 from the sale of the options. You also made money because your stock increased in value by $2.50 per share. If you are assigned, that's a good result, since you both sell stock at your price and keep the option premium. If you are not assigned, that's also a good result because it leaves you well placed next Monday when the market opens. You can either sell your stock or continue to hold it. If you decide to hold, you can write call options again, collecting another premium.

When the stock closes very near the strike price, you must wait to learn whether you get to keep your stock or must sell it. That decision is not yours to make. The option owner must make that decision on (or before) expiration Friday, and your broker learns of that decision when notified by the Options Clearing Corporation (OCC).[4] Your broker must pass the information along to you before the market opens on the next business day.

Once you learn if you are assigned, your situation is identical to that of someone whose options finished out of the money (not assigned) or in the money (assigned). Thus, in the next examples, we ignore the possibility that the option is at the money when the market closes on expiration day.

Scenario 3   BCD is above $35. You are assigned an exercise notice and must sell your 500 BCD shares at the strike price. If the stock is above, but very close to, the strike price, you are not *always* assigned. (Why this is possible is discussed in Chapter 16.) Be certain to check with your broker.

This is a satisfactory result and the result you hoped to achieve from the position, as it provides your maximum possible profit. You earned $2.50 per share on 500 shares (stock was $32.50 when you initiated this position, and you sell at $35) *plus* you keep the option premium ($450). Your total profit is $1,700. That represents a return of 10.8 percent in one month (129.1 percent annualized) on your $15,800 investment.

Note: The investment is $15,800 because:

You placed 500 shares at $32.50 into the position. That's an investment of $16,250.

You collected $450 from the sale of the options. This cash is used to reduce the cost of your investment, making the net investment $15,800.

All possible results appear to be satisfactory. So, why doesn't everyone do this? What can go wrong? What are the risks? These are good questions. Before looking at the answers, let's discuss additional covered call writing examples.

STRATEGY 2:
WRITING-IN-THE-MONEY CALLS

Writing in-the-money calls is the most conservative covered call writing strategy and is for investors who have two main investment objectives:

1. Increase the chances of earning a profit.
2. Gain protection against loss, in addition to earning a profit.

Why Writing in-the-Money Calls Produces Frequent Profits

When you own shares of stock, in order to earn a profit, the stock must increase in value. When you own any covered call position, to earn a profit, the stock must be above the downside break-even point when expiration day arrives. The lower the break-even point, the greater the likelihood that the stock is above that price on any given date. Here's why.

Let's consider two different stock prices, one lower than the other. Every time the stock is above the higher price, it is *also* above the lower price. But some of the time the stock is between the two prices. Therefore, the stock is above the lower price more often. If those two prices represent break-even points, then the stock is above the lower break-even point more often, and the investor with the lower break-even point earns a profit more often.

From this we can conclude two things:

1. Any covered call position is more likely to be profitable when compared with buying and holding stock without writing covered calls because the break-even point is lower.
2. Writing in-the-money options reduces the break-even point more than writing at-the-money or out-of-the-money options (the option premium is higher) and produces profits more often.

More Likely Profits *and* Additional Safety?

Writing in-the-money options provides increased protection against loss.[5] If this strategy reduces risk by providing more downside insurance, and if it produces more frequent profits, what's the catch?

In return for the benefits associated with writing in-the-money call options, some of your profit potential is reduced. Thus, choosing which option to write depends on your personal investment objectives. It's important to select a strategy that makes you comfortable and meets your objectives.

This point is discussed further in Part IV, when we get to the specifics of writing covered calls on exchange traded funds.

Writing in-the-money call options enables you to earn a good profit, and that profit comes with the bonus of owning a safer position. Use this strategy whenever you believe that earning a larger profit is less important than reducing the chances of losing money.

Example

You buy 500 shares of BCD, paying $32.50 per share.

You write 5 Sep 30 calls (expiring in one month) and receive $330 for each.

Downside break-even point: $29.20 (32.50 – 3.30)

Maximum profit (per 100 shares): $80 (cost = 29.20; sell at 30)

Do I Really Want to Sell Stock for Less than I Paid?

Does it seem strange to buy stock at $32.50 and immediately sell someone else the right to buy that same stock from you at only $30 per share? Relax. That's not what you are doing. Here's why.

You can look at this situation in two different ways:

1. Use the premium received from writing the call option to reduce your cost. Thus, you are paying only (in this example) $29.20 per share of stock, not $32.50. When you sell the stock at $30, you have a profit of $0.80 per share.

2. When you write an in-the-money option, the premium you receive can be divided into two parts: the intrinsic value and the time premium. The intrinsic value is a *refund* of part of your purchase price and the time premium represents your potential profit.

   In this example, the intrinsic value of the option is $2.50 per share (stock price minus strike price) and the time premium is $80. Thus, you can think of this as a situation in which you pay $32.50 for stock and receive a rebate of $2.50, making your net purchase price $30. The $80 time premium represents your profit potential.

Expiration Possibilities

When expiration day arrives, there are two possibilities:

Scenario 1   BCD is below the strike price, and the options expire worthless. By writing the calls, you are better off (by the $1,650 you collected from the option sale) compared with the investor who simply holds the stock. That investor has a loss, but you have a profit if the stock is above the break-even point ($29.20). Even if the stock is below that price, your loss is reduced by $3.30 per share because you had the foresight to write the call options. This may not be a profitable trade for you, but it is a satisfactory result considering how much the stock has declined.

Scenario 2 BCD is above the strike price, and you are assigned an exercise notice. This is your best result. You earn the maximum profit ($0.80 per share) attainable when using this strategy. Your return is 2.7 percent for one month, or 32.9 percent annualized.[6] This maximum reward is far less than that available from writing out-of-the-money call options, but it comes with a much greater amount of protection against loss. This book will help you to choose among the possibilities to find a combination of risk and reward that is comfortable for you.

STRATEGY 3: WRITING AT- OR NEAR-THE-MONEY CALLS

Writing at-the-money calls is an attractive compromise strategy and is suitable for investors who want to earn a good profit and gain a small amount of downside protection. Typically, investors who have a neutral outlook on the market write at-the-money options. These options have a greater time premium in their price than either in- or out-of-the-money options. Thus, the potential profit to be derived from the option sale is greatest for at-the-money options.[7] The potential for profit based on stock price movement is greater when selling out-of-the-money options.

At-the-money options are priced lower than in-the-money options but higher than out-of-the-money options. Thus, they afford the covered call writer an intermediate amount of protection to the downside.

Example

You buy 500 shares of BCD at $32.50.

You write 5 BCD Sep 32½ calls (expiring in one month) and receive $180 for each.

Downside break-even: $30.70 (32.50 − 1.80)

Maximum profit per 100 shares: $180

Expiration Possibilities

Scenario 1 BCD is below the strike price, and the options expire worthless. This is a satisfactory result. Once again, you are better off by the amount you received for writing the calls than the investor who simply owns stock.

Scenario 2 BCD is above the strike price, and you are assigned on your call options. You earn the maximum possible profit from this position, or $900 (180 times 5) on an investment of $15,350 for a return of 5.9 percent (70.4 percent annualized).

STRATEGY 4: WRITING OPTIONS WITH MORE DISTANT EXPIRATION DATES

This strategy is more conservative than writing options with shorter expirations because you receive a higher option premium, affording a greater amount of protection to the downside. Remember, options with more time remaining until expiration are worth more and trade for higher prices than shorter-term options. You can combine this technique with writing either in-the-money, at-the-money, or out-of-the-money options.

As a general guideline, the *time premium* in the price of an option is related to the square root of the time remaining until the option expires. Simply, this means that an option with four months until expiration often has twice the time premium of an option with one month remaining. A nine-month option contains roughly three times as much time premium as a one-month option. Because other factors come into play in determining the price of an option, this is merely a reasonable estimate.[8]

As with other covered call writing strategies, when safety increases, some profit potential must be sacrificed. Options with more distant expiration dates provide a greater potential profit per option—but provide a smaller potential profit on an annualized basis. The next examples illustrate this point. Because most discussions concerning portfolio returns are based on annualized earnings, it's important to be aware of the annualized profit potential for each of your covered call positions.

Assume you buy 500 shares of BCD, paying $32.50 per share.

In-the-Money Example

You write 5 BCD Dec 30 calls (expiring in four months) and receive $500 for each.

Downside break-even point: $27.50 (32.50 – 5)

Maximum profit (per 100 shares): $250 (cost = 27.50; sell at 30)

At-the-Money Example

You write 5 BCD Dec 32½ calls and receive $370 for each.

Downside break-even point: $28.80 (32.50 – 3.70)

Maximum profit (per 100 shares): $370

Out-of-the-Money Example 1

You write 5 BCD Dec 35 calls and receive $280 for each.

Downside break even point: $29.70

Maximum profit (per 100 shares): $530

Out-of-the-Money Example 2

You write 5 BCD Mar 35 calls (expiring in seven months) and receive $400 for each.

Downside break-even point: $28.50

Maximum Profit (per 100 shares): $650

Scenario 1   The options expire worthless. In each case, if the stock is above the downside break-even point, you earn a profit. As always, when the stock declines in price, you are better off than an investor who does not write covered call options.

Scenario 2   If assigned an exercise notice on your calls, you achieve the maximum possible profit from the position.

Summarizing the examples used in this chapter, the data in Table 10.1 compare the results of writing longer-term options with writing shorter-term options. Because so many variables come into play when determining the price of an option in the marketplace, you cannot predict what option prices will be available when you are ready to write a covered call. But you can use the data from the table to get a feel for how the profit potential is altered when you change from writing near-term options to writing options with longer expirations. Of course, don't expect to find these exact sample returns duplicated in the real world.

The data presented in Table 10.1 illustrate some points that are important for you, as a potential option writer, to understand.

TABLE 10.1 Comparing Profit Potential: Writing Longer- versus Shorter-term Options; Stock Trading @ 32.50 per share

	Strike Price	Months to Exp	Premium	Intrinsic Value	Time Value	Break-Even	Max ($) Profit	Max (%) Profit	Annualized Profit (%)
In the Money	30	1	$330	$250	$ 80	29.20	$ 80	2.74%	32.88%
	30	4	$500	$250	$250	27.50	$250	9.09%	27.27%
	30	7	$620	$250	$370	26.30	$370	14.07%	24.12%
At the Money	32½	1	$180	$ 0	$180	30.70	$180	5.86%	70.36%
	32½	4	$370	$ 0	$370	28.80	$370	12.85%	38.54%
	32½	7	$500	$ 0	$500	27.50	$500	18.18%	31.17%
Out of the Money	35	1	$ 90	$ 0	$ 90	31.60	$340	10.76%	129.11%
	35	4	$280	$ 0	$280	29.70	$530	17.85%	53.54%
	35	7	$400	$ 0	$400	28.50	$650	22.81%	39.10%

Time Value and Profit Potential

(Reminder: Time Value = Option Premium – Intrinsic Value)

- The time value of an option increases as time to expiration increases.
- The time value of an option is greatest for at-the-money options.
- The time value of an option represents your maximum potential profit from the option part of a covered call position.

Protection (Insurance against Loss)

- The lower the strike price of a call option, the lower the downside break-even point and, thus, the more protection against loss.
- The more time remaining until the option expires, the greater the amount of downside protection.
- Increased protection comes at the expense of lower annualized profit potential.

Annualized Profits

- As the time to expiration increases, the maximum dollar amount you can earn from a covered call position increases.
- As the time to expiration increases, the maximum annualized return on your investment decreases.
- As the strike price of the call option increases (and becomes an out-of-the-money option), the greater the amount of potential profit. Of course, that increased profit potential is derived from a hoped-for increase in the price of the underlying stock and is not directly related to writing the call option.

It's a good idea to examine bid-ask options data online.[9] Doing so allows you to get familiar with option pricing and practice calculating the potential profit for a myriad of possible covered call positions. Gaining experience with the calculations before you begin trading makes you better prepared when you enter your first option order.

NOTE TO NONBELIEVERS

If you are an investor who doesn't accept the premise that it's extremely difficult for an individual investor to outperform the market (see Part I), and if you still believe the correct strategy is to build a portfolio of individual stocks, you still can profit from a thorough understanding of covered call writing. It's a strategy that you can use to enhance your investment returns. By all means, continue to select your own investments, but seriously consider writing out-of-the-money options. That method allows you to continue to rack up capital gains from your own stock picks—if you truly are a successful stock picker—and at the same time collect option premiums to add to your earnings. If you are wrong and your stocks don't perform as anticipated, the option premium you earn will be a welcome consolation.

Can You Make Enough Money to Bother Writing Covered Calls?

When adopting more conservative strategies, the potential profits may appear to be anything but spectacular. Most books touting an investment methodology claim extraordinary profit potential to lure readers into adopting suggested methods. That is not the method here. The money you can earn writing covered calls is limited, but it's still possible to earn extraordinary returns. This book illustrates an investment method that provides ample returns and still reduces the risk of owning investments in the stock market.

Yet if your objective is to double your money every year, you have the chance to achieve that goal by buying stocks that undergo substantial price increases *and* by writing out-of-the-money calls. Doing so allows you to capture a good portion of those capital gains as well as to collect option premiums. Of course, finding those great stocks to buy may present a problem.

Some investors may find the potential profits cited in Table 10.1 to be too small to be worth the effort involved in adopting a covered call writing strategy. To those investors, I offer two comments:

1. If you earn "only" 2 percent per month on a consistent basis, and if you allow the money to remain in the account and compound, your money doubles every three years. (Earning 2.0 percent per month for 36 months turns $1,000 into $2,040.) This return is not only substantially better than the historical stock market return of approximately 11 percent per year, but this method makes it more likely you will outperform the market averages on a consistent basis.

2. In today's investment world, the premium level of listed options is lower than it has been through much of options' history. Although option premiums may decrease further, it's reasonable to expect they will be higher, on average, in the coming years. (See Chapter 12 for an examination of historical option premium levels.) If that's true, then returns available from writing covered call options will increase as those premiums increase.

CHOOSING THE CALL
TO WRITE: SUMMARY

Table 10.2 summarizes the picture of covered call writing from the point of view of selecting an option to write. Usually each investor chooses an option to write that provides the best combination of profit potential and risk management. To learn which strategy suits you best, write some covered calls in the real world, and see if you are comfortable with the positions and if they are helping you meet your investment objectives. I suggest that you begin with short-term at-the-money options on stocks you already own. If you like the strategy, start building your ETF portfolio and writing covered calls on your new investments.

TABLE 10.2   Which Option to Write

Option Description	Profit Potential	Downside Protection	Market Outlook
Strike Price			
Out of the money	Highest	Least	Bullish
At the money	Intermediate	Intermediate	Neutral to bullish
In the money	Least	Most	Neutral to bearish[a]
Time to Expiration			
Front 2 months	Highest	Least	
Few months (3–5 months)	Intermediate	Intermediate	
Longer term (6–8 months)	Least	Most	Long-term investment

[a]All covered call writing strategies are bullish. But if short-term bearish, writing in-the-money calls is a viable alternative to selling stock.

WHAT ARE THE RISKS
OF COVERED CALL WRITING?

Although writing covered call options is a more conservative strategy than simply buying and holding individual stock market investments, as with any investment involving the stock market, it is not risk free. There are four major risks associated with this strategy.

1. If the stock undergoes a severe price decline, you may lose money. The premium received from the option sale provides some insurance against loss and reduces any loss, but there is no guarantee against losing money.

Note: If you are an investor who is likely to continue to hold your stock positions during a market decline, then this is not a risk factor for you. In fact, writing options reduces your losses during the decline.

2. If your primary objective is to sell stock at the strike price, it's possible that writing a covered call option will cause you to lose the sale.

   Here's how: If the stock price climbs above the strike price during the lifetime of the option and subsequently falls below that price when expiration arrives, the call owner does not exercise the option and you do not sell your stock. If instead of writing the call option, you enter a limit order with your broker to sell the stock, the stock would be sold when it reaches your price. Thus, by accepting the call premium, you run the risk of still owning the stock after it reaches your target selling price. If you have no interest in selling the stock, then this is not a risk factor for you.

3. If your stock rises through the strike price and advances through your upside break-even price, you lose the opportunity to sell stock at the higher price, as writing the call places a cap on your selling price. You still earn a good profit (some investors mistakenly believe they lose money in this situation), but this profit is less than you could have made without the option sale. However, keep this in mind: Most investors don't know whether a stock is going to continue to go higher or if it's about to reverse direction. Most investors sell their positions well before the ultimate high. Thus, even if you don't write a call option, it doesn't mean you can earn the maximum profit available from the position.

4. If you own a dividend-paying stock, it's possible to fail to collect the dividend. The call owner has the right to exercise the call at any time and may choose to do so before the stock goes ex-dividend. If that happens, you do not receive the dividend. It's not all bad news: You sell stock at the strike price earlier than expected (before expiration), and you can put the money back to work early by reinvesting the proceeds of the sale.

Another risk associated with selling call options is impossible to quantify, for it's a psychological risk. Some investors want the best of all possible worlds every time they make a trade and are never satisfied with less. As you have seen, covered call writing enhances the returns of an investment in the vast majority of the cases. When the stock declines, remains unchanged, or increases by a limited amount, covered call writing allows investors to earn additional profits. The only time it does not improve results occurs when the underlying stock undergoes a substantial price increase. For some investors that's not good enough. If you fit into this category and always must achieve the best possible results, you may have some difficulty adopting a strategy that includes covered call writing.

CONFLICTING INFORMATION?

If you learned about covered call writing elsewhere, it's likely you've been advised that this strategy is designed for investors and traders who believe the stocks they own are not likely to advance in price in the near future. It's true that the best *psychological* result occurs when the stock holds steady and the option you write expires worthless. Remember, predicting that a stock is not going to increase in value is against the teachings of MPT.

This strategy is suitable for much more than just stable markets, and the best *financial* result occurs when you are assigned an exercise notice. Covered call writing provides protection during market downturns and is extremely profitable during bull markets. This strategy is suitable for most investors who want to own positions in the stock market, regardless of market conditions.[10]

Remember that modern portfolio theory teaches us that trying to time the market is not a winning strategy. Thus, I believe that covered call writing is a suitable investment strategy in any market condition—for that portion of your assets allocated to investing in the stock market.

Authors who recommend that covered call writing be adopted only when a stable stock market is expected are speaking to traders rather than to investors. Traders have a much shorter time horizon and often hold positions for only a few days (or minutes). Although short-term traders can use covered call writing, this strategy is much more effective for investors and their longer-term outlooks.[11]

SUMMARY

When comparing the writing of covered calls with the strategy of simply buying and holding stocks:

- Writing calls allows you to *make money* (or lose less) if your stock goes down.
- Writing calls allows you to make *more* money if your stock is unchanged.
- Writing calls allows you to make *more* money if your stock increases in value by a limited amount (up to the upside break-even point).

- Writing calls earns *less* money if your stock increases in price beyond the upside break-even point. You still do well; you still earn good profits, but not as much as you could have made without the call sale.

There is a saying on Wall Street that sums up the rationale behind adopting a covered call writing approach to your investments: "Sometimes the bulls win, sometimes the bears win, but the pigs always lose." Don't be greedy. Invest according to the teachings of MPT and allow your enhanced earnings to compound over time. You have a much better chance of beating the market with this approach than with attempting to choose your own investments or to put your faith in the professionals who manage traditional mutual funds.

Each investor must make an individual decision concerning the suitability of writing covered calls, but I strongly believe the rewards more than compensate for the risks.

This option writing strategy produces a better result the vast majority of the time and is an appropriate investment strategy for a great many investors. Yet the *possibility* of making a killing on any one investment often prevents an investor from adopting the covered call writing strategy. If you accept the precepts of MPT and recognize that it's exceedingly difficult to outperform the market on a consistent basis, then adding covered call writing to your investment methods is likely to improve your results. In Part IV we'll discuss how you can use this strategy when investing in exchange traded funds.

CHAPTER 11

Option Strategies You Can Use to Make Money

Uncovered Put Writing

C overed call writing and uncovered put writing are very similar strategies. They have identical risk parameters (see Table 11.1) and are different investment vehicles for achieving the same investment
objectives. Each has its own advantages, and many investors achieve satisfactory results using both strategies.

UNCOVERED PUT WRITING: THE STRATEGY IN A NUTSHELL

The writing of uncovered, or naked, puts is an investment strategy in which
you enter into an agreement with another party (the option buyer). You accept an obligation, for a limited time, that grants the other party the right to
force you to buy stock at an agreed-on price (strike price). As with covered
call writing, you have no say in whether (or when) that other person will
choose to exercise the put option and force you to buy the stock. That decision rests entirely with the put owner. Because the price you can be
forced to pay is known, the most you can lose is the cost of the shares
(strike price times the number of shares) minus the option premium you
collect. This maximum loss is similar to (but less than) that of an investor
who owns stock outright.

Uncovered put writing is a bullish strategy, and the profit potential is
limited to the option premium you receive for writing (selling) the put.

TABLE 11.1 Comparing Risk

	Covered Call Writing	Uncovered Put Writing
Covered Call Writing versus Uncovered Put Writing		
Stock	Buy 100 shares @ 42	None
Write	1 Nov 40 call	1 Nov 40 put
Option Premium	$3.50	$1.50
Intrinsic Value	$200	None
Time Premium	$150	$150
Cash Outlay	$3,850 debit	$150 credit
Cash Backing	None	$3,850
Max Profit	$150	$150
Max Loss	$3,850	$3,850
Downside B/E	38.50	38.50
Advantages/ Disadvantages	All brokers allow	Not always allowed
	Can't overspend	May sell too many puts
	2 commissions	Only 1 commission
	Difficult to close	Easy to close

The person who buys your put wants the stock price to plunge. If that happens, the option owner makes a sizable profit by buying stock at a much lower price in the open market and forcing you to buy that same stock at the much higher price. That unhappy scenario is probably going to happen to you on occasion. Writing uncovered put options is a strategy that can be used intelligently to increase the probability of earning a profit, but this strategy does not guarantee a winning result on *every* trade. The situation is the same as when you write covered call options: If option buyers didn't earn a profit at least some of the time, there would be no buyers of put options when you want to write them.

When expiration day arrives, if the stock price is above the strike price, then the put option expires worthless and you are under no further obligation to buy stock. Your profit is the cash you received when writing the option. If the price of the stock is below the strike price, you are assigned an exercise notice and must fulfill the obligations of the contract—namely you must buy the stock at the strike price. This is something you were willing to do when writing the option, so it should not be considered an unhappy event.

When you are assigned, you have several alternatives in terms of what to do next. You can write covered call options against the stock (recommended), hold the stock without writing call options (hoping it goes up in price (this is against the teachings of modern portfolio theory), or sell the stock.

What do you get in exchange for accepting both a limited potential profit and the obligation to buy stock at the strike price? You are paid a cash premium to accept that obligation. You receive this money up front, and it's yours to keep, regardless of whether the other party ever forces you to buy stock.

When writing covered calls, you must spend cash to buy stock. When you write uncovered puts, cash is kept in reserve in case you are required to buy stock later. When interest rates are high, that reserve cash earns enough interest to boost your annual profits. This is not important in today's interest rate environment, but is something to keep in mind.

Questions

Three questions always arise in the minds of those who are considering adopting uncovered put writing.

1. Isn't it foolish to accept the option premium in exchange for accepting the risk that the stock might undergo a severe price decline?
2. If I'm bullish, wouldn't I be better off trying to buy stocks that can provide much larger returns on my investment?
3. If my goal is to accumulate wealth over the years, is this a winning strategy?

Answers

For most investors, the answers are *no, no,* and *yes.*

1. When you buy stock, you take the same risk. If the stock undergoes a rapid price decline, you suffer a substantial loss. But the put writer is better off than the investor who simply buys stock. Sure, they both lose, but the put writer keeps the put premium to reduce (and sometimes even eliminate) the loss.
2. If you have the ability to find those stocks, more power to you. The evidence suggests neither public investors nor professionals have that ability on a consistent basis. Writing uncovered put options enhances your investment returns and gives you an excellent chance of beating the averages most of the time.[1]
3. This strategy can produce consistent market-beating returns. Allowing those earnings to compound over time is an excellent path to accumulated wealth.

GOALS OF WRITING
UNCOVERED PUT OPTIONS

There are two major objectives for uncovered put writers: You either earn a profit (keep the option premium) or you buy your stock (or exchange traded fund [ETF]) at a favorable price.

When you write a naked put option, there are only two possible results when expiration day arrives.

1. If the stock or ETF is higher than the strike price, the put option expires worthless, and your profit is the cash you received for writing the put option.
2. If the stock or ETF is below the strike price, you are assigned an exercise notice and buy shares of stock at a predetermined price. That price is the strike price reduced by the amount of the option premium. For example, if you write an ETFQ Nov 40 put for $1.50 and are assigned on that put option, you pay a net of $38.50 for each ETFQ share.

Investors who should consider writing uncovered put options fall into two categories:

1. Investors who want to buy the underlying asset (stock or ETF) at a price below the current market price. Those investors have a further choice:
   a. Wait and hope the stock declines to the desired level, so it can be bought.
   b. Write a put option. You either buy the stock at your price or earn a profit as a consolation prize. That prize is the option premium.
2. Investors who want to earn a profit if the stock (or ETF) either increases in price or remains relatively unchanged in price. That profit is represented by the option premium.

Thus, this strategy may be appropriate for you when you want to buy shares of stock but are unwilling to pay the current market price. It's also appropriate for investors who want to earn a profit if they are unable to buy stock at their target price. Investors who place bids below the market, hoping to acquire shares at a later date and at a lower price, do not earn any profit if the stock does not decline to a price level they are willing to pay. When the put writer fails to purchase stock because it does not decline to an acceptable price level, a consolation profit is earned. That's surely a better result than having a bid go unfilled. Imagine—this is equivalent to earning a profit just because you entered a bid to buy shares at a price below the market.

Writing a put option may obligate you to purchase shares at a later date, so be certain you have the cash available in the event you are forced to buy stock.

NAKED PUT WRITING IN ACTION

Choosing Which Put to Sell

Let's look at an example. ABCD is a volatile stock you have been interested in buying for some time. Your target buy price is somewhere in the low $14s and it's currently trading near $15.50. Because it's a volatile stock, the option premiums are attractive for writing.[2] When you check current option prices online, you note there are several options you can write that enable you to meet your investment objective. Let's look at several possibilities and consider the benefits and disadvantages associated with each in an effort to select which put option to sell. Note that different investors make different choices, and none is making a mistake.

Assume it is currently the first week of August and expiration is three weeks in the future.

- ABCD Aug 15 put is $0.60 bid.
- ABCD Sep 15 put is $1.25 bid.
- ABCD Sep 12½ put is $0.30 bid.

If you write the Aug 15 put, you receive $60 per put option. If the put expires worthless, your profit is $60 for a three-week investment. Assuming your uncovered put positions are always cash backed, you must maintain $1,500 in the account for each put sold. Because you can use the cash generated from the sale of the put, your investment is $1,440 (plus commissions). The $60 profit represents a return of 4.16 percent (over 70 percent annualized) (4.16 percent return for three weeks is [4.16 × 52] ÷ 3, or 72.22 percent).

If the stock declines in price and eventually you are assigned an exercise notice, then you own the stock at $14.40 per share. If that is an acceptable purchase price, then writing the Aug 15 put is a good investment choice for you. Investors who demand an even lower purchase price can consider writing a put option with additional time premium.

If you decide to write the Sep 15 put, you receive $125 per option. This time there are seven weeks before expiration day. When expiration day arrives, there are two attractive possibilities:

1. You earn a seven-week profit of $125, or a return of 9.09 percent (67 percent annualized).

2. You own the shares, at $13.75 per share. (You pay 15 and deduct the option premium of 1.25.)

Of course, there is no guarantee of earning a profit, and it's possible ABCD stock will be trading considerably below $13.75 per share when you are assigned an exercise notice and forced to purchase the shares. Looking at the stock from today's perspective, and knowing the outcome is either a profit of $125 or a reduced purchase price ($13.75), writing the ABCD Sep 15 put option is an excellent investment choice.

There is one other alternative to consider. If your main goal is to earn a profit and you are less inclined to become an owner of ABCD shares, writing the Sep 12½ put option may appeal to you. You collect a significantly lower option premium, but, in return, it's far more likely that the option expires worthless and you do not become a shareholder. Writing this put can produce either of two outcomes when expiration day arrives in seven weeks:

1. The option expires worthless and you earn $30 on an investment of $1,220. That represents a return of 2.46 percent (18 percent annualized). This provides a lower return than writing the Sep 15 put, but it is much more likely you will earn that return.

2. You own the shares, paying $12.20. If you were eyeing the shares at a price in the low $14s, then this must be an acceptable purchase price.

If expiration day finds you owning the shares because you were assigned an exercise notice on puts you sold, you have the choice of holding and hoping for a price increase (this choice goes against the teachings of MPT) or writing covered call options (recommended) to earn additional income. The investment objective is eventually to be assigned an exercise notice by the owner of a covered call option you write. When that happens, you should have a good profit, as represented by the put and call option premium(s) you collected while waiting to sell the stock.[3] Here's how it works:

1. You write an ABCD Sep 12½ put and collect a premium of $0.30.

2. At expiration, you are assigned an exercise notice. You now own ABCD stock at a cost of $12.20.

3. You write an Oct 12½ call and collect a premium of $0.25, reducing the cost of your ABCD shares to $11.95.

4. When October expiration arrives, assume ABCD is below the strike price and the call option expires worthless.

5. You write a Nov 12½ call option and collect a premium of $0.30, reducing the cost of your ABCD shares to $11.65.

6. Finally, good news. The stock rallies and when November expiration arrives you are assigned an exercise notice on the call option and sell your stock at the strike price.

7. You sold ABCD at $12.50 and bought at a net cost of $11.65. You are where you wanted to be when you started: You have a profit and own no shares of ABCD. The profit is $0.85 on an original investment of $1,220, or 7.0 percent in three months.

Choosing the Expiration Month

As with writing covered call options, selling near-term options allows you the opportunity to earn the highest annualized profits. Writing options with more time remaining allows you to collect higher premiums, providing you with a lower break-even price if you are assigned and must buy stock. Your target price for buying the shares (if assigned) helps determine the proper expiration month to choose. There are two ways you can get a lower purchase price for the stock (if assigned): Write an option with either additional time before expiration or a lower strike price. By practicing with pretend trades ("paper trading"), you can gain a good feel for how these uncovered put positions perform in the real world. As you become comfortable with the process, you soon gain the confidence to choose the specific put option that best suits your needs.

When option premiums are low, as they are in today's market (compared to average prices dating back to 1988), writing options with shorter expirations is desirable so you can boost your potential annualized returns. When option premiums are higher, as surely they will be again one day, writing options with more time to expiration provides the comfort of additional safety and lower break-even points. As with all aspects of options trading, each investor must adjust the strategy of writing naked put options to suit personal preferences.

Choosing a Put to Sell Summary

When you are eager to own the stock, choose a put that is more likely to be in the money when expiration day arrives. Thus, choose at-the-money or slightly in-the-money puts.

If your paramount consideration is the price at which you buy stock, then choose a put whose premium allows you to own the shares at your target price (or lower). Of course, you may never buy the shares, but you keep the put premium as your profit and consolation prize.

If your investment objective is to earn a profit and you are *willing* to own the shares (but would rather not), then choose an out-of-the-money put, as there is less chance you will be forced to buy stock when expiration day arrives. But don't sell just any put—be certain there is enough time premium in the option to allow you to earn a minimum return on your investment. Each investor has to establish a minimum target, but the suggestion here is that the minimum should not be less than 0.5 percent per month (after commissions). (Personally I currently aim for a minimum return of $1\frac{1}{2}$ percent per month.)

RISK AND MARGIN CONSIDERATIONS

Writing uncovered put options is a very attractive strategy. One major reason is risk. This investment method is slightly less risky than simply buying and holding stocks, and every investment advisor tells the world that owning a diversified portfolio of stocks is a prudent investment choice. As an added bonus, the chances of earning a profit are increased (compared with buy and hold) when you write uncovered put options (or covered call options).

An investor who buys 1,000 shares of stock at $20 per share is investing $20,000. When you write 10 put options with a strike price of 20, you are accepting the obligation to buy 1,000 shares of stock at $20 per share at a later date. You may never have to honor that obligation, but if you do, your risk becomes the same as the investor who buys the shares now. But you have the advantage of having sold 10 put options, and the cash you received lowers the cost of your investment. Of course, your maximum profit is limited to the cash you receive when writing the puts.

If your position is cash backed—that is, if you have $20,000 cash in your account in case you are called on to honor the obligation to buy stock—then you are in the same position as any other stockholder when share prices decline.

Warning

Sometimes put writers make careless decisions and find themselves in trouble. This occurs when investors sell too many put options. Investors with $20,000 to invest know that $20,000 is the maximum possible loss (unless they *choose* to trade on margin and borrow cash from their brokers). When buying stock, investors know how much cash to spend and do not buy extra shares.

However, put writers might erroneously think that it isn't a big deal to sell 20 or 30 put options, instead of only 10. After all, they might mistakenly believe, "What's the harm in selling an option that costs only $50 per contract? That's a pretty small trade. If I can make $500 selling 10 puts, why don't I just sell 30 and make $1,500?" This mind-set must be avoided. When writing put options, always think about what you are going to do if you are assigned an exercise notice. If you are assigned on 30 puts with a strike price of 20, you must purchase 3,000 shares at $20 for a net cash outlay of $60,000. If you don't have sufficient cash in your account and cannot either transfer that cash into your account immediately or borrow it from your broker, you are going to receive a margin call.[4] That's an event you don't want to happen and something that is easily avoided.

Advice: Don't overextend yourself. When you begin your put-writing strategy, be certain you are fully cash backed. Later, when you have more experience, you can begin to use a small amount of margin. But the more margin you use, the greater the risk. Please don't be careless.

The main risk with adopting a strategy of writing uncovered put options for unwary investors is not the strategy itself, but their inability to recognize that it is easy to sell too many put options. This cannot happen to you if you are constantly aware of the cash you need, just in case you are assigned an exercise notice on each and every put option you sell. Such an assignment is unlikely before expiration day, but if you are aware, then you will not sell too many put options.

It's true that you can avoid being assigned an exercise notice if you repurchase any options you sold previously—*before* you are assigned. But sometimes an assignment notice arrives unexpectedly, and it's too late to repurchase the puts once you receive the assignment notice. Each broker

---

The Importance of Being Earnestly Cash-Backed

Note: The covered call writer does not have the problem of writing too many covered calls because that strategy uses cash to buy stock. The covered call writer understands the necessity of not opening new positions when out of money. It is less obvious when the uncovered put writer who uses margin is out of money. Thus, it's important to keep track of the amount of cash required, if you are assigned on all of the puts you sold.

handles this sticky situation differently, so be certain you know what your broker does when you don't have enough cash to cover an assignment.

Write uncovered puts. Collect those premiums. Buy stocks you want to own at favorable prices. But don't sell more put options than your financial condition allows. Be aware that each option you sell may obligate you to purchase 100 shares of stock, so always know how you will pay for that stock if and when you receive an assignment notice. To repeat: The main risk of this strategy is writing too many put options and not knowing what to do if assigned on each of the put options you sell.

One further risk is worth considering when you write an uncovered put. It's possible to miss out on a surge in the value of the shares you want to buy, but an unlikely combination of events is required before this risk comes into play.

- The stock drops in price to a point where you would have bought it.
- The stock then rallies substantially beyond the strike price of the put option.

If these events happen, then the investor who buys shares easily outperforms the investor who writes the uncovered put option. Although this scenario occasionally occurs, it is far more likely that the put writer achieves a better financial result than the investor who enters a low bid in an attempt to buy stock. After all, the put writer outperforms whenever the shares decline in price, remain relatively unchanged, or increase in value up to the break-even point (see box). This investment strategy is very similar to covered call writing in that it produces better results the vast majority of the time.

Break-Even Points for Put Writers

Break-even points for put writers are the same as those for call writers (see Chapter 9). The *upside break-even point* is the stock price at which you make the same profit as the investor who is simply long stock. That point equals the strike price plus the put premium. Above that price, the investor who owns stock makes additional profits and the put writer does not.

The *downside break-even point* is the stock price below which selling the put option is no longer profitable. That price equals the strike price minus the put premium.

COMPARING RISK: COVERED CALL
WRITING AND UNCOVERED PUT WRITING

As mentioned earlier, the risks associated with covered call writing and uncovered put writing are identical. When you adopt covered call writing, you buy stock and collect the premium from writing a call option now. When you adopt uncovered put writing, you agree to buy stock later (if called on to do so) and collect the premium from writing a put option now.

The data in Table 11.1 illustrates the cost and risks associated with either position. In our example, the stock is priced at $42 per share, and you write an option with a strike price of 40.

- An identical investment ($3,850) is required, either in cash for the covered call or cash kept in reserve (so the put option is cash backed) for the uncovered put.
- Maximum profit occurs when the stock is above the strike price (40) when expiration arrives.
- Maximum profit equals the time premium of the option.
- Maximum loss (stock goes bankrupt) is $3,850.

SUMMARY

Uncovered (naked) put writing is a bullish strategy for investors who want to reduce the downside risk of owning stocks. When adopting this strategy, investors either collect a profit when the put expires worthless or buy the shares they want to own at a reduced price when assigned an exercise notice. Profits are limited to the premium collected when writing the option.

Despite opinions to the contrary, this strategy is more conservative than that of simply owning stock and increases the chances of outperforming the market over an extended period of time. Just remember not to overextend your resources.

CHAPTER 12

Historical Data

BuyWrite Index and Volatility Index

I t's one thing to read about an options strategy, but I'm sure you want to know if the strategy really performs as advertised. Does it really enhance returns for stock market investments? Fortunately evidence shows it does.

BUYWRITE INDEX

The Chicago Board Options Exchange (CBOE) publishes data for BXM, or BuyWrite index, a benchmark designed to track the performance of a hypothetical covered call writing strategy. BXM is based on a portfolio that approximates ownership of each of the stocks in the S&P 500 index (SPX) and writing covered call options on the index. Data for this index are available beginning in June 1988.

The performance of the BXM is based on the following five-step investment strategy. (*Note:* This description is presented to enable you to understand how the BXM works; this investment methodology is not recommended for readers to follow.)

1. Buy and maintain ownership of a portfolio of stocks that mimics the S&P 500 index. An investor does not have to own the entire index, as long as the stock portfolio has a very high correlation with that index.
2. Write the near-term SPX call option early in the morning on the third Friday of each month.[1]

3. To provide a constant methodology, the call that is sold always has one month remaining to expiration. The strike price is always just above the current index level (the first call option that is out of the money).

4. The call is held through expiration and is *cash settled* (see box) based on prices at the opening of the market on the third Friday of the month. *Note:* The strategy used to calculate the BXM does not allow for any adjustments. In the real world, the results of an investor who adopts this methodology may differ from that of the official BXM if that investor makes an adjustment to the position. Chapters 15 and 16 provide examples of how and why investors may want to make such adjustments.

5. Every month, a new one-month call option is written, based on the identical strategy. Because assignments are cash settled, an investor who adopts this strategy never has to worry about selling and repurchasing stocks, except for making an occasional change in portfolio makeup (when the composition of the index changes). If the investor is assigned an exercise notice, no shares of stock change ownership.

Now that the BXM exists, an important question remains: What does it tell us about the financial results of adopting a covered call writing strategy? If writing covered calls is an advantageous strategy, would following that strategy produce meaningful benefits in the real world? The existence of the BXM index provides information needed to answer the question.[2]

Cash-Settled Exercises and Assignments

Because SPX options are cash settled, the portfolio owner never has to relinquish shares. When a cash-settled option expires in the money, the option owner's account is credited, and the option writer's account is debited, the proper amount of cash. The cash amount is equal to the number of points by which the option is in the money, multiplied by 100.

For example, if the investor using the BXM strategy writes an SPX call with a strike price of 1,110 and if the settlement price of the SPX (based on opening prices of each of the stocks on the third Friday of the month) is $1,117.35, then the writer of the call option must deliver cash to the owner of the option. That cash amount is $1,117.35 − $1,110.0, or $7.35 × 100. That translates into $735 per contract.

If an option is out of the money at expiration, it simply expires worthless and no cash is transferred.

It's possible to compare investment returns when owing a diversified portfolio of stocks (index mutual funds) with returns using a covered call writing strategy. Keep in mind that the BXM strategy has a slightly bullish bias, because the option written is always slightly out of the money. Index mutual funds have a totally bullish bias, as they are fully invested in stocks and earn profits when stock prices increase and suffer losses when they decrease. Figure 12.1 illustrates the comparison.

The figure clearly shows that the option-writing strategy easily outperformed an investment plan of simply buying and owning stocks over this 16-year period. It's also noteworthy that this was a bullish period for the market, with the S&P rising from the mid-260s in June 1988 to over 1,100 in mid-2004. As discussed in Chapter 10, covered call writing outperforms a buy-and-hold strategy through most stock market conditions, but compares less well in strongly rising markets. Even though these 16 years were primarily bullish, covered call writing significantly enhanced investors' returns on investments.

Table 12.1 presents the year-by-year comparison of investment results. The buy-write strategy enhanced investment returns in only 9 of the 16

**BuyWrite Index versus S&P 500 Index
June 1, 1988–March 2004**

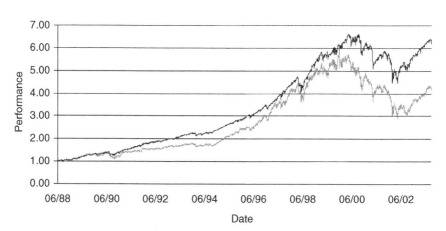

FIGURE 12.1   BuyWrite Index versus S&P 500 Index June 1988–March 2004
Source: Chicago Board Options Exchange

SPX and BXM were set to a value of $1.00 as of June 1, 1988. Actual SPX was 266.69. Upper line represents BXM, worth 6.30 times its initial value as of March 2004. Lower line represents SPX, worth 4.20 times its initial value as of March 2004.

TABLE 12.1 Year-by-Year Profit Comparison

			BXM versus SPX		
Year Ending	BXM	1-Year Gain	SPX	1-Year Gain	Diff
Start	100.00		266.69		
1988	108.13	**8.13%**	277.72	4.14%	3.99%
1989	135.17	25.01%	353.40	**27.25%**	−2.24%
1990	140.56	**3.99%**	330.22	−6.56%	10.55%
1991	174.85	24.39%	417.09	**26.31%**	−1.91%
1992	195.00	**11.52%**	435.71	4.46%	7.06%
1993	222.50	**14.10%**	466.45	7.06%	7.05%
1994	232.50	**4.50%**	459.27	−1.54%	6.04%
1995	281.26	20.97%	615.93	**34.11%**	−13.14%
1996	324.86	15.50%	740.74	**20.26%**	−4.76%
1997	411.41	26.64%	970.43	**31.01%**	−4.37%
1998	489.37	18.95%	1,229.23	**26.67%**	−7.72%
1999	592.96	**21.17%**	1,469.25	19.53%	1.64%
2000	636.81	**7.40%**	1,320.28	−10.14%	17.54%
2001	567.25	**−10.92%**	1,148.09	−13.04%	2.12%
2002	523.92	**−7.64%**	879.82	−23.37%	15.73%
2003	625.38	19.37%	1,111.92	**26.38%**	−7.01%
	Total Gain (Compounded)	**525.38%**		**316.93%**	

Source: Chicago Board Options Exchange

BXM: BuyWrite index
SPX: S&P 500 index
Start: Data from June 1, 1988
Diff: BXM One-Year Gain Minus SPX One-Year Gain
Total Gain Compounded: From June 1, 1988 to December 31, 2003

periods (15 full years and 1 partial year), but as Table 12.1 shows, in some years those additional profits were substantial (more than 17.5 percent in 2000 and almost 16 percent in 2002). The purpose of adopting a covered call writing strategy is to improve the probability of outperforming the market over an extended period of time. As the results show, this anticipated enhancement was a reality for the period for which data are available. From June 1988 through June 2004, BXM returned 525 percent and SPX returned 317 percent.

There are going to be years when you may wish you never heard of covered call writing. For example, notice how the S&P index easily outperformed the BXM during the very bullish years of 1995 to 1998. But over the longer term, this strategy is very likely to continue to provide substantial benefits—reduced volatility and additional profits—when compared with simply buying and holding a diversified stock portfolio.

Before you decide to rush into adopting an investment approach that duplicates the BXM strategy, consider some drawbacks. If you want to own a basket of stocks that attempts to mimic the performance of the S&P 500 index, you must determine the proper number of call options to sell to obtain the best possible hedge. Here is an example of how to make the calculation:

If the current price of the SPX index is $1,100, the formula for the quantity of index options contracts needed to hedge the entire portfolio is:

Amount to be hedged (the current market value of the portfolio)
÷ strike price of the SPX options contract × 100

For example, if the portfolio you construct in an attempt to mimic the performance of the S&P 500 is worth $250,000, and if you write an SPX option with a strike price of 1100, then to hedge the portfolio properly, you want to sell

$$250,000 \div (1100 \times 100) \text{ contracts}$$

That's 2.27 contracts. Fractional contracts are not allowed, so you would write two contracts to provide the best possible hedge. This process hedges $220,000 of your portfolio, leaving the remaining $30,000 unhedged. That's great when the market rises, but it is not as good when the market falls. Fortunately, it's not necessary to leave yourself exposed to that degree of market risk. Although adopting this methodology does allow you to minimize commissions (because the options are cash settled, you don't have to constantly buy or sell the underlying shares), it's inconvenient and adds unnecessary risk when you cannot hedge your *entire* portfolio.

Thus, I recommend that you do not attempt to mimic the returns of the BXM index by adopting the methodology just described. There is a much simpler, much more efficient method available to you. The method involves constructing a diversified portfolio from among the many optionable exchange traded funds and then writing covered call options on those shares. Be sure to buy ETFs in increments of 100 shares. To match the returns of the BXM most closely, you can write call options that are slightly out of the money.[3] The details are discussed in Part IV.

Although worthwhile to understand how the performance of the BXM index is calculated, trying to match that index's performance is not an efficient methodology for the vast majority of investors. Stick with a covered call writing program in which you can easily hedge your entire portfolio.

FURTHER EVIDENCE THAT COVERED CALL WRITING WORKS

The data for BXM presents compelling evidence that covered call writing is a viable strategy. Those who disapprove of writing covered calls argue that the limited upside potential makes the strategy unattractive. What the naysayers fail to mention is that it's much more common for markets to make small directional movements rather than to be strongly bullish. It is just those small movements that produce outstanding results for the strategy of covered call writing. It is well worth taking the chance of missing out on part of a huge upward move, because such moves are uncommon. But even when those sharp upswings happen, the covered call writer makes out very well, as the strategy has a bullish bias. In Table 12.1 you can see how much better the S&P performed during the bullish run from 1995 to 1998, but the performance of the BXM was pretty impressive also, averaging a return of 20.51 percent (versus 28.01 percent).

There is additional evidence to support the superiority of adopting covered call writing. Richard Croft, an investment counselor and portfolio manager, and associates have constructed a buy-write index based on the Standard & Poor's Toronto Stock Exchange 60 index (TSE60). It is named the Montreal Exchange Covered Call Writers index (symbol: MCWX). Data are available beginning in late December 1993.[4] The covered call strategy outperformed the buy-and-hold strategy in 8 of the 10 years of data availability. Table 12.2 shows that while the TSE60 index approximately doubled, the covered call index nearly tripled.

The investment methodology used by Croft is slightly different from that used by the CBOE and the BXM index. The TSE 60 index portfolio is comprised of an ETF, the Standard & Poor's Toronto Stock Exchange 60 Index Participation Fund. At expiration, options are cash settled, so it is never necessary to buy or sell shares of the ETF. The strategy calls for writing a call option that is *closest* to the money (rather than the first out-of-the-money option) at the end of the trading day (rather than early in the morning) on the Monday following expiration. Thus, this strategy leaves the investor naked long (unhedged) all day Monday following expiration. (Croft does not explain why the option trades are not made early Monday morning.) These statistics provide additional evidence supporting the idea that covered call writing enhances portfolio performance.

Not only are returns on an investment enhanced, an additional benefit of the covered call writing strategy is those returns are achieved with a reduction in volatility. Croft notes that the annual returns achieved by covered call writers are more consistent than those achieved by owners of the ETF.[5] The CBOE publishes a graph showing the standard deviation of the

TABLE 12.2   Year-by-Year Profit Comparison

			MCWX versus TSE60		
Year	MCWX	1-Year Gain	TSE60	1-Year Gain	Diff
1993	102.0		221.49		
1994	105.0	2.94%	221.84	0.16%	2.78
1995	119.0	13.33%	250.51	12.92%	0.41
1996	156.0	31.09%	321.59	28.37%	2.72
1997	191.0	22.44%	378.09	17.57%	4.87
1998	193.0	1.05%	375.98	−0.56%	1.61
1999	231.0	19.69%	495.86	31.88%	−12.20
2000	269.0	16.45%	528.72	6.63%	9.82
2001	268.0	−0.37%	442.55	−16.30%	15.93
2002	247.0	−7.84%	373.15	−15.68%	7.85
2003	287.0	16.19%	458.72	22.93%	−6.74
	10–Year Gain (Compounded)	**181.37%**		**107.11%**	

Source: Montreal Stock Exchange

MCWX: Montreal Exchange Covered Call Writers Index
TSE60: the Toronto Stock Exchange 60 Index
Diff: BuyWrite Index minus TSE60

annualized returns is reduced by 33 percent when the buy-write strategy is utilized.[6] In layman's terms, the annual profit (or loss) differs from the average profit by a smaller amount when the covered call strategy is adopted—hence, the portfolio value is less volatile.

VOLATILITY INDEX

The CBOE Volatility index (VIX) was originally designed to track the implied volatility (IV) of the Standard & Poor's 100 index (OEX). A change was made in 2003, and the VIX now tracks the IV of the SPX (S&P 500 index). The methodology used to calculate the value of the index was updated at the same time. The calculation includes options with a variety of strike prices in the front two expiration months.[7] Information is available online for those interested in details of the calculation method.[8]

Originally introduced in 1993 (using data dating back to 1986), the VIX soon became the benchmark for measuring implied volatility. VIX is a measure of future volatility *expectations*, rather than of actual historical

How Implied Volatility Affects Option Prices

High implied volatility (IV) translates into high option prices. For example, consider a call option (stock is 50) with six months until expiration and a strike price of 50:

When the implied volatility is 15, the option trades at $2.35

When the implied volatility is 30, the option trades at $4.40

When the implied volatility is 49 (as in September 2001), the option trades at $7.00

When the implied volatility is 150 (as in October 1987), the option trades at $20.10

It may be difficult to believe, but the bid for options that routinely trade for less than $3 today were more than $20 for a few days in October 1987. And people were desperate to buy those options to protect their remaining assets. In addition, asking prices were much higher than bid prices as few people were willing to sell options.

volatility. High implied volatility (high option prices) means there is an expectation that the market is going to be more volatile than usual before options expiration. But the index represents more than that to some traders and has come to represent a measure of market sentiment, with high VIX measurements indicating "fear" and low measurements indicating "complacency." That fear represents concern about a large market decline, and high VIX readings are considered bearish for the market. The highest readings ever recorded occurred during and immediately after the stock market crash of October 1987, when the VIX reached an incomprehensible 150. (For comparison, in mid-2004, the VIX is near 15.) When the market reopened a few days after the terrorist attacks of September 11, 2001, the VIX reached a level of "only" 49.

Figure 12.2 presents VIX data from 1990 through year-end 2003. The data in the figure begins in 1988 because the 1987 data (VIX 150 in October) would dwarf all other VIX values.

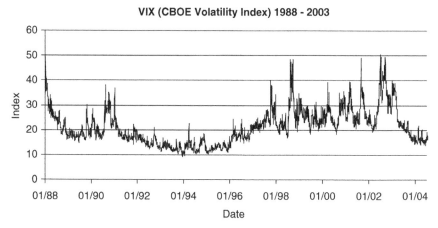

FIGURE 12.2 CBOE Volatility Index (VIX), January 1, 1988–June 30, 2004
Source: Chicago Board Options Exchange

WHAT DO ALL THESE DATA MEAN FOR COVERED CALL WRITERS?

You have seen the evidence demonstrating the viability of writing options as part of a conservative strategy. The future is unknowable, but:

- BXM data show covered call writers earned a higher return than buy-and-hold investors over a 16-year period.
- VIX is cyclical and periodically turns higher, then lower. It is difficult to predict when these ups and downs will occur. The BXM data tell us that it pays to stay with covered call writing during both highs and lows in the VIX.
- The VIX is currently below its recent range but well above the record lows. If it eventually turns higher, covered call writing should produce even better returns than it offers today.

Let's move on to the specific recommendations of how you can construct a portfolio according to the teachings of modern portfolio theory and enhance your expected profits by writing covered calls or uncovered puts.

PART IV

Putting It All Together

CHAPTER 13

Building a Portfolio

You know that modern portfolio theory (MPT) stresses the importance of owning a well-diversified portfolio. You've seen how exchange traded funds (ETFs) offer many advantages over traditional mutual funds for investors who have (or can accumulate) at least several thousand dollars to invest. You've learned about options and how they can be used to enhance the returns on your portfolio. It's time to tie it all together and develop an investment methodology that increases the probability of beating the market on a consistent basis.

BUILDING A WELL-DIVERSIFIED PORTFOLIO

The first step is deciding what constitutes a proper portfolio for you. You don't have to be married to that portfolio; you can make changes whenever you deem it advisable. To get started, select the types of investments you want to own. Some sample portfolios follow, but they are merely examples. One may be suitable for you, but the purpose of using examples is to illustrate how easy it is to compile your own portfolio.

Begin by allocating your assets. This is not an easy task for many investors; they simply invest all their available money in the stock market. Although it is not the best way to proceed, if you fall into that category, or if you *want* to invest all your assets in stocks, it's your money and you are entitled to make that choice.

After deciding how much to invest in the stock market, use that money to purchase a suitable mix of ETFs. Choose only ETFs that have listed options (see Tables 13.1 and 13.2 at the end of this chapter) and buy in round lots (increments of 100 shares). You may decide that one broad-based ETF is sufficient diversification, or you may prefer to tweak your portfolio to include several types of ETFs.

You can buy ETFs that invest in domestic or foreign companies. You can choose those that invest in small, medium, or large companies. You can invest in specific sectors of the market. Of course, you can build your portfolio out of any combination of ETFs that suits you.

Keep in mind:

- Trading expenses are important. Each ETF purchase requires the payment of a commission to your broker. Writing options on each ETF requires paying another commission. Thus, concentrating your holdings into fewer ETFs minimizes expenses. More important, using the services of a deep-discount broker makes a significant difference in the performance of your investment portfolio. You don't ever want to find yourself in a position where you want to make a trade but decide not do so because trading expenses are too high.
- To use options efficiently, you want to own round lots (100-share increments) of each ETF in your portfolio.[1]

Each sample portfolio assumes an investment of $100,000, but you can make adjustments to fit your financial condition. It's easier to see how the method works when real prices are used, and the prices throughout this chapter were current in mid-2004.

SAMPLE PORTFOLIOS, ASSUMING AN INVESTMENT OF $100,000

Sample Portfolio #1: Based on a Single Broad-Based Index   If you want to limit your portfolio to a single ETF and if you are interested in owning shares in the American stock market, VTI provides the broadest possible diversification. VTI is the symbol for the Vanguard Total Stock Market VIPERs. This ETF tries to replicate the performance of the Wilshire 5000 index by owning a *sampling* of the stocks representing that index. As of year-end 2003, according to the Vanguard Group, VTI represented ownership in 3,651 different stocks. It's inefficient for this ETF to own shares of each stock in the Wilshire 5000 index because many of those stocks are difficult to buy or sell in any reasonable quantity. Because sampling comes very close to mimicking the performance of the entire index, it's sufficient to own these 3,600+ different stocks.

VTI is priced at approximately $110, so buy 900 shares spending $99,000.

Sample Portfolio #2: Based on a Different Broad-Based Index
An alternative investment is the Russell 3000 index, consisting of the 3,000 largest publicly listed U.S. companies, representing about 98 percent of the total capitalization of the entire U.S. stock market. According to Barclays Global Investors, the ETF owned 2,946 of the 3,000 stocks early in 2004. The symbol for the iShares Russell 3000 Index is IWV.

Priced near $65, you can buy 1,500 shares, investing $97,500.

Portfolios Based on Size of Companies

Sample Portfolio #3: Small-Cap Lover's Portfolio Some investors prefer to own a portfolio consisting of smaller, faster-growing companies, believing these stocks can provide better returns. During most periods in our history, small-caps have outperformed the stocks of larger companies, but this has not always been true.

To emphasize small caps, you can add shares of IWM to your portfolio. IWM is the symbol for the iShares Russell 2000 index, which is comprised of the smallest 2,000 companies in the larger Russell 3000 index. In other words, it holds no shares of any of America's largest 1,000 companies. Obviously, the more shares of IWM you add, the more your portfolio emphasizes smaller capitalization stocks.

One possible portfolio:

Buy 1,000 shares of IWV (price approximately $65; cost $65,000).

Buy 300 shares of IWM (price approximately $117; cost $35,000).

Sample Portfolio #4: Mid-Caps You can build a portfolio consisting of mid-cap stocks by purchasing shares of MDY, the S&P MidCap 400 index, or IJH, the iShares representing the same index. As of this writing, MDY is a better choice because the options are more actively traded.

Buy 900 MDY at $109, investing $98,100.

Sample Portfolio #5: Larger Companies Diamonds (DIA), the ETF representing ownership of the 30 stocks in the Dow Jones Industrial

Average, is a good choice for an investor who wants to concentrate on owning shares of large, well-known companies.

If you prefer to own an ETF that has more than 30 stocks in its portfolio and is better diversified then OEF, the iShares S&P 100 index fund may be appropriate. This ETF tracks the performance of the Standard & Poor's 100 index (OEX).

Buy 400 DIA at $105, investing $42,000.

Buy 1,000 OEF at $56, investing $ 56,000.

Sample Portfolio #6: Portfolio Avoiding Smaller Companies

If you prefer to own a mix of larger and mid-size companies and omit small-capitalization stocks from your portfolio, consider:

Buy 500 MDY at $109, investing $54,500.

Buy 800 OEF at $56, investing $44,800.

Concentrating on Growth Stocks or Value Stocks

When investing in ETFs, you have the choice of buying a balanced portfolio or a portfolio emphasizing either growth stocks or value stocks. For example, several of the iShare ETFs that match the performance of a specific index *also* offer ETFs that divide the stocks in the index into a growth sector and a value sector. These ETFs include the Russell 1000, Russell 2000, Russell 3000, S&P MidCap 400 index, and S&P SmallCap 600 index.

Thus, you can buy shares of an ETF representing the entire index, or just the growth or value portion of the indexes.

Here's how it works: The stocks in a given index are ranked by their price-to-book ratios. To determine the ratio, each stock's price per share is divided by its book value.[2] This ratio compares how the stock market values the shares of a company compared with the value of the company on its financial statements.

The stock list is then divided into two parts. The stocks with the highest price-to-book ratios are placed in the growth index and those with the lowest price-to-book ratios are placed in the value index.

The growth and value component indexes based on the Russell indexes contain some duplication of stocks, as the fund managers consider some stocks suitable for both the value and growth portfolios. The growth and value components of the MidCap 400 and SmallCap 600 indexes do not have any duplication of stocks.

The bottom line is that you have the choice of investing in only part (approximately half) of each of these indexes, if you prefer to emphasize either growth or value stocks.

Sample Portfolio #7: Emphasizing Growth Stocks

Buy 400 VTI (Wilshire 5000) at $110, investing $44,000.

Buy 200 IJK (MidCap 400 Growth) at $123, investing $24,600.

Buy 300 IJT (SmallCap 600 Growth) at $93, investing $27,900.

Sample Portfolio #8: Emphasizing Value Stocks

Buy 300 DIA at $105, investing $31,500.

Buy 300 IJK (MidCap 400 Value) at $115, investing $34,500.

Buy 300 IJS (SmallCap 600 Value) at $105, investing $31,500.

Note: This portfolio is balanced between large-, mid- and small-capitalization stocks and places two-thirds of the capital into value stocks.

Sample Portfolio #9: Includes Investments in Foreign Stocks

It's not necessary to limit your investments to American companies. Good asset allocation suggests investing internationally. EFA is an ETF that attempts to mimic the performance of the MSCI EAFE index—the Morgan Stanley Capital International Europe, Australasia, and Far East—the benchmark used in the United States to measure international equity performance. EFA invests in stocks from Europe, Australia, Asia, and the Far East.

Priced near $140, shares of EFA can be added to any portfolio to provide additional diversification.

Sample portfolio stressing American mid-caps and foreign stocks:

Buy 100 EFA at $140, investing $14,000.

Buy 400 MDY at $109, investing $43,600.

Buy 400 VTI at 109, investing $43,600.

Sample Portfolio #10: Investment in Specific Market Sectors

If you are willing to go against the teachings of MPT (this is not recommended, but if it suits your investment style, you certainly are allowed to make this type of investment) and accept the risks and potential rewards that come with a less-diversified portfolio, you can apportion some of your capital to specific industries. You can do this by owning shares of either sector SPDRs or HOLDRs.

If you believe that proper asset allocation includes investing in real estate, one path to achieving that goal is to own shares of real estate investment trusts (REITs). You easily can invest in a suitable group of REITs by owning shares of the iShares Cohen & Steers Realty Majors Index Fund (ICF). This ETF seeks investment results corresponding to the performance of large, actively traded U.S. real estate investment trusts, as represented by the Cohen & Steers Realty Majors index.

Adding real estate investments helps diversify your portfolio. If you believe that one or two specific sectors of the market (e.g., biotechnology) represent the wave of the future and will outperform other types of investments, you may decide to allocate some of your investment capital to those industries. A sample portfolio might contain:

Buy 100 BBH (Biotech HOLDRs) at $140, investing $14,000.

Buy 300 XLF (Financial Sector SPDR) at $29, investing $8,700.

Buy 100 ICF (Cohen & Steers REITs) at $106, investing $10,600.

Buy 100 MDY (MidCap 400 SPDR) at $109, investing $10,900.

Buy 500 VTI (Vanguard Total Market VIPERs) at $109, investing $54,500.

SUMMARY

Although most ETFs do not have listed stock options, the variety of ETFs that are optionable is sufficiently diverse to allow you to build a portfolio that meets almost everyone's needs. Table 13.1 contains the current list of optionable ETFs. Table 13.2 lists the optionable HOLDRs and sector SPDRs.

Now that you know how to build a portfolio that meets your requirements, it's time to think about the type of option strategy to adopt when managing your portfolio.

TABLE 13.1 Optionable ETFs

Underlying Exchange Traded Fund	Symbol
DIAMONDs (DJIA)	DIA
Nasdaq 100 Index Tracking Stock	QQQ
FORTUNE 500 Index Tracking Stock	FFF
iShares Cohen & Steers Realty Major	ICF
iShares Dow Jones US Utilities Sector	IDU
iShares Dow Jones US Energy Sector	IYE
iShares Dow Jones US Financial Sector	IYF
iShares Dow Jones US Healthcare Sector	IYH
iShares Dow Jones US Technology Sector	IYW
iShares Dow Jones US Telecommunications Sector	IYZ
iShares Russell 1000	IWB
iShares Russell 1000 Growth	IWF
iShares Russell 1000 Value	IWD
iShares Russell 2000	IWM
iShares Russell 2000 Growth	IWO
iShares Russell 2000 Value	IWN
iShares Russell 3000	IWV
iShares Russell 3000 Growth	IWZ
iShares Russell 3000 Value	IWW
iShares Russell MidCap	IWR
iShares Russell MidCap Growth	IWP
iShares Russell MidCap Value	IWS
iShares S&P 100 Index Fund	OEF
iShares MidCap 400 Index	IJH
iShares MidCap 400 BARRA Growth Index	IJK
iShares MidCap 400 BARRA Value Index	IJJ
iShares SmallCap 600 Index	IJR
iShares SmallCap 600 BARRA Growth Index	IJT
iShares SmallCap 600 BARRA Value Index	IJS
MidCap SPDRs	MDY
PowerShares Dynamic Market Portfolio	PWC
PowerShares Dynamic OTC Portfolio	PWO
Vanguard Total Market VIPERs	VTI
iShares Goldman Sachs Networking Index	IGN
iShares Goldman Sachs Semiconductor Index	IGW
iShares Goldman Sachs Software Index	IGV
iShares Goldman Sachs Technology Index	IGM
iShares MSCI EAFE Index	EFA
StreetTRACKS Dow Jones Global Titans Index	DGT
Fidelity NASDAQ Composite Index	ONQ

Source: American Stock Exchange

TABLE 13.2 Optionable HOLDRs and Sector SPDRs

Underlying Exchange Traded Fund	Symbol
Biotech HOLDRs	BBH
Broadband HOLDRs	BDH
Europe 2001 HOLDRs	EKH
Internet Architecture HOLDRs	IAH
Internet HOLDRs	HHH
Market 2000+ HOLDRs	MKH
Oil Service HOLDRs	OIH
Pharmaceutical HOLDRs	PPH
Regional Bank HOLDRs	RKH
Retail HOLDRs	RTH
Semiconductor HOLDRs	SMH
Software HOLDRs	SWH
Telecom HOLDRs	TTH
Utilities HOLDRs	UTH
Wireless HOLDRs	WMH
iShares NASDAQ Biotechnology Sector	IBB
Select SPDR—Health Care	XLV
Select SPDR—Materials	XLB
Select SPDR—Consumer Staples	XLP
Select SPDR—Energy	XLE
Select SPDR—Financial	XLF
Select SPDR—Industrial	XLI
Select SPDR—Technology	XLK
Select SPDR—Utilities	XLU
Select SPDR—Consumer Discretionary	XLY

Source: American Stock Exchange

CHAPTER 14

Finding Your Style

Choosing an Option to Write

You now own a diversified portfolio consisting of exchange traded funds (ETFs), or are ready to purchase such a portfolio. For those readers who do not yet have enough in savings to justify the brokerage commissions involved in beginning this process, you can begin a savings program by paying yourself first. This means investing some money from every paycheck before you tackle any of your other bills. Go for passive investing and choose an index fund that charges very low fees. Periodically, as you amass sufficient funds to benefit from the recommended program, you can cash in your index funds to purchase ETFs and begin writing covered calls against them. Depending on the ETFs you want to own, $10,000 may be enough to get started. Thus, even if you are not yet ready to begin this program, by mastering the investment methods described here, you will be prepared to do so when your financial situation allows.

Once you own your ETF portfolio, the next step is selecting which call option to write against each of your holdings. Sometimes you have a myriad of choices; other times there may be just two or three options from which to choose. It's important to understand how to think about making a final decision. There are no wrong decisions, but you have much to gain by making the choice that provides the best fit for your investing style. In this chapter we'll go through an example, in detail, showing the thought processes involved in considering each of the choices. That puts you in position to make an intelligent decision when selecting the option to write. In the next chapter we'll take an even closer look at the covered call writing strategy as we follow a hypothetical portfolio for an entire year.

To some readers, this attention to detail may seem tedious, but if you take the time to study the material carefully, you will be better placed to make decisions appropriate for both your pocketbook and your psyche.

It's important to have confidence in your investing methods and to own a portfolio that makes you feel comfortable—from the expectation of being able to meet both your investment objectives and your psychological needs. The following discussion includes an example of how psychology fits into this picture.

As you proceed with the process of selecting specific options to sell, you develop a certain style. That is, you may choose to adopt a very conservative style that focuses primarily on portfolio protection and less on generating profits. You may choose to be very aggressive, seeking to earn the majority of your income by picking winning stocks. (Remember, modern portfolio theory [MPT] tells you how difficult that is to accomplish.) I believe that a compromise strategy seeking some portfolio protection coupled with a good profit potential is a winning style. Regardless of your choice, once you select a specific style, you don't have to remain married to it. You can modify your investing strategy every time an expiration day arrives, seeking a system for writing covered call options that gives you the most satisfaction. Some investors prefer to choose one style and remain with it for consistency; others frequently make subtle changes. The more you accept the premise that's it's unlikely that you can profitably predict the timing and direction of stock market moves, the more likely you are to remain consistent in your style—after you discover what it is.

DETERMINE YOUR INVESTMENT OBJECTIVE

If you invest without writing any covered call options, your potential gains are unlimited and you own your investments unhedged. If, instead, you decide to limit your potential profits by adopting a covered call writing strategy, you are compensated for accepting those limited profits by gaining some portfolio protection and an increased probability of earning a profit. The track record of the BuyWrite index (BXM) discussed in Chapter 12 shows that adopting this investment strategy under a variety of market conditions is expected to provide enhanced earnings.

Many investors believe they have the ability to successfully time the market. But we have already discussed one of the conclusions of MPT: that attempting to do so is a poor method of investing over the long term. Because the methods illustrated here are based on the findings of MPT, let's assume you want the portion of your assets allocated to investing in equities to remain fully invested at all times. To remain fully invested, write new options immediately after expiration when you sell options that expire worthless. If you are assigned an exercise notice and sell some of your holdings, reinvest the proceeds by buying more ETFs (the same or different ones) as soon as possible. "As soon as possible" means the morning of the first business day after expiration.

FIRST DECISIONS

Before implementing a covered call writing campaign, two decisions must be made.

1. What portion of your portfolio do you want to dedicate to this strategy? The recommendation here is to write covered call options on your entire portfolio of ETFs. (If you choose to own shares of individual stocks, you also can write covered call options against them.)

2. How do you expect to make the bulk of your profits?

   a. Is your primary objective to make as much money as possible from a rising stock market? Then you want to be writing out-of-the-money (OTM) call options. You collect some premium from the options, but your primary source of income depends on your ability to select stocks that increase in value. This style provides very little portfolio protection and is most successful in strongly rising markets. This is not the ideal scenario for covered call writing and goes against the precepts of MPT, but it does allow you to aim for additional profits.

   b. Are your primary objectives to earn significant profits from writing options and to gain some insurance against loss? Then you want to write at-the-money (ATM) and/or in-the-money (ITM) options and occasionally options that are *slightly* out of the money. The greatest advantage of adopting this style is that it leads to earning profits from a much greater percentage of your positions. This is the recommended investment style for covered call writers, and it does not leave you depending on a bull market to make money from your equity investments. Writing ATM or ITM options provides greater (but limited) protection against a market decline and works well in either neutral or rising markets. It also helps to reduce, or eliminate, losses in markets that undergo small declines.

Choosing the Call Option to Write

To get a clearer understanding of how important your investment objectives are in choosing which call to write, let's consider an example. Assume you purchase shares of a generic ETF (whose symbol is ETFQ) at $40. Let's further assume when writing a covered call option, you have the choice of selling a call option with strike prices ranging from 36 to 44, in 1-point increments. How do you determine which to sell?

Options are always available with at least four different expiration months. For this discussion, let's assume you always write the option that expires in the front month—which means the month with the nearest expiration date. We'll consider selling each of the options in turn, indicating the advantages or disadvantages of each. By seeing why writing each call is appropriate for some investors under some circumstances, you will gain some insight on which option you would choose to sell under similar circumstances.

Table 14.1 lists the strike price of each option, the premium (price of the option) you collect when selling, the amount of protection against loss it provides, and your maximum potential profit. That profit potential is divided into two parts. The time premium in the option is the maximum profit you can earn as a result of writing the call. The second part of the potential profit represents the maximum capital gain you can earn, if the stock increases in value and you are assigned an exercise notice at expiration.

TABLE 14.1   Option Premium for Hypothetical ETFQ Options

Price = 40; Time to Expiration = 4 Weeks

Strike Price	Option Premium	Downside Protection[a]	Profit Potential	
			Option Time Premium	ETFQ above Strike Price
36	$4.00	10.00%	$ 0	$ 0
37	$3.20	8.00%	$ 20	$ 0
38	$2.35	5.88%	$ 35	$ 0
39	$1.65	4.13%	$ 65	$ 0
40	$1.10	2.75%	$110	$ 0
41	$0.65	1.63%	$ 65	$100
42	$0.35	0.85%	$ 35	$200
43	$0.20	0.50%	$ 20	$300
44	$0.10	0.25%	$ 10	$400

[a]Amount stock can decline before break-even point is reached.

If you insist (contrary to MPT) that you have a good feel for the direction the market is going to move next, then:

- If you have a bullish outlook, write OTM calls, giving yourself the opportunity to earn a profit if the ETF price increases. Be careful not to choose an option that is too far out of the money, because the premium you receive is too small and it's not worth the effort
- If you have a neutral market outlook (per MPT), write an option that is close to the money, allowing yourself to collect the maximum time value.
- If your outlook is mildly bearish, you can gain extra protection against a market decline by writing ITM options.
- If you are very bearish, don't adopt a bullish strategy (such as covered call writing).

The following represents some of the thoughts you may have when deciding which option to write. The discussion is in the first person and may seem repetitive, but once you go through the process once or twice, you will find it much easier to make the necessary decisions each time. By taking the time to understand the process now, decision making becomes a much simpler process.

Thought Process Involved in Considering Each Option as a Sale Candidate

Let's consider writing each option in turn and consider the arguments for and against choosing each specific option. Investors following different agendas can make a good case for choosing any of several of the options listed. Consider the reasons stated for selecting each option. The argument that makes the most sense to you provides a good hint as to how you should begin when you get started with this investment method.

Writing the 44 Call The $10 I can earn is a tiny potential return. When I deduct the cost of making the trade, there's not much left for me and little to recommend this action. I don't want to write calls for such a small premium. It's extremely likely that this option is going to expire worthless because it's so far out of the money, but the reward for selling it is simply too small to consider.

Writing the 43 Call This choice is a bit better. Making $20 (before commissions) on an investment of $4,000 represents a return of only 0.5 percent. Although nothing to get excited about, if I earn an equivalent return month after month, my annual return is boosted by about 6 percent. That's the equivalent of collecting a healthy dividend. In addition to earning this $20, I have the opportunity to gain another $300 if the underlying ETF increases in value by at least three points before expiration. That's a rise of 7.5 percent and not a likely occurrence. If I write the 43 call, I must give up the opportunity to earn even more than $300, but I'm willing to do that because it is so unlikely. I'm willing to accept the $20 as payment for giving up that opportunity.

Conclusion: This is a reasonable option to write, but only when I'm strongly bullish. It's not a good choice when I have no opinion on market direction because the premium is pretty small. I doubt I'll ever want to write an option to earn a smaller return than this.

Writing the 42 Call   This choice is pretty similar to writing the 43 call. I collect a slightly higher option premium and sacrifice the chance of making an extra $100 in the event of a big rally. In this case, the potential profit of $35 from the option sale represents a return of almost 1 percent. Again, that's not enough to get me excited about the prospect of writing covered calls, but it does allow me to maintain a bullish posture and collect a nice extra premium this month. I think it's a good trade-off to take the extra $15 up front and give up on the chance of making an extra $100 if there is a big rally. After all, if ETFQ rises to 42, that's a 5 percent increase for the month and a pretty significant move. I'll be quite pleased with my profits if that happens, and it's not necessary to hope ETFQ moves all the way to 43. This is a long-term investment strategy, and I don't have to make the maximum possible profit every month. My goal is to accumulate steady profits over the long term.

Writing the 41 Call   The strategy followed by the BXM calls for writing a call option with the first OTM strike price. For ETFQ this month, that's the 41 call. If it's good enough for the Chicago Board Options Exchange (CBOE) to use as their model, perhaps it should be good enough for me. The potential profit of $65 per option represents a return of 1.65 percent for a one-month holding period, or 19.6 percent annualized (without considering the benefits of compounding). There's even the possibility of earning an additional $100, if ETFQ closes above the strike price of 41 on expiration Friday. Writing this call option is an excellent choice for me as it allows me to collect a decent option premium and still participate in a market rally. My downside protection is reasonable (0.65 per share, or 1.65 percent).

Writing the 40 Call   Writing an ATM option has three things to recommend it.

1. This call option has more time premium than any of the other options. (Reminder: total option price equals time premium plus intrinsic value, if any). And it's the time premium in an option that represents my potential profit when I sell it.

2. It provides a decent amount of protection in case the market drifts lower (2.75 percent).

3. It provides a nice profit when the market moves sideways for a period of time. If ETFQ is unchanged on expiration day, I'll earn 2.75 percent, and that's a great return when my money is invested in a position that goes nowhere. Of course, that 2.75 percent also represents my maximum potential profit for the next month, but I'm willing to accept that in exchange for gaining some downside insurance and the chance to profit if my holdings are flat for the month.

Selling this option is a good compromise strategy and I find it quite attractive. In fact, I may choose to alternate between selling the call that is just out of the money in some months and the ATM call in other months.

Writing the 39 Call   I notice the 39 call has the same time premium as the 41 call. This is not always going to be the case, but it does happen. If earning a profit of $65 on an investment of $3,835 appeals to me, then I have two choices. When I write the ITM call, I cannot earn any additional profit if the market goes higher. But, in return, I get 1.65 points of downside protection. Writing the 41 call gives me the opportunity to earn the same time premium from the option, plus an extra $100 if ETFQ increases in value, but provides insurance of only $65. My choice is between having an extra 1 point of downside protection or the possibility of earning an extra 1 point of possible profit. I'll choose the 39 call if I am an investor who prefers extra safety.

Writing the 38 Call   This is a pretty conservative play. If I sell the 38 call for $235, I'm protected all the way down to 47.65, a drop of 5.88 percent. Of course, in return for this "free" insurance, my profit potential is only $35 per contract, or 0.88 percent, and that's before commissions. This is not the type of call I want to sell on a regular basis, yet for those times when I am deeply concerned about the direction of the stock market, it presents me with an opportunity to remain fully invested (something I decided I want to do, as trying to time the market is not a winning strategy) and earn some income for the coming month. I'll usually want to write options with a greater profit potential, but writing the 38 call allows me to sleep at night during my current uncertainty about the stock market.

Writing the 37 Call   The potential return is a pretty dismal $20 per contract, and that's only 0.5 percent. I'd have to be very worried about the market to accept such a small return. It's true that I would be protected against loss if ETFQ drops 8 percent, but I won't usually require that much protection for only one month. Conclusion: This is not a good choice for me.

Writing the 36 Call   This option trades at parity. That means the total option premium is equal to the option's intrinsic value, and there is zero time value. Because my potential profit is the time value, writing this option is not a possibility because there is no potential profit. As options get deeper and deeper in the money (i.e., as the strike price decreases for call options), time value decreases. If the option is deep enough in the money, time premium approaches zero and there is no reason to write such an option in a covered call writing portfolio.

Summary: Which Call to Write?

When you begin writing covered calls, the way you feel about your positions gives you a great deal of insight. If you are comfortable with your positions, then your choice of which call option to write is probably appropriate for you. If you are nervous and literally lose sleep worrying about your investments, then your choice is not appropriate. It's impossible to measure the psychological importance of being confident with your investment choices, as constant worry is not good for you. The good news is that covered call writing provides a reduction in the overall risk of being invested in the stock market and, thus, should help reduce anxiety. That alone provides sufficient reason for many investors to find a place in their portfolios for writing covered calls on ETFs.

When expiration arrives, there are only two possible outcomes for each of your ETF positions.

1. The options expire worthless.
   a. Next Monday, in order to remain fully hedged, write new options against your holdings. Expiration weekend is a good time to study the various choices available. That minimizes the time you must spend making the final decision on Monday.
   b. You probably will maintain ownership of ETFs you currently own, but if you prefer to own different ETFs, immediately after expiration is a convenient time to sell some of your holdings and switch into different ETFs.
2. The options expire in the money. You are going to be assigned an exercise notice. You will be forced to sell your ETFs.
   a. Next Monday reinvest the proceeds of the sale and write call options. You can reinvest in the same ETFs or buy new ones. You plan to remain fully invested at all times. The weekend is a good time to decide which ETFs you want to own.

There is no better time than the next trading day—generally the Monday morning after expiration—to write new calls on your existing positions or to reinvest cash in a new covered call position.[1] We'll talk more about this process later, including how you can avoid being assigned an exercise notice by taking action prior to expiration.

CONSISTENCY OR FLEXIBILITY?

After you find the general style that fits both your investment objectives and your comfort level, there is a decision to be made. You can choose to follow the same strategy every month, unless there is a compelling reason to make a change. Alternatively, you can decide at the last minute which option writing style to follow: from the most aggressive (writing OTM options) to the most conservative (writing ITM options). Being consistent is suggested by the teachings of MPT, which tells you that guessing market direction or trying to time the market is inefficient. However, human nature is not always easy to ignore, and you may find yourself being overly bullish (write OTM calls) or bearish (write ITM calls). It's your money, and you make these decisions. There is no right or wrong way to make covered call writing work for you. Satisfying your psychological self is an important aspect of investing. You do not want to be second-guessing your decisions, so it's important to be able to accept those decisions, once you make them. One of the objectives in adopting this strategy is to feel good about your portfolio and the potential profits.

HISTORICAL RESULTS

Because the BXM adopts the strategy of always writing an option with a strike price that is just out of the money, you may feel comfortable adopting that strategy as well. It's only slightly bullish and allows you to participate in market rallies. Because the general trend of the stock market has been higher over any extended period of time, it's reasonable to adopt a stance that makes good money in rising markets.

Of course, there are many alternatives. For example, you may want to be more bullish on specific ETFs and more conservative on others. Or you may want to change your strategy after each expiration date to suit your current market outlook. There is no single correct way to use covered call writing. With my personal investing, I remain consistent and almost always choose a conservative approach, writing options that are slightly in the money. But that might not be suitable for you.

Thus, you must decide whether to accept a consistent strategy every month or to vary your technique. There's no hurry in making this decision.

You'll get to know more about covered call writing and how well it suits you with each passing expiration period.

If you do your homework over expiration weekends, this investment method doesn't take much of your Monday morning. You may prefer to allow someone else to enter your trades for you. One important point must be made. If you appoint someone else (broker or financial planner perhaps) to enter your trades, it's best to determine, *in advance*, which style you want to use. I strongly suggest you allow that advisor almost no discretion when entering orders and do not allow your agent to determine overall strategy or to time investments. This prevents misunderstandings and bad feelings, and allows you to invest as you see fit.

GETTING STARTED

If these ideas appeal to you, you may be eager to begin. But please read the next two chapters carefully before taking the plunge. This advice is especially important if you are new to options trading. It takes you through the process by building a fictional portfolio and managing it through an entire year of trading. There are some winning months as well as some losers. You learn the types of trades you can make before expiration to avoid selling your underlying ETFs and how to adjust a position to reduce risk. When adopting this strategy, your results are going to depend on the performance of the overall market, but this method increases your chances of beating the market when compared with picking stocks or mutual funds on your own.

CHAPTER 15

Covered Call Writing in Action

A Year of Trading

Theory's great, but how does all this work in the real world? What kind of results can you expect? How do you handle the month-to-month decisions? Are there going to be special situations for which you must make decisions? Is this investment method as simple as it appears to be?

In this chapter we'll take a detailed look at how an investor works with a real portfolio and handles a variety of trading decisions. The results described are all fictional, but realistically represent the types of situations you face and the decisions that must be made when managing a portfolio of exchange traded funds (ETFs) and hedging those positions with covered calls. This chapter is important and introduces issues not covered elsewhere.

Even though we discussed how writing uncovered puts can achieve the identical results with more efficiency, this chapter considers only covered call writing because many brokerage houses do not allow their clients to sell uncovered put options, even when they are cash backed. Chapter 16 provides a similar discussion on put writing—but please don't skip this chapter, as it provides guidance for situations you are certain to face. If you learn how to write covered calls successfully, then making the adjustment to writing uncovered puts is not going to be a problem for you.

CHOOSING YOUR PORTFOLIO

For our study, let's select one of the hypothetical portfolios created in Chapter 13.

Important note: There is no recommendation that this portfolio is appropriate for any investor. It was chosen because it contains a mix of three different ETFs, and trading this portfolio over a one-year period presents many different decision-making opportunities. The purpose of this section is for you to encounter the types of real-life choices that occur when you use the recommended strategy. When you understand the trading techniques that support the strategy, it becomes much easier to make winning decisions. This is especially true for those readers who are new to options trading.

A sample portfolio stressing American mid-caps and foreign stocks might include:

100 EFA (an investment in European, Australasian, and Far Eastern stocks)

400 MDY (S&P MidCap 400 index)

400 VTI (Vanguard Total Stock Market VIPERs)

TAKING THE PLUNGE

For simplicity, let's make these trading assumptions:

- All trades are made online, except where noted. If you prefer to call your broker to place orders, bear in mind that it takes longer for those orders to be executed and the additional cost reduces your profits.
- The commissions used are typical of fees charged by some deep-discount brokers. Both lower and higher rates are common.
  - The commission to buy or sell ETFs is $10 per order.
  - The commission for options is $10 per order plus $1.50 per contract.
  - Exercise and assignment fees are $20 each.[1]
- The preferred method is to write options expiring in the front month, but there may be exceptions.

It's a brand-new year and you are eager to begin using options. Let's assume it's a Wednesday in mid-January, and expiration is two days in the future. You have carefully considered your investment choices and are ready to proceed.

The following narrative is written in the first person, as it represents the thought process of the trader who owns the portfolio. That trader is new to covered call writing and is gaining experience as time passes.

A great deal of information is packed into the following discussion. To gain the maximum benefit, go through the trades slowly, and determine if the trading decisions make sense to you. This is where you can get a better feel for the trading style that appeals to you. If the trades illustrated feel right, you can begin your option writing program by adopting a similar style. If you would be more comfortable writing out of the money (OTM) options and seeking higher potential profits, that provides a hint as to how you should treat your own investments. Similarly, if you would prefer the additional safety that comes with writing in-the-money (ITM) options, that's the style you should adopt when you begin writing covered calls. It won't take long for you to become proficient with making the decisions, entering the orders, and managing your positions.

TERMINOLOGY

Each month investments are made on the Monday following expiration Friday. In our examples, the initial trades are made in January, but the options sold expire in February. For the purposes of this discussion, let's refer to these trades as February expiration trades even though the positions are initiated during January.

FEBRUARY EXPIRATION

I have $100,000 to invest and, after careful consideration, I'm going ahead with the covered call writing program. To have a well-diversified portfolio, I'm including an investment in overseas stocks. Between 10 and 15 percent of my available capital is used to buy 100 shares of EFA. I'm investing the balance of my money in 400 shares of VTI, as it tracks the entire U.S. stock market, and 400 shares of MDY, because I like the idea of owning mid-cap stocks. Mid-caps are small enough for future growth, yet they are not as volatile as smaller capitalization stocks. For each 100 shares of an ETF purchased, I'm writing one at-the-money (ATM) call option.

OK, I'm in. I paid $109.00 for 400 shares of VTI and wrote the Feb 109 calls for $1.80. The shares cost $43,610, including commissions and I received $704 ($720, less $16 commission) from the option sale.

Likewise, I bought 400 shares of MDY (coincidentally trading at the same price of $109 this month) and 100 shares of EFA (paid $134) and wrote the Feb 109 and Feb 134 calls respectively.

I was able to put almost all my money to work, and I'm leaving the residual $986.50 in my brokerage account until I have enough to reinvest in additional ETF shares. In today's environment of very low interest rates, brokerage houses pay a minuscule rate of interest—one-tenth of 1 percent annually on idle cash, so let's assume this cash earns no interest (to minimize calculations and make the discussion easier to follow).

My initial trades are listed in Table 15.1A.

I've decided to begin my option writing program by adopting a middle-of-the-road style. That's why I've written calls that expire in the front month (February) and are at the money for each of my three positions. This gives me the chance to collect the maximum time premium from writing options.[2] My positions are summarized in Table 15.1B. The table also lists the maximum possible profit I can earn from each position, and that occurs if I am eventually assigned an exercise notice.

I realize I don't have much protection against loss if the market declines, but the good news is that I'd have no protection at all if holding an unhedged stock portfolio.[3] My maximum gain occurs if I am assigned on all three positions. If that happens, I'll earn 1.57 percent on my money, after expenses. Not exciting, but a decent annualized return (18.84 percent).

I'm going to take the time to watch my positions closely as I enjoy watching the day-to-day fluctuations of the stock market. I know other investors are better off not thinking about their positions until a day or two before expiration, but my personality requires me to constantly be aware of how my investments are performing.[4] I truly believe this investing method is going to produce good results.

TABLE 15.1A February Expiration Trades

B/S/W	Qty	SYM	Price	Call	Prem	Comm	Invested
B	400	VTI	109.00			10.00	($43,610.00)
W	4	VTI		Feb 109	1.80	16.00	$704.00
B	400	MDY	109.00			10.00	($43,610.00)
W	4	MDY		Feb 109	1.85	16.00	$724.00
B	100	EFA	134.00			10.00	($13,410.00)
W	1	EFA		Feb 134	2.00	11.50	$188.50
				Total	**Invested**		**($99,013.50)**
					Cash		**$986.50**
				Acct	**Value**		**$100,000.00**

B/S/W: Buy, sell, or write.
Qty: Shares of ETF or number of option contracts.
SYM: ETF trading symbol.
Price: Price paid for ETF, per share.
Call: Expiration and strike price of option sold.
Prem: Option price.
Comm: Commission for trade $10 to buy or sell ETF; $10 + $1.50 per contract for options.
Invested: Cost to buy ETF or cash received from selling calls.
Total Invested: Sum of individual position costs.
Cash: Residual cash, not invested.
Acct Value: Sum of cash and investments in account.

TABLE 15.1B February Expiration Positions

ETF	Qty	Price	Call	Opt Sale	Invested	Break-Even	Profit Potential	Down Protect	Return
VTI	400	109.00	Feb 109	$704.00	$42,906.00	107.27	$684.00	1.59%	1.59%
MDY	400	109.00	Feb 109	$724.00	$42,886.00	107.22	$704.00	1.64%	1.64%
EFA	100	134.00	Feb 134	$188.50	$13,221.50	132.22	$158.50	1.33%	1.20%
			Total Invested		**$99,013.50**		**$1,546.50**		**1.56%**
			Cash		**$986.50**				
			Total Account		**$100,000.00**				
			MAX Value		**$101,546.50**				

Opt Sale: Proceeds from selling options

Invested: Cost of ETF minus premium received from option sale

Break-Even: Position is profitable if above this price at expiration

Profit Potential: Maximum profit, after deducting $20 assignment fee

Down Protect: % ETF can decline before reaching break-even price

Return: % return on investment, if maximum profit is achieved

MAX Value: Future account value if assigned on all options

145

Time passes and nothing dramatic happens during the month. Looking at my positions after the markets are closed on expiration Friday, I see that two of the call options I sold are expiring worthless, but I am going to be assigned on the EFA call. (For convenience, I'll use the past tense, assuming I have already been assigned on options that are in the money and that OTM options have already expired. In the next chapter, we'll see that these assumptions are reasonable but not 100 percent accurate.) The results for the January investments (February expiration) are listed in Table 15.1C. *Note:* I no longer own any shares of EFA, but have $13,380 cash instead.[5]

For the past month, the S&P 500 index was down by 1.0 percent, the markets abroad were about 1 percent higher, and I earned 0.78 percent on my holdings. Earning any profit when the market declines makes me feel pretty good about my investment methodology. Of course, this is the result of only one month, and I'll need more time to determine how satisfying writing covered calls on a portfolio of ETFs really is.

Two of my options expired worthless, so on Monday I'll simply write new options. Both MDY and VTI are currently priced midway between two strike prices. If these ETF open essentially unchanged on Monday, I'll have to choose between writing slightly ITM or the slightly OTM options for each. I'll make my decision quickly, so I don't remain naked long (unhedged) these ETFs for too long. Of course, if the market is heading higher, the longer I wait to sell calls, the better. Conversely, if the market is declining, the longer I wait, the less I'm going to receive when writing the call option.[6] Because I don't want to get involved with trying to time the market, I'll get this trade executed within 10 minutes of the opening bell.

EFA is a different situation. That ETF increased in value this month, and I no longer own any shares. I have the choice of investing the proceeds of the sale in a different ETF or maintaining my exposure to foreign markets. For now I'll stick with owning 100 shares of EFA.

Overall, February expiration was not an exciting month, but I'm very satisfied with the results. No major investing decisions were necessary, and my portfolio didn't require too much of my time.

MARCH EXPIRATION

It's Monday morning and I've made my decisions; I am ready to trade online as soon as the market opens.

One word of warning: Be absolutely certain you know whether your options have expired and whether you have been assigned per your expectations. If you can view your account online, that information should be available to you sometime on Sunday. But if you do not have access to the Internet or if your broker does not provide that service, you must call your

TABLE 15.1C February Expiration Results

ETF	Opening Price	Ending Price	Assigned	Current Position	Cost	Current Value	Sale Proceeds	P/L	% P/L
VTI	109.00	107.50	No	400	$42,906.00	$43,000.00		$94.00	0.22%
MDY	109.00	108.52	No	400	$42,886.00	$43,408.00		$522.00	1.22%
EFA	134.00	136.13	Yes	0	$13,221.50		$13,380.00	$158.50	1.20%
Total					**$99,013.50**	**$86,408.00**	**$13,380.00**	**$774.50**	**0.78%**
Cash Start					$986.50				
Cash End					$14,366.50				
Account Value Start					$100,000.00				
Account Value End					$100,774.50				

Opening Price: Price paid for ETF shares

Ending Price: ETF closing price at expiration

Assigned: Was this account assigned an exercise notice?

Cost: Original cost of position

Current Value: Value of shares at ending price

Sale Proceeds: Cash received if assigned ($20 assignment fee deducted)

P/L: Profit or loss for current month

% P/L: Net return on investment for current month

Cash Start: Cash in account to begin month

Cash End: Cash in account after expiration (idle cash plus sale proceeds) broker early enough on Monday morning to allow you to verify your current positions and make your trading plans accordingly. Every once in a while, you are going to have an expiration surprise. It is not likely, but sometimes an option that is in the money by a few pennies does not get assigned. It's even possible to be assigned an exercise notice when an option finishes out of the money by a penny or two. Take nothing for granted, and verify your positions *before* you begin trading on Monday.

Note: If you are planning to call your broker to place orders, you can do it either before or after the market opens. But if you plan on discussing your trades with your broker, call early to allow extra time. I recommend that you be prepared to tell your broker what you want to do, rather than ask a broker who has not had any time to carefully consider your holdings or your overall strategy for an opinion.

I'm not thrilled that my ETFs closed midway between two strikes, forcing me to choose between writing a slightly ITM or a slightly OTM option. I'd prefer the chance to write an ATM option, but there's nothing I can do about this situation. Waiting for the market price of the underlying ETF to change so that it's near the money is a losing strategy, and I am not going to play that game.[7] I've decided to adopt the more conservative style this month and write options that are about a half point in the money rather than those that are a half point out of the money.

The S&P futures are almost unchanged this morning, so I anticipate my two ETFs will open relatively unchanged. That's good news, because one of the risks of adopting a covered call writing strategy occurs if I choose to hold unhedged positions over the weekend. In other words, once my options expired worthless, I owned the underlying assets (in this case VTI and MDY) outright, with no opportunity to write new call options until the market opened on the Monday following expiration. I could have avoided this risk: Last Friday I could have repurchased the soon-to-be worthless expiring calls and written new calls that expire in March. However, I chose not to do so. (An example of how to roll a position to a later month is presented later.)

It takes about 20 minutes to make the final decisions and make the trades. I'm sure it will take less time as I gain more experience with the procedure.

VTI opened 5 cents higher ($107.55) than Friday's close, and I was able to write the Mar 107 call for $2.15. MDT opened 3 cents lower ($108.49), and I wrote the Mar 108 call for $1.85. I bought 100 shares of EFA, paying $136.12, and wrote one Mar 136 call for $2.00. The trades are summarized in Table 15.2A.

I spent $11,865.50 on new investments for the month and now have $2,501.00 in idle cash. Table 15.2B lists my current positions and the profit potential for the month. *Note:* The value of the account is $8 more than it was last Friday because today's opening prices and last Friday's closing prices are not identical. For the purposes of our discussion, the monthly

TABLE 15.2A March Expiration Trades

B/S/W	Qty	SYM	Price	Call	Prem	Comm	Invested
		VTI	107.55				
W	4	**VTI**		Mar 107	2.15	16.00	$844.00
		MDY	108.49				
W	4	**MDY**		Mar 108	1.85	16.00	$724.00
B	100	**EFA**	136.12			10.00	($13,622.00)
W	1	**EFA**		Mar 136	2.00	11.50	$188.50
				Total	**Invested**		**($11,865.50)**
			Cash	Start			$14,366.50
			Cash	**Now**			**$2,501.00**

profit/loss (P/L) is calculated based on opening prices on Monday, the day the new positions are opened. The year-to-date totals are based on the $100,000 starting investment.

Because I adopted a more conservative approach by writing (slightly) ITM options, my potential profit is reduced. That's a price I'm willing to pay for the extra downside protection.

The March expiration period turned out to be a pretty good month for the American stock market, and the S&P rallied by more than 2 percent. Overseas, the markets held steady. I made my maximum possible profit this month, since all my ETF options finished in the money. I'll have no positions when the market opens next Monday and I'm back where I started, except there is more cash in my account now. So far I'm ahead by $2,041.00. The results are listed in Table 15.2C. Again, nothing exciting, but I now understand this process better and am able to make my decisions and enter my trades with greater assurance that I know what I'm doing.

APRIL EXPIRATION

I've thought about it over the weekend, and I'm going to make a change in my underlying portfolio. I've decided I have too much invested in the mid-cap index so will decrease my investment to only 200 shares. I'll buy additional shares of VTI with the extra money.

The S&P futures are down fractionally Monday morning, and my plan is to write options as close to the money as possible. I could have earned additional profits if I had chosen to sell OTM calls last time, but that's no reason for me to lose my discipline and abandon my objectives. I chose covered call writing because it provides some downside protection along with more frequent profits, and that insurance is valuable to me.

TABLE 15.2B March Expiration Positions

ETF	Qty	Price	Call	Opt Sale	Invested	Break-Even	Profit Potential	Down Protect	Return
VTI	400	107.55	Mar 107	$844.00	($42,176.00)	105.44	$604.00	1.96%	1.43%
MDY	400	108.49	Mar 108	$724.00	($42,672.00)	106.68	$508.00	1.67%	1.19%
EFA	100	136.12	Mar 136	$188.50	($13,433.50)	134.34	$146.50	1.31%	1.09%
		Total Invested			**($98,281.50)**		**$1,258.50**		**1.28%**
		Cash			**$2,501.00**				
		Total Account			**$100,782.50**				
		MAX Value			**$102,041.00**				

Invested: Today's ETF value, minus proceeds from option sale

Total Account: Total is not identical with value at February expiration because today's (Monday) opening prices differ from last Friday's closing prices

TABLE 15.2C March Expiration Results

ETF	Opening Price	Ending Price	Assigned		Current Position	Cost	Current Value	Sale Proceeds	P/L	% P/L
VTI	107.55	109.89	Yes		0	$42,176.00		$42,780.00	$604.00	1.43%
MDY	108.49	111.03	Yes		0	$42,672.00		$43,180.00	$508.00	1.19%
EFA	136.12	136.15	Yes		0	$13,433.50		$13,580.00	$146.50	1.09%
			Total			**$98,281.50**	**$0.00**	**$99,540.00**	**$1,258.50**	**1.28%**
			Cash	**Start**		$2,501.00				
			Cash	**End**		$102,041.00				
			Beginning Account Value			**$100,782.50**				
			Ending Account Value			**$102,041.00**				

As predicted by the futures, the market opened calmly this morning and I had no trouble executing my trades. The results are listed in Table 15.3A.

I now have more money invested in the broad-based Wilshire 5000 and less in mid-cap stocks. For my three positions, I wrote one option that was out of the money and two that were in the money by a small amount. The positions are listed in Table 15.3B.

March turns out to be one of those dreary months for the market. The averages begin the month lower and slowly continue lower with no conviction. By the time expiration arrives, the S&P 500 is down almost 3 percent, and the options I wrote on VTI and MDY expired worthless. The bright spot for the month was the overseas markets, which increased in value, and my EFA calls finished in the money. The investment results are listed in Table 15.3C.

This was one of those months that illustrates the value of diversification in reducing overall market risk. My small EFA profit partially offset my other losses. Of course, asset allocation won't always work this way. I'm sure there will be times when my U.S. investments outperform those from overseas. But my purpose is minimization of risk, and investing a portion of my assets in foreign markets is one method of accomplishing that goal.

Overall, I lost just over $500 this month, or about one-half of 1 percent. I'm not happy, but I did outperform the market by a wide margin, so have nothing to complain about. For the first three months of the year my profits are just over 1.5 percent. I had hoped to do much better, but it's not easy to make money from bullish positions with the market down 2 percent for the year.

TABLE 15.3A   April Expiration Trades

B/S/W	Qty	SYM	Price	Call	Prem	Comm	Invested
B	600	VTI	109.89			10.00	($65,944.00)
W	6	VTI		Apr 110	2.30	19.00	$1,361.00
B	200	MDY	111.05			10.00	($22,220.00)
W	2	MDY		Apr 111	2.05	13.00	$397.00
B	100	EFA	136.20			10.00	($13,630.00)
W	1	EFA		Apr 136	2.25	11.50	$213.50
			Invested				**($99,822.50)**
			Cash Start				$102,041.00
			Cash Now				**$2,218.50**

TABLE 15.3B April Expiration Positions

ETF	Qty	Price	Call	Opt Sale	Invested	Break-Even	Profit Potential	Down Protect	Return
VTI	600	109.89	Apr 110	$1,361.00	($64,583.00)	107.64	$1,397.00	2.05%	2.16%
MDY	200	111.05	Apr 111	$397.00	($21,823.00)	109.12	$357.00	1.74%	1.64%
EFA	100	136.20	Apr 136	$213.50	($13,416.50)	134.17	$163.50	1.49%	1.22%
		Total	**Invested**		**($99,822.50)**		**$1,917.50**		**1.92%**
		Cash			**$2,218.50**				
		Total	**Account**		**$102,041.00**				
		MAX	**Value**		**$103,958.50**				

TABLE 15.3C April Expiration Results

ETF	Opening Price	Ending Price	Assigned	Current Position	Cost	Current Value	Sale Proceeds	P/L	% P/L
VTI	109.89	106.85	No	600	($64,583.00)	$64,110.00		(473.00)	−0.73%
MDY	111.05	108.12	No	200	($21,823.00)	$21,624.00		(199.00)	−0.91%
EFA	136.20	139.17	Yes	0	($13,416.50)		$13,580.00	163.50	1.22%
			Total		**($99,822.50)**	**$85,734.00**	**$13,580.00**	**(508.50)**	**−0.51%**
			Cash Start		**$2,218.50**				
			Cash End		**$15,798.50**				
			Beginning Account Value		**$102,041.00**				
			Ending Account Value		**$101,532.50**				

MAY EXPIRATION

Over the weekend I considered my investment program and my portfolio and decided to maintain my positions. I plan to repurchase the 100 shares of EFA I was forced to sell.

On Monday morning things are looking better. There were a few good earnings surprises this morning—companies' quarterly earnings reports were better than analysts expected—and the futures predict a higher opening for the market. I got a bit lucky this time: My holdings increased in value since last Friday's closing prices. That gives me the chance to earn a bit more money this month, but of course the results depend on where the market is when expiration arrives in four weeks.[8]

My trades are summarized in Table 15.4A.

I maintained my overall style by writing VTI and MDY options as close to the money as possible. However, I decided to take a small chance and write the call that is 1 point out of the money for my EFA shares. The foreign markets have been doing pretty well lately, and I thought I'd attempt to make a bit extra this time. My positions are summarized in Table 15.4B.

Note the total value of my account is higher than it was at the previous expiration (Table 15.3C) because the market opened higher this morning and my VTI and MDY positions increased in value.

The market, ever full of surprises, did a complete about-face this month and more than recovered its losses for the year. This was the month where the more bullish investors did very well. I can't complain, however, as I made the maximum possible from each of my covered call positions, or 1.74 percent. The results of my May expiration trades are listed in Table 15.4C.

May was one of those months that tests investors' ability to stick with a covered call writing program. Even though my investment portfolio easily

TABLE 15.4A May Expiration Trades

B/S/W	Qty	SYM	Price	Call	Prem	Comm	Invested
		VTI	107.25				
W	6	**VTI**		May 107	2.25	19.00	$1,331.00
		MDY	109.01				
W	2	**MDY**		May 109	1.90	13.00	$367.00
B	100	**EFA**	139.20			10.00	($13,930.00)
W	1	**EFA**		May 140	1.60	11.50	$148.50
			Total	**Invested**			**($12,083.50)**
				Cash Start			$15,798.50
				Cash Now			**$3,715.00**

TABLE 15.4B May Expiration Positions

ETF	Qty	Price	Call	Opt Sale	Invested	Break-Even	Profit Potential	Down Protect	Return
VTI	600	107.25	May 107	$1,331.00	($63,019.00)	105.03	$1,161.00	2.07%	1.84%
MDY	200	109.01	May 109	$367.00	($21,435.00)	107.18	$345.00	1.68%	1.61%
EFA	100	139.20	May 140	$148.50	($13,781.50)	137.82	$198.50	0.99%	1.44%
		Total Invested Cash			($98,235.50) $3,715.00		$1,704.50		1.74%
		Total Account MAX Value			$101,950.50 $103,655.00				

TABLE 15.4C May Expiration Results

ETF	Opening Price	Ending Price	Assigned	Current Position	Cost	Current Value	Sale Proceeds	P/L	% P/L
VTI	107.25	111.50	Yes	0	($63,019.00)		$64,180.00	$1,161.00	1.84%
MDY	109.01	114.18	Yes	0	($21,435.00)		$21,780.00	$345.00	1.61%
EFA	139.20	142.96	Yes	0	($13,781.50)		$13,980.00	$198.50	1.44%
		Total			**($98,235.50)**	**$0.00**	**$99,940.00**	**$1,704.50**	**1.74%**
		Cash Start			**$3,715.00**				
		Cash End			**$103,655.00**				
		Beginning Account Value			**$101,950.50**				
		Ending Account Value			**$103,655.00**				

Why Covered Call Writing Is Wrong for Some Investors

If you own shares of an ETF (or individual stock) and write a covered call option, how will you react if your investment starts to rally and you watch the price rise steadily? If you are pleased to see the market rally and recognize that a rising market allows you to earn the maximum profit this investment method can produce, then covered call writing is suitable for you.

However, if you are going to tell yourself that writing the call was a mistake and if you blindly fix that mistake by buying back the call you sold earlier (at a substantial loss), hoping the underlying ETF continues to increase in value, then covered call writing is not for you.

Of course, you can buy back the call written earlier when the underlying is rising in price. Repurchasing a call previously sold is not only acceptable, but can be part of an intelligent strategy that involves changing your position. The dangerous part arises when the call is bought out of frustration at having sold it in the first place, with no follow-up plan of action. If your plan is to buy back the option and simply hold onto your ETF shares (unhedged) in an attempt to recover the loss resulting from the original option sale, then you are attempting to time the market, a most difficult undertaking. Many beginners fall into this trap because they simply cannot tolerate seeing the option they sold increase in price. You may wish you had waited before writing the call options, but it's important to recognize that a rising market is good for you. After all, you are a bullish investor, you have a significant portion of your assets invested in the stock market, and a rising market allows you to earn decent profits. If you can't get it out of your mind that you want to make a fortune in the market—and make it immediately—then covered call writing, an investment methodology that requires some patience, is not for you. That's OK, as not all investment methods suit every investor. Find what works for you, both financially and psychologically.

A prudent investor does not base investment methods on hoping for the best.

Later we'll take a closer look at how investors can buy back an option sold earlier, when we examine how to roll a position to take advantage of rising prices.

performed better than the overall market during the first few months this year, I could have made more money during May if I owned ETFs outright and did not write covered call options. Of course, I recognize that underperforming during the most bullish months represents one of the risks of adopting this strategy and am willing to accept that occasional underperformance. I believe that over an extended period of time I'll earn enough extra money to more than compensate for my reduced (compared with the averages) earnings during those strongly upward markets by outperforming those averages under other market conditions. (In reality, I'll do very well when the market is strongly bullish. But I'll earn *less* than the investor who is unhedged.)

I'm very pleased with my May results. It's a good feeling to make the maximum possible profit, but the rising market leaves me feeling uncomfortable. I hope the market continues to rally, but I'm afraid of a decline. My account now contains all cash and no remaining positions. Of course I'll reinvest the entire amount next Monday, nervous about the future or not, and I'll use the weekend to decide if I want to change my mix of investments.

Note: A problem can arise for investors who cannot accept less than the best possible results. Even though these investors may recognize covered call writing performs well over time and represents a realistic method for outperforming the market averages, if they cannot do better than the averages *every* year, they are unhappy. As noted in Chapter 12, covered call writing returned smaller profits than the market averages during the most bullish years at the close of the twentieth century, when the technology bubble was growing. Even with that several-year period of underperformance, over the history of the BuyWrite index, covered call writing made more money than simply owning the S&P 500 index. If you are one of those investors who *must* have the best of all possible results every time, think twice about using covered call writing as a method of enhancing your returns.

JUNE EXPIRATION

The rally continues on Monday morning, and all the ETFs I want to buy are slightly higher than last Friday's closing prices. Again, I'm going for the extra profit on my overseas investments and am writing the 1-point OTM call on my 100 shares of EFA.

I've decided to make a minor change in my investment portfolio. My new portfolio consists of this mix of ETFs:

100 EFA

200 MDY

500 VTI

200 OEF (tracks the S&P 100 index)

I added OEF to my portfolio for three reasons:

1. It's a broad-based index and tracks the performance of 100 large companies.

2. Coupled with MDY, it allows concentration in market segments that exclude the more volatile small-cap stocks.

3. It allows me to put virtually all my idle cash to work. I don't want several thousand dollars sitting in my brokerage account uninvested.

My trades for the month are summarized in Table 15.5A.

My positions and potential profits are listed in Table 15.5B.

I bought my 500 VTI shares at a price of $111.65, making it difficult to choose the appropriate strike price to sell. Maintaining my philosophy of writing the call that is closest to the money, I chose the Jun 112 call. Choosing the option to write for my other positions was much simpler.

June was a dreadful month for the market.

After a day or two of higher prices, there was some political unrest in the Middle East. Using that as an excuse, nervous traders sent the market lower. Within two weeks the market was down over 4 percent, and expiration is still two weeks in the future. I decided it was time to protect my portfolio and to sacrifice some potential profits. The options I sold earlier are trading at low prices (example: VTI Jun 112 call can be bought for $0.30). Thus, they provide very little downside protection. I am going to buy back those calls and simultaneously write new calls with lower strike prices. Because there is only a short time to the June expiration, I'm also going to move the position to the following month by writing calls that expire in July. This process is called rolling down and out.

TABLE 15.5A June Expiration Trades

B/S/W	Qty	SYM	Price	Call	Prem	Comm	Invested
B	500	VTI	111.65			10.00	($55,835.00)
W	5	VTI		Jun 112	1.95	17.50	$957.50
B	200	MDY	114.25			10.00	($22,860.00)
W	2	MDY		Jun 114	2.15	13.00	$417.00
B	100	EFA	143.06			10.00	($14,316.00)
W	1	EFA		Jun 144	1.60	11.50	$148.50
B	200	OEF	57.08			10.00	($11,426.00)
W	2	OEF		Jun 57	0.90	13.00	$167.00
			Total Invested				**($102,747.00)**
			Cash Start				$103,655.00
			Cash Now				**$908.00**

TABLE 15.5B June Expiration Positions

ETF	Qty	Price	Call	Opt Sale	Invested	Break-Even	Profit Potential	Down Protect	Return
VTI	500	111.65	Jun 112	$957.50	($54,877.50)	109.76	$1,102.50	1.70%	2.01%
MDY	200	114.25	Jun 114	$417.00	($22,443.00)	112.22	$337.00	1.78%	1.50%
EFA	100	143.06	Jun 144	$148.50	($14,167.50)	141.68	$212.50	0.97%	1.50%
OEF	200	57.08	Jun 57	$167.00	($11,259.00)	56.30	$121.00	1.38%	1.07%
		Total	**Invested**		**($102,747.00)**		**$1,773.00**		**1.73%**
			Cash		906.50				
		Total	**Account**		103,653.50				
		MAX	**Value**		105,426.50				

Rolling a Position Type I. Rolling for Protection

The term "rolling" refers to moving a position from one option to another. The term is used when the new option has a different strike price, a different expiration month, or when both are changed. When rolling a position, there are many choices. The recommended method for choosing the new option to write is to pretend you are opening a new position. Write the option that meets your criteria for profit potential *and* protection.

Two trades are required to roll a position: (1) repurchase the option sold earlier, then (2) immediately (to avoid remaining unhedged) write a new call option. The newly sold call has a lower strike price and expires in a later month. For example, with VTI trading at $107.50, I bought 5 VTI Jun 112 calls, paying $0.30 for each, and sold 5 VTI Jul 108 calls, collecting $3.05. Table 15.5C shows the trades made to roll each position.

Note: When rolling, I can call my broker and enter a *spread* order. Such an order consists of (at least) two separate trades that are tied together, with the condition that both portions of the order must be filled or neither portion is to be filled.

> **Example:** I could call my broker and say: "Buy 5 VTI Jun 112 calls and sell 5 VTI Jul 108 calls for a net credit of $2.75 or better." This means that I want to collect at least $275 (five times) when making these two trades. If the broker is unable to make both trades at prices that meet my conditions, then no trades are made. That leaves me with my original position.

Note: It's not necessary to call your broker if you trade online. Simply buy the previously sold option and quickly sell the new option.

TABLE 15.5C June Expiration: Trades to Roll Positions

ETF	Qty	Current Price	Bought Calls	Buy Price	Sold Calls	Sell Price	Spread Credit	Cash Collected
VTI	5	107.50	Jun 112	0.30	Jul 108	3.05	$2.75	$1,340.00
MDY	2	109.90	Jun114	0.15	Jul 110	2.70	$2.55	$484.00
EFA	1	141.75	Jun 144	0.55	Jul 142	2.05	$1.50	$127.00
OEF	2	54.99	Jun 57	0.05	Jul 55	0.80	$0.75	$124.00
							Cost to Roll	**$2,075.00**
							Old Cash	**$906.50**
							New Cash	**$2,981.50**

Cash Collected: After commissions ($10 per trade + $1.50 per contract)
Cost to Roll: The amount is positive because I collected cash to make the trades

Because I'm anxious to make the trade and reduce the chances of my sustaining further losses, I chose to trade online without taking the time to telephone the order to my broker. Besides, if I try to place this limit order through a broker, there is always the chance the order will go unfilled.[9] I am unwilling to use a market order, so I quickly make the trades by myself online.[10]

My new positions are listed in Table 15.5D.

There are several points of interest in these trades:

- By writing a call with a lower strike price, I collect additional option premium. This extra cash provides additional protection in case the market heads even lower.
- By writing calls with a lower strike price, I'm giving up my chance to earn a decent profit this month. My best possible result this month is a profit of only $446. Still, I'd be thrilled to do that well, considering how far the market has declined in these past two weeks.
- I have one position (OEF) that is not only under water (losing money), but there is no chance it can make any money. Note in Table 15.5D that my best result for OEF is a loss of $155. And I'll do that well only if OEF is above the strike price when expiration arrives in six weeks.
- It's far more important for more conservative investors to preserve capital than to worry about making a profit every month. More bullish investors might prefer to take their chances and not roll the position, but that's not a risk I am willing to take.
  Note: The BXM methodology never rolls a position.
- By writing July calls instead of June calls, I collect additional time premium.[11] This means that unless I want to roll to different strike prices, I may not have any trades to make when June expiration arrives, as I've already sold my July options.
- The premium I received for writing the VTI Jul 108 calls is higher than might have been expected. One reason for this is that declining markets (and especially rapidly declining markets) tend to make investors afraid that a much larger price drop is possible. Thus, more people are eager to buy put options—either to hedge their portfolios or to profit from a market decline. This increase in the number of put buyers also pushes call prices higher.[12] The phenomenon of rising option prices is the result of an increase in the implied volatility (IV) of the options.[13]

I feel more comfortable with my positions after rolling, but the market continued its decline. When June expiration arrived, the S&P 500 was lower by more than 6 percent for the month. Rolling saved me from incurring a large loss, but I still lost money this month. The only good news that comes from this market decline is that fear has gripped some investors and option

TABLE 15.5D June Expiration: Positions after Rolling

ETF	Qty	Current Price	New Calls	Cash Collected	Invested Now	Break-Even	Profit Potential	Down Protect	Return
VTI	5	107.50	Jul 108	$1,340.00	($53,537.50)	107.08	$442.50	0.40%	0.83%
MDY	2	109.90	Jul 110	$484.00	($21,959.00)	109.80	$21.00	0.10%	0.10%
EFA	1	141.75	Jul 142	$127.00	($14,040.50)	140.41	$139.50	0.95%	0.99%
OEF	2	54.99	Jul 55	$124.00	($11,135.00)	55.68	($155.00)	None	-1.39%
		Invested			($100,672.00)				
		Cash From	Rolling		$2,075.00		$448.00		0.45%
		Old Cash			$906.50				
		New Cash			$2,981.50				
		Account	Value		$103,653.50				
		MAX	Value		$104,101.50				

New Calls: Description of newly written calls

Cash collected: Cash collected from roll, after commissions

Invested Now: Current cost of position, after rolling

Break-Even: Break-even price for entire month

Profit Potential: Maximum profit (for entire month) if assigned at expiration

Down Protect: Amount ETF can decline from *current* price to reach break-even price

Return: Maximum profit for entire month

prices are higher than they have been in recent months. If that holds true for another month, I'll be able to collect better prices when I write new call options for the August expiration. None of my options expired because I rolled all of them to July.

My results for the June expiration are summarized in Table 15.5E.

I suffered a setback this month with the market decline. But once again, covered call writing came to the rescue, reducing my losses. For example, if I had owned my ETFs unhedged, I would have lost $5,290: $2,885 on 500 VTI + $1,092 on 200 MDY + $703 on 100 EFA + $610 on 200 OEF. Instead, my losses were reduced to about half that amount ($2,865). Like any other investor who owns stocks, I'd be much happier with a rising market, but I must admit I feel pretty good about having a profit for the year (less than 1 percent) when the market is down more than 8 percent.

Note: This is the first month my options still have time remaining when an expiration day arrives. Thus, the value of those outstanding options must be deducted from the value of my ETFs to determine the total value of my account (see Table 15.5E).

I'm already fully invested for next month since I rolled the positions out to July. No trading is necessary Monday morning. I'll miss my trading activity, as it's something I look forward to every month. But I do have one important decision to make, and I'll work on it over the weekend: Am I going to maintain the positions as they are, or should I roll the positions again by buying back options I am currently short and replacing them with lower strike options? It's very tempting to maintain my current OTM call positions in an attempt to make extra money if the market stages a comeback. But I must remember that my goal is to make money month after month, and I don't want to be in the business of predicting which way the market is going to move in the future.

JULY EXPIRATION

I've decided to maintain my current positions in VTI, MDY, and OEF because

- The options are not too far out of the money (just over 2 points for VTI, just over 1 point for MDY, and about 1 point for OEF).
- I can't collect enough extra cash (after paying both a buy and sell commission) to make it worthwhile to roll to a different July option with a lower strike price.

However, EFA is sufficiently OTM that I'm going to repurchase my short Jul 142 call and substitute an appropriate option—either the 137 or 138 call. I'll know more when the market opens and I can see the current option prices.

TABLE 15.5E June Expiration Results

ETF	Opening Price	Ending Price	Assigned	Current Position	Cost	Current ETF Value	Current Call	Opt Price	Opt Value	P/L	% P/L
VTI	111.65	105.88	No	500	($53,537.50)	$52,940.00	Jul 108	$1.50	$750.00	($1,347.50)	-2.52%
MDY	114.25	108.79	No	200	($21,959.00)	$21,758.00	Jul 110	$1.95	$390.00	($591.00)	-2.69%
EFA	143.06	136.03	No	100	($14,040.50)	$13,603.00	Jul 142	$1.00	$100.00	($537.50)	-3.83%
OEF	57.08	54.03	No	200	($11,135.00)	$10,806.00	Jul 55	$0.30	$60.00	($389.00)	-3.49%
				Total	($100,672.00)	$99,107.00			$1,300.00	($2,865.00)	-2.85%
				Cash	$2,981.50						
				Starting Account Value	$103,654.50						
				Ending Account Value	$100,788.50						

Cost: Amount invested, after rolling position

Current ETF Value: Value of ETF shares at June expiration

Opt Price: Current price of July calls (sold earlier)

P/L: ETF cost minus ETF value minus option value

Ending account value: Value of ETFs plus cash minus value of short option positions

On Monday morning the markets are quiet and open essentially unchanged from last week's closing prices. I decided to roll the EFA to the 137 strike. The trade is listed in Table 15.6A. My positions are listed in Table 15.6B.

The profit potential for this month is higher than usual, but that's a result of being short OTM call options. If the market recovers some of its recent losses, I'll also recover. I don't know what to expect, but I decided to maintain my positions. In this respect I'm in the same boat as any unhedged investor who owns stocks or mutual funds. It's tough (for me) to hold during periods when the market is declining, but I am committed to remaining fully invested.

June turns out to be a dull month, but that's not a bad thing. At least the slide has ended for the time being. The American stock market stages a mild 1 percent comeback, but the markets around the rest of the world are fairly flat. All my options expire worthless. Next month I'll be in position to write ATM options again.

The results for the month of July are listed in Table 15.6C.

The account made a decent recovery this month, and I'm ahead 3 percent for the first seven months of the year. Since the market is down roughly 7 percent over the same time period, that's a satisfying result.

AUGUST EXPIRATION

There was not much to ponder this past weekend, and I've decided to sell the options that are a fraction of a point out of the money for my domestic ETFs and the next higher strike for EFA. That's consistent with my style of writing options whose strike price is nearest to the money.

The market is poised to open just a bit higher this morning, according to the S&P futures market. I'm going to waste no time writing options and

TABLE 15.6A July Expiration Trades

B/S/W	Qty	SYM	Price	Call	Comm	Net Cost
		EFA	136.02			
B	1	EFA	1.00	Jul 142	11.50	($111.50)
W	1	EFA	2.70	Jul 137	11.50	$258.50
			Invested			**$147.00**
			Cash Start			$2,981.50
			Cash Now			**$3,128.50**

TABLE 15.6B July Expiration Positions

ETF	Qty	Price	Call	Opt Sale	Invested	Break-Even	Profit Potential	Down Protect	Return
VTI	500	105.90	Jul 108	$0.00	($52,950.00)	104.40	$1,780.00	1.42%	3.36%
MDY	200	108.75	Jul 110	$0.00	($21,750.00)	106.80	$620.00	1.79%	2.85%
EFA	100	136.02	Jul 137	$147.00	($13,455.00)	135.02	$225.00	0.74%	1.67%
OEF	200	54.04	Jul 55	$0.00	($10,808.00)	53.74	$232.00	0.56%	2.15%
			Invested		($98,963.00)		$2,857.00		2.89%
			Cash		$3,128.50				
		Total	Account		$102,091.50				
		MAX	Value		$104,948.50				

Opt Sale: Proceeds from sale, *after* expiration
Profit Potential: Maximum for entire month, if assigned on calls

TABLE 15.6C July Expiration Results

ETF	Opening ETF Price	Ending Price	Assigned	Current Position	Cost	Current Value	P/L	% P/L
VTI	105.90	106.92	No	500	($52,950.00)	$53,460.00	$1,260.00	2.38%
MDY	108.75	109.80	No	200	($21,750.00)	$21,960.00	$600.00	2.76%
EFA	136.02	135.97	No	100	($13,455.00)	$13,597.00	$242.00	1.80%
OEF	54.04	54.53	No	200	($10,808.00)	$10,906.00	$158.00	1.46%
			Total		**($98,963.00)**	**$99,923.00**	**$2,260.00**	**2.28%**
			Cash		**$3,128.50**			
		Beginning Account Value			**$100,788.50**			
		Ending Account Value			**$103,048.50**			
		Total Cash			**$3,128.50**			

P/L: ETF value minus cost

should complete my trades within the first few minutes after the market opens.

I'm getting more and more efficient at this process. It took me only three minutes to complete the sale of four different options expiring in August. The trades are listed in Table 15.7A.

My excess cash is building, and I want to put it to work as soon as possible. My current positions are listed in Table 15.7B.

The August expiration period begins with one of those bullish markets that investors love. Prices rise steadily day after day. By Wednesday of the second week, all my short option positions are significantly in the money, and there are still two and one-half weeks until August expiration. I can simply wait for expiration to arrive, and I'll probably collect the maximum possible return my positions allow (when assigned an exercise notice on each call). Instead, I'm making an adjustment to each position. These trades have a bullish bias.

Earlier, I rolled down and out to a lower strike price when the options I sold became significantly out of the money. The goal was to gain additional protection against loss. This time I'm making the mirror-image trades (rolling up and out) because the options I sold are now significantly in the money. I'm rolling up to a higher strike price and out to a more distant expiration date in an attempt to earn extra profits. The new options I write are going to be near the money, per my usual investment style. I'm buying back August options and substituting September options with higher strike prices.

TABLE 15.7A August Expiration Trades

B/S/W	Qty	SYM	Price	Call	Prem	Comm	Invested
		VTI	106.97				
W	5	VTI		Aug 107	2.05	17.50	$1,007.50
		MDY	109.85				
W	2	MDY		Aug 110	2.10	13.00	$407.00
		EFA	136.10				
W	1	EFA		Aug 137	2.20	11.50	$208.50
		OEF	54.60				
W	2	OEF		Aug 55	0.70	13.00	$127.00
			Invested				**$1,750.00**
			Cash	Start			$3,128.50
			Cash	**Now**			**$4,878.50**

TABLE 15.7B August Expiration Positions

ETF	Qty	Price	Call	Opt Sale	Invested	Break-Even	Profit Potential	Down Protect	Return
VTI	500	106.97	Aug 107	$1,007.50	($52,477.50)	104.96	$1,002.50	1.88%	1.91%
MDY	200	109.85	Aug 110	$407.00	($21,563.00)	107.82	$417.00	1.85%	1.93%
EFA	100	136.10	Aug 137	$208.50	($13,401.50)	134.02	$278.50	1.53%	2.08%
OEF	200	54.60	Aug 55	$127.00	($10,793.00)	53.97	$187.00	1.16%	1.73%
		Total	**Invested Cash**	**$1,750.00**	**($98,235.00)** $4,878.50		**$1,885.00**		**1.92%**
		Total MAX	**Account Value**		$103,113.50 $104,998.50				

171

Rolling a Position Type II. Rolling to Make Money

This time I'm entering my orders as spread transactions and having my broker execute the orders. I don't want to take the chance that I will have difficulty executing the trades. I tell the broker, "I have four spread orders.

"First, in a spread transaction, buy 5 VTI Aug 107 calls to close (buy an option sold earlier) and sell 5 VTI Sep 111 calls to open (write an option to establish a new position) for net a debit of $2.40." A net debit of $2.40 means to pay no more than $2.40 *more* to buy the August call than you receive when selling the September call.

"Second, as a spread, buy 2 MDY Aug 110 calls to close and sell to open 2 MDY Sep 113 calls for a net debit of $1.50.

"Next, as a spread, buy to close 1 EFA Aug 137 call and sell to open 1 EFA Sep 141 call for a net debit of $1.90.

"Last, take a spread order. Buy to close 2 OEF Aug 55 calls and sell to open 2 Sep 57 calls for a net debit of $1.15."

After entering the orders, I monitor the markets, trying to judge how easily my orders can be executed. Some brokers are much more efficient than others in getting spread orders filled, so I want to be certain my broker is good. If not, I can change brokers or enter individual orders online. Using the broker eliminates the risk of getting a fill at bad prices but increases the risk of failing to complete the roll.

It turns out that I had nothing to worry about. Within the hour I've been notified by e-mail that all my spread orders are filled. The trades are listed in Table 15.7C.

When making the decision to maintain my current positions or roll them, I must consider risk versus reward. Conservative investors may prefer to hold, locking in their profits. More aggressive investors are more willing to roll the position up and out in an effort to earn more money. The

TABLE 15.7C August Expiration: Trades to Roll Positions

ETF	Qty	Current Price	Bought Calls	Buy Price	Sold Calls	Sell Price	Spread Debit	Cash Paid
VTI	5	110.71	Aug 107	$4.00	Sep 111	$1.60	$2.40	$1,235.00
MDY	2	113.00	Aug 110	$3.30	Sep 113	$1.80	$1.50	$326.00
EFA	1	141.00	Aug 137	$4.40	Sep 141	$2.50	$1.90	$213.00
OEF	2	56.65	Aug 55	$1.80	Sep 57	$0.65	$1.15	$256.00

	Cost to Roll	($2,030.00)
	Old Cash	$4,878.50
	New Cash	$2,848.50

Cost to roll: Cash is negative because I paid cash to make the trades.

possibility of extra profits comes with the risk of losing profits already earned this month. There is no right decision here. Either choice is reasonable.

Note: It cost over $2,000 to roll my positions. I would have been unable to make these trades if my idle cash reserves were not sufficient.

Rationale for Rolling a Position

Before rolling, my positions were very safe and it was very likely I would earn the maximum. Is there any reason to abandon these relatively safe positions in an attempt to earn additional profits? Yes, there is.

Let's assume the market stabilizes between now and August expiration. I'll be assigned on all my August calls, achieving the maximum profit. The following Monday I'll buy the same ETFs I currently own, paying the then current market price. If the price remains steady, I'll be paying 111 for my VTI shares and writing VTI Sep 111 calls.

By rolling the position today, I'm also reinvesting in VTI at its current price near 111. I'm writing the same Sep 111 call that I'd be writing if I waited a few weeks. Thus, I'm not taking any more risk now than I would be taking later. Thus, the question becomes: What do I have to gain or lose by rolling my positions to September now?

If I roll now, I give up some downside protection. If the market reverses direction and heads lower before August expiration, I'll be worse off because I rolled the position. I'm currently protected against losing any money in my VTI position if the market turns down, as long as it stays above 107 (the strike price of the August call I wrote earlier) when expiration arrives. Once I roll to the VTI Sep 111 call, that four points of protection disappears.

If I roll now, I'll have the opportunity to earn additional profits from the September expiration cycle because I'll receive a higher price selling my September calls now (see box). It's true I must pay some time premium to buy back my August calls,[14] but because they are a few points in the money, that time premium is minimal compared with the extra time premium I can gain from writing September options now.

The rolling decision comes down to this:

- Am I willing to exchange extra protection for the next two and a half weeks in exchange for the opportunity to earn extra profits from September expiration?
- By rolling now, I'll lose money if the market retreats before expiration. But if the rally continues, I'll earn additional profits because the September calls carry significant time premium, and that time premium represents my profit.

Rolling Now: What I Have to Gain

It is a simple matter to calculate the theoretical value of an option using widely available calculators.[15] For our purposes that theoretical value is a good estimate of actual option prices, but one never knows in advance if special circumstances will affect those prices.

Assume VTI is 111.00 and the implied volatility is 13 percent

45 days to September expiration (rolling now)
VTI Aug 107 call theoretical value: $4.20
VTI Sep 111 call theoretical value: $2.15
Cost to roll: $2.05 (Buy Aug 107 and sell Sep 111)

26 days to September expiration (waiting until Monday, after expiration)
VTI Aug 107 call price: expired with a value of $4.00
VTI Sep 111 theoretical value: $1.65
Cost to roll: $2.35

By waiting until after expiration, I save $0.20 per option when buying back my August calls. But I'll receive $0.50 less when writing the September calls. That difference represents my *estimated* gain by rolling now. There is no way to know what market conditions will obtain when expiration day arrives, but these calculations provide a reasonable guess.

- Because I don't have any idea if the market is going to head higher or lower, rolling now allows me to maintain my overall strategy of owing ETF shares and writing options that are at the money. This is the deciding factor for me.

In making the decision to roll, I must make the same decision covered call writers face constantly: Do I want to give up the safety of my current position seeking extra profits? Each investor faces this problem occasionally. Because I agree with the teachings of modern portfolio theory and accept the fact that I have no ability to predict the direction of the next stock market move correctly, I choose to roll the position because the risk/reward outlook is favorable. Being a conservative investor, I usually choose the more conservative path and hold the position. But this time I'm rolling. Rolling not only gives me the position I want (short the ATM call), but it also gives me some experience handling the decisions required in the rolling process. That experience ought to be helpful when I next face a similar problem.

Note: In June, when I rolled the position down and out, the purpose was to gain protection for my portfolio. To me that's a prudent choice. This month I'm rolling the position in an attempt to gain additional profits because the risk-to-reward factor is favorable. I don't expect to make this type of roll often.

The Trades (Rolling)

Let's look at each of the four positions and compare the potential gain with the possible loss from rolling the positions now.

VTI Position I moved the strike price 4 points higher (from 107 to 111). Because I paid $240 for each spread (plus $35 in commissions), I've increased my investment in VTI by $1,235 ($240 × 5 + $35). If VTI is above 111 when September expiration arrives, that $1,235 turns into $2,000. (I'll earn 4 extra points on each of my 500 shares by selling at the strike price of 111 instead of 107.)

MDY Position I invested an additional $150 per option to roll the strike prices up by 3 points. I'm putting that additional investment at risk trying to turn that $326 (including commissions) into $600 (three points on 200 shares.

EFA Position I rolled my position 5 points higher, investing $190 plus $23 in commissions to do so. The potential profit is $310 less commission. Commissions are more significant when rolling the EFA position because I have only 100 shares.

OEF Position My OEF options were less than 2 points in the money, and rolling this position is less attractive than the others. I had to choose between maintaining this position, thereby providing a small amount of protection for my investment, and rolling to make it consistent with the others. I voted for consistency, and it cost $256 to roll the position. If these options are in the money at expiration, I'll earn an extra $144–$200 for each option, less the $256 cost to roll.

Summary: Rolling the Positions

If the market declines over the next few weeks, rolling the positions is going to cost me because I'll lose all or part of the extra money I just added to my investments. However, if the market continues to advance, or even if it remains relatively unchanged from its current price level, then rolling the position is going to prove to be profitable because I'll keep the extra time premium I received for writing the September options early. I'm comfortable with rolling because I don't want to place bets on the direction of future stock market moves.

Is It Better To Wait Rather than Roll Now?

When trading options, you are at the mercy of how options are priced in the marketplace. The professional traders who make markets in those options determine those prices, and they in turn are influenced by order flow. When there are many more buyers than sellers, option prices move higher. Conversely, when there are many more sellers, prices move lower. In addition, world events drive option prices. Anything that creates fear in the minds of option traders (professionals *and* public investors) causes option prices to jump higher—because of the uncertainty of the future. For example, the attack on September 11, 2001, or the crash of October 1987.[16] When investors are complacent about the future, or when markets are calm, option prices slowly decline. Because I don't have any way of knowing whether option prices will be relatively high or low when August expiration day arrives, I don't know whether it is best to roll now or wait. I don't want to be in the prediction business, and I made the decision to roll without making a guess as to future option pricing.

The new positions are listed in Table 15.7D.

The market continued to rally during the final weeks of the August expiration period, but the rate of increase slowed. By the time the third Friday of August arrived, all my options were in the money. Over the weekend I'll have to decide between maintaining my positions and rolling again. I was not assigned on any options, as they still have one month remaining in their lifetimes. Table 15.7E lists my positions at expiration.

August was a good month, as it should be when the markets rally. I'm now ahead over 5 percent for the year.

SEPTEMBER EXPIRATION

There are no decisions to be made after all, as the options are only slightly in the money. I am going to maintain all positions for now. The markets open near the levels of last Friday. There are no trades to list, and the current positions are shown in Table 15.8A.

September is a great month for covered call writers. The markets are nearly unchanged for the month, with the exception of the foreign markets, which did not hold up as well. When expiration arrives, only the EFA option is out of the money, and I'll be assigned an exercise notice on my other three positions. My investment results for September are listed in Table 15.8B.

My return for the month is only 1.40 percent. There are two reasons for that: (1) my EFA position did not return the maximum, and (2) I started the month with two options positions that were already in the money. ITM options do not produce as much profit as ATM options, but it was not appropriate to roll my positions.[17]

TABLE 15.7D August Expiration: Positions After Rolling

ETF	Qty	Current Price	New Calls	Cash Paid	Invested Now	Break-Even	Profit Potential	Down Protect	Return
VTI	500	110.71	Sep 111	$1,235.00	($53,712.50)	107.43	$1,767.50	2.97%	3.29%
MDY	200	113.00	Sep 113	$326.00	($21,889.00)	109.45	$691.00	3.15%	3.16%
EFA	100	141.00	Sep 141	$213.00	($13,614.50)	136.15	$465.50	3.44%	3.42%
OEF	200	56.65	Sep 57	$256.00	($11,049.00)	55.25	$331.00	2.48%	3.00%
			Invested		($100,265.00)		$3,255.00		3.25%
			Cash From Rolling	($2,030.00)					
			Old Cash	$4,878.50					
			New Cash	$2,848.50					
			Account Value	$103,113.50					
			MAX Value	$106,368.50					

Cash Paid: Cost to roll, including commissions

TABLE 15.7E August Expiration Results

ETF	Opening Price	Ending Price	Assigned	Current Position	Cost	Current ETF Value	Current Call	Opt Price	Opt Value	P/L	% P/L
VTI	106.97	111.44	No	500	($53,712.50)	$55,720.00	Sep 111	$1.85	$925.00	$1,082.50	2.02%
MDY	109.85	114.09	No	200	($21,889.00)	$22,818.00	Sep 113	$2.50	$500.00	$429.00	1.96%
EFA	136.10	141.66	No	100	($13,614.50)	$14,166.00	Sep 141	$3.00	$300.00	$251.50	1.85%
OEF	54.60	57.02	No	200	($11,049.00)	$11,404.00	Sep 57	$0.85	$170.00	$185.00	1.67%
Total					**($100,265.00)**	**$104,108.00**			**$1,895.00**	**$1,948.00**	**1.94%**
Cash					**$2,848.50**						

Beginning Account Value	**$103,654.50**
Ending Account Value	**$105,061.50**

Assigned: Note: Still one month before expiration; option owner did not exercise

Cost: Amount invested, after rolling position in midmonth

Current ETF Value: Value of ETF shares at August expiration

Opt Price: Current price of Sep calls sold earlier

P/L: ETF cost minus ETF value minus option value

Ending account value: Value of ETFs plus cash minus value of short option positions

TABLE 15.8A September Expiration Positions

ETF	Qty	Price	Call	Opening Opt Val	Invested	Break-Even	Profit Potential	Down Protect	Return
VTI	500	111.40	Sep 111	$925.00	($54,775.00)	109.55	$705.00	1.66%	1.29%
MDY	200	114.11	Sep 114	$500.00	($22,322.00)	111.61	$458.00	2.19%	2.05%
EFA	100	141.70	Sep 141	$300.00	($13,870.00)	138.70	$210.00	2.12%	1.51%
OEF	200	56.99	Sep 57	$170.00	($11,228.00)	56.14	$152.00	1.49%	1.35%
			Total Invested	$1,895.00	($102,195.00)		$1,525.00		1.49%
			Cash		$2,828.50				
			Total Account		$105,023.50				
			MAX Value		$106,548.50				

Opening Opt Val: Value of open option positions
Total Account: Value of ETFs, plus cash, less value of open option positions

179

TABLE 15.8B September Expiration Results

ETF	Opening Price	Ending Price	Assigned	Current Position	Cost	Current Value	Sale Proceeds	P/L	% P/L
VTI	111.40	111.35	Yes	0	($54,775.00)		$55,480.00	$705.00	1.29%
MDYM	114.11	114.20	Yes	0	($22,322.00)		$22,780.00	$458.00	2.05%
EFA	141.70	139.86	No	100	($13,870.00)	$13,986.00		$116.00	0.84%
OEF	56.99	57.05	Yes	0	($11,228.00)		$11,380.00	$152.00	1.35%
		Total			**($102,195.00)**	**$13,986.00**	**$89,640.00**	**$1,431.00**	**1.40%**
		Cash Start			**$2,828.50**				
		Cash End			**$92,468.50**				
		Beginning Account Value			**$105,023.50**				
		Ending Account Value			**$106,454.50**				

I intend to reinvest in the same mix of ETFs next month, but I'll watch my cash closely as I'll buy another 100 shares of OEF as soon as I have enough cash.

OCTOBER EXPIRATION

The S&P futures were steady before the market opened Monday morning, correctly predicting a flat opening. My trades are listed in Table 15.9A. Option prices are a bit higher this month because there are five weeks to expiration.

I'm reinvesting in the identical portfolio, but this month I'm writing the call options that are slightly out of the money. My current positions along with the potential profits are listed in Table 15.9B.

October is an exciting month for investors—that is, if not being sure of what is going to happen next is exciting for you. The market is up about 3 percent within the first three days, and I have to think about rolling my positions up. But before I can make the final decision, the market drops 5 percent the next day. There are still more than four weeks remaining until expiration, and the market has already experienced a decent-size rally followed by an even larger decline. Uncertainty abounds, and option prices are higher across the board as buyers are willing to pay higher prices to place bets on market direction. At the same time, option writers are demanding higher premiums.

I'm certainly lucky that I did not roll my positions, or I would have been whipsawed and forced to roll down.[18] At current price levels, rolling down is a serious consideration, but I'm going to wait it out for now, even though I'm nervous about my positions.

The market never finds a direction and spends the rest of the month rallying and then stumbling, only to rally again. At month end, the market has eked out a gain of less than 0.5 percent. The markets overseas fared better, gaining 1 percent. It turned out to be a good month for our strategy and I'll be assigned on two of my four option positions.

This was a very fortunate month for me, but it does represent one of the potential dangers of covered call writing. Whipsaws can occur, wiping out several months' worth of profits. It's never easy to roll a position when the market is volatile. The two previous times I rolled this year, it was not difficult to make the decision, as markets were moving in one direction without being too volatile. This month the volatility made decision-making precarious. As already noted, I was lucky. I cannot expect to be so lucky next time.

The October expiration results are listed in Table 15.9C.

For the November expiration, I'm going to maintain my current portfolio.

TABLE 15.9A October Expiration Trades

B/S/W	Qty	SYM	Price	Call	Prem	Comm	Invested
B	500	**VTI**	111.40			10.00	($55,710.00)
W	5	**VTI**		Oct 112	1.50	17.50	$732.50
B	200	**MDY**	114.15			10.00	($22,840.00)
W	2	**MDY**		Oct 115	1.75	13.00	$337.00
W	1	**EFA**	140.01	Oct 141	2.50	11.50	$238.50
B	200	**OEF**	57.04			10.00	($11,418.00)
W	2	**OEF**		Oct 57	1.20	13.00	$227.00
					Invested		**($88,433.00)**
					Cash	Start	**$92,468.50**
					Cash	Now	**$4,035.50**

TABLE 15.9B October Expiration Positions

ETF	Qty	Price	Call	Invested	Break-Even	Profit Potential	Down Protect	Return
VTI	500	111.40	Oct 112	($54,967.50)	109.94	$1,012.50	1.32%	1.84%
MDY	200	114.15	Oct 115	($22,493.00)	112.47	$487.00	1.48%	2.17%
EFA	100	140.01	Oct 141	($13,762.50)	137.63	$317.50	1.70%	2.31%
OEF	200	57.04	Oct 58	($11,181.00)	55.91	$399.00	1.99%	3.57%
		Total	**Invested**	**($102,404.00)**		**$2,216.00**		**2.16%**
			Cash			**$4,035.50**		
		Total	**Account**	**$106,439.50**				
		MAX	**Value**	**$108,655.50**				

183

TABLE 15.9C October Expiration Results

ETF	Opening Price	Ending Price	Assigned	Current Position	Cost	Current Value	Sale Proceeds	P/L	% P/L
VTI	111.40	112.03	Yes	0	($54,967.50)		$55,980.00	$1,012.50	1.84%
MDY	114.15	114.80	No	200	($22,493.00)	$22,960.00		$467.00	2.08%
EFA	140.01	142.13	Yes	0	($13,762.50)		$14,080.00	$317.50	2.31%
OEF	57.04	57.25	No	200	($11,181.00)	$11,450.00		$269.00	2.41%
		Total			**($102,404.00)**	**$34,410.00**	**$70,060.00**	**$2,066.00**	**2.02%**
		Cash Start			**$4,035.50**				
		Cash End			**$74,095.50**				
		Beginning Account Value			**$106,439.50**				
		Ending Account Value			**$108,505.50**				

NOVEMBER EXPIRATION

The overseas markets are lower this morning, but since I was assigned on my short call position, I currently don't own any shares of EFA. I'll repurchase this morning and write my slightly OTM call option, as usual.

The markets are quiet and I am now fully invested. I used my idle cash and now own 300 shares of OEF. But in order to have enough cash, I was forced to write the slightly ITM OEF Nov 57 call because the Nov 58 call would not have generated enough cash to enable me to buy that extra 100 shares of OEF. As it is, I barely made it; my idle cash is now only $8. Because I have so little cash, I will be unable to roll my positions up, if I were inclined to do so.

The November expiration trades are listed in Table 15.10A.

Positions are listed in Table 15.10B.

November was a strong month for small-capitalization stocks, but unfortunately my portfolio is underweighted in them. I was able to participate to a small extent because my holding in VTI includes companies of all sizes. But small-cap stocks rose over 3 percent in November while the rest of the market drifted over a narrow trading range. The overseas markets continued to slide, and my EFA option expired worthless. All things considered, it was a fine month and my year-to-date profits continue to increase.

Note: Diversifying the portfolio to include overseas stocks worked against me this month. But owning such investments reduces risk. Earlier this year owning overseas investments worked in my favor. Overall, diversifying has been a benefit. Perhaps I should consider further diversification when I reallocate my assets for the coming year. It's something to think about, but for now, I'll stick with my current portfolio and won't try to chase the latest trend in the market by loading up on smaller stocks. The results for November are listed in Table 15.10C.

TABLE 15.10A November Expiration Trades

B/S/W	Qty	SYM	Price	Call	Prem	Comm	Invested
B	500	VTI	112.01			10.00	($56,015.00)
W	5	VTI		Nov 112	1.70	17.50	$832.50
B		MDY	114.77				
W	2	MDY		Nov 115	1.80	13.00	$347.00
B	100	EFA	140.08			10.00	($14,018.00)
W	1	EFA		Nov 141	2.20	11.50	$208.50
B	100	OEF	57.18			10.00	($5,728.00)
W	3	OEF		Nov 57	1.00	14.50	$285.50
			Invested				**($74,087.50)**
			Cash Start				$74,095.50
			Cash Now				**$8.00**

TABLE 15.10B November Expiration Positions

ETF	Qty	Price	Call	Invested	Break-Even	Profit Potential	Down Protect	Return
VTI	500	112.01	Nov 112	($55,172.50)	110.35	$802.50	1.49%	1.45%
MDY	200	114.77	Nov 115	($22,607.00)	113.04	$373.00	1.51%	1.65%
EFA	100	140.08	Nov 141	($13,799.50)	138.00	$280.50	1.49%	2.03%
OEF	300	57.18	Nov 57	($16,868.50)	56.23	$157.50	1.66%	0.93%
			Total Invested	**($108,447.50)**		**$1,613.50**		**1.49%**
			Cash	**$8.00**				
			Total Account	**$108,455.50**				
			MAX Value	**$110,069.00**				

TABLE 15.10C November Expiration Results

ETF	Opening Price	Ending Price	Assigned	Current Position	Cost	Current Value	Sale Proceeds	P/L	% P/L
VTI	112.01	112.15	Yes	0	($55,172.50)		$55,980.00	807.50	1.46%
MDY	114.77	114.97	No	200	($22,607.00)	$22,994.00		387.00	1.71%
EFA	140.01	137.35	No	100	($13,799.50)	$13,735.00		(64.50)	–0.47%
OEF	57.18	57.22	Yes	0	($16,868.50)		$17,080.00	211.50	1.25%
		Total			**($108,447.50)**	**$36,729.00**	**$73,060.00**	**1,341.50**	**1.24%**
		Cash	**Start**		**$8.00**				
		Cash	**End**		**$73,068.00**				
		Beginning Account Value			**$108,455.50**				
		Ending Account Value			**$109,797.00**				

Note that something very interesting happened this month in my MDY position. I made more money than I thought I could possibly make from this position. When I calculate my best possible return, I assume the ETF rises above the strike price and I am assigned an exercise notice. When that happens, I pay an assignment fee of $20. This time MDY closed at 114.97, or only 3 cents below the strike price. Thus, I did not receive an exercise notice, did not pay the $20 fee, and my 200 shares are worth only $6 less than they would be if they were priced at the strike price. I have $6 less but saved $20 for an increased profit of $14. Not a lot of money, but a great result!

My year-to-date profit is almost 10 percent while the S&P 500 index is barely 3 percent ahead.

DECEMBER EXPIRATION

The markets are mixed this morning, and I reinvested my cash. Call option prices are a bit lower than they have been recently. Not a lot lower, but five to ten cents less for each option I'm selling. I could wait a day or two and hope that option prices rebound, but I won't do so for three important reasons:

1. Not only do I want to be fully invested at all times, *but* I also want those investments to be hedged at all times.

2. There is no guarantee that option prices will rebound, and they might even decline further.

3. Because options are a wasting asset, the price I expect to receive when writing a call declines daily (all things being equal).

The trades are listed in Table 15.11A.

My positions for December are listed in Table 15.11B.

December is a good month for the market. The holiday rally is in full force both here and overseas. I never reach the point where I want to roll my positions to higher strikes.

I did not participate in a portion of the rising market. The S&P 500 index moves 5 percent higher in December and I settle for my maximum profit, which is 1.41 percent for the month. I'm still doing better than the overall market for the year, but this result illustrates one of the risks involved when using a covered call writing program—upside profits are limited unless I roll my positions in a timely manner. I've decided that making my target profit each month is more than acceptable, and if others do better when the bull market is alive, that's OK. I know I'll do better than other

TABLE 15.11A December Expiration Trades

B/S/W	Qty	SYM	Price	Call	Prem	Comm	Invested
B	500	VTI	111.94			10.00	($55,980.00)
W	5	VTI		Dec 112	1.55	17.50	$757.50
		MDY	115.02				
W	2	MDY		Dec 115	1.80	13.00	$347.00
		EFA	137.01				
W	1	EFA		Dec 138	1.95	11.50	$183.50
B	300	OEF	57.20			10.00	($17,170.00)
W	3	OEF		Dec 57	0.90	14.50	$255.50
			Invested				**($71,606.50)**
			Cash Start				$73,068.00
			Cash Now				**$1,461.50**

investors when markets move lower or are stagnant. Besides, I'm not in competition with anyone else. I'm managing my money to fit my needs.

My results for the month of December are listed in Table 15.11C.

I see no reason to alter my investment style and will continue on the same path for the final month of the year.

JANUARY EXPIRATION

The recent rally means I must repurchase my ETFs at much higher prices than before. I was assigned on all positions and have only cash remaining in my account. This is the equivalent of being forced to roll my positions to higher strike prices. Of course, I can refuse to roll the positions by stubbornly writing ITM calls. I won't succumb to that trap because (I have to repeat it to myself often to make sure I resist the temptation) I know I am not good at predicting in which direction the market is going to move next. Thus, I'll stay with writing options that are at the money for domestic investments and one point out of the money for my foreign holdings.

The high prices present another problem. I no longer have enough cash to repurchase the full positions I owned last month. I'm cutting back my OEF investment to 200 shares.

TABLE 15.11B December Expiration Positions

ETF	Qty	Price	Call	Invested	Break-Even	Profit Potential	Down Protect	Return
VTI	500	111.94	Dec 112	($55,212.50)	110.43	$767.50	1.35%	1.39%
MDY	200	115.02	Dec 115	($22,657.00)	113.29	$323.00	1.51%	1.43%
EFA	100	137.01	Dec 138	($13,517.50)	135.18	$262.50	1.34%	1.94%
OEF	300	57.20	Dec 57	($16,904.50)	56.35	$175.50	1.49%	1.04%
		Total	Invested	($108,291.50)		$1,528.50		1.41%
			Cash	$1,461.50				
		Total	Account	$109,753.00				
		MAX	Value	$111,281.50				

TABLE 15.11C December Expiration Results

ETF	Opening Price	Ending Price	Assigned	Current Position	Cost	Current Value	Sale Proceeds	P/L	% P/L
VTI	111.94	117.44	Yes	0	($55,212.50)		$55,980.00	767.50	1.39%
MDY	115.02	120.99	Yes	0	($22,657.00)		$22,980.00	323.00	1.43%
EFA	137.01	145.22	Yes	0	($13,517.50)		$13,780.00	262.50	1.94%
OEF	57.20	58.88	Yes	0	($16,904.50)		$17,080.00	175.50	1.04%
		Total			**($108,291.50)**	**$0.00**	**$109,820.00**	**1,528.50**	**1.41%**
		Cash	**Start**		**$1,461.50**				
		Cash	**End**		**$111,281.50**				
	Beginning Account Value				**$109,753.00**				
	Ending Account Value				**$111,281.50**				

January trades are listed in Table 15.12A.

My positions are listed in Table 15.12B.

The year-end rally continues for a few days, but after the New Year's break, the market heads lower. The downward move is without conviction, and January expiration arrives with the market losing less than one-half of 1 percent for the expiration period. This represents another good month for my covered call writing program. For the past 12 months I've been working on my new investment strategy. I've learned a great deal and am going to continue writing covered calls next year.

The results for January expiration are listed in Table 15.12C.

My profits for the year are 12.32 percent, while the S&P 500 index gained 9.0 percent over the same time period. I have a busy weekend ahead. Besides making the usual decision about which ETFs to own, it's time to make my annual decision on how to allocate my assets. I want to decide just how much of my overall portfolio should be invested in the stock markets of the world. Thus, I'll either be adding some additional cash to my covered call writing program or removing some for investment elsewhere. I'm looking forward to another profitable year with my newfound investment methodology.

In Chapter 16 we'll take a similar (but less detailed) look at how writing uncovered put options works. There are educational points of interest, even for investors who intend to stay with the covered call strategy.

TABLE 15.12A January Expiration Trades

B/S/W	Qty	SYM	Price	Call	Prem	Comm	Invested
B	500	**VTI**	117.49			10.00	($58,755.00)
W	5	**VTI**		Jan 118	1.45	17.50	$707.50
B	200	**MDY**	121.00			10.00	($24,210.00)
W	2	**MDY**		Jan 121	2.00	13.00	$387.00
B	100	**EFA**	145.48			10.00	($14,558.00)
W	1	**EFA**		Jan 147	2.00	11.50	$188.50
B	200	**OEF**	58.91			10.00	($11,792.00)
W	2	**OEF**		Dec 59	0.85	13.00	$157.00
				Invested			**($107,875.00)**
			Cash	Start			$111,281.50
			Cash	**Now**			**$3,406.50**

TABLE 15.12B January Expiration Positions

ETF	Qty	Price	Call	Invested	Break-Even	Profit Potential	Down Protect	Return
VTI	500	117.49	Jan 118	($58,047.50)	116.10	$932.50	1.19%	1.61%
MDY	200	121.00	Jan 121	($23,823.00)	119.12	$357.00	1.56%	1.50%
EFA	100	145.48	Jan 147	($14,369.50)	143.70	$310.50	1.23%	2.16%
OEF	200	58.91	Jan 59	($11,635.00)	58.18	$145.00	1.23%	1.23%
		Total Invested		($107,875.00)		$1,745.00		1.62%
		Cash		$3,406.50				
		Total Account		$111,281.50				
		MAX Value		$113,026.50				

TABLE 15.12C January Expiration Results

ETF	Opening Price	Ending Price	Assigned	Current Position	Cost	Current Value	Sale Proceeds	P/L	% P/L
VTI	117.49	116.98	No	500	($58,047.50)	$58,490.00		442.50	0.76%
MDY	121.00	120.35	No	200	($23,823.00)	$24,070.00		247.00	1.04%
EFA	145.48	146.13	No	100	($14,369.50)	$14,613.00		243.50	1.69%
OEF	58.91	58.71	No	200	($11,635.00)	$11,743.50		107.00	0.91%
			Total		($107,875.00)	$108,916.50	$0.00	1,040.00	0.96%
			Cash		$3,405.00				
		Beginning Account Value			$111,281.50				
		Ending Account Value			$112,321.50				

CHAPTER 16

Uncovered Put Writing in Action

Writing uncovered puts has some advantages over writing covered calls:

- It is less expensive because commissions are reduced. The trade involves writing one put option. Covered call writing consists of two trades: buying exchange traded fund (ETF) shares and writing one call option.
- Initiating a position does not require legging into the position you want to own because writing the put option is a single transaction.[1]
- It is easier to close a position when locking in a profit. Buying a put to close a position is a simple one-step process.

However, there is one disadvantage to writing uncovered puts that is more important than the advantages: Some brokers do not allow their customers to write naked put options under any circumstances. If your broker prohibits this strategy, it's strongly recommended that you find a more cooperative broker. However, if you wish to maintain your account with that broker, covered call writing is an equivalent investment strategy. (See Chapter 15.)

One word of caution is required. When writing naked put options, if your positions are cash backed then you never have to worry about receiving a margin call from your broker. A position is cash backed when there is sufficient cash in the account to pay for stock if you are assigned an exercise notice for the put options you sold. If the cash is in your account, the maximum risk for the position is known (and is essentially equivalent to that of any other shareholder).[2]

If you do not have enough cash, and if you are assigned an exercise notice on puts you wrote, it's possible your broker will issue a margin call, requiring you to (immediately) deposit additional cash or securities into your account. This is a situation you want to avoid. Some brokers don't provide any warning and simply close positions (of their choosing) to raise the needed cash.

If you are writing naked puts for the first time, begin by having cash to back all your positions. As you become more acquainted with writing uncovered puts and the risks involved,[3] you may decide to borrow money from your broker and own uncovered put positions that are only partially backed by cash. Using margin provides an opportunity to increase your profits, but it also enhances risk.[4] Trading on margin is not for everyone, and a discussion of this topic is beyond the scope of this book.

You must be certain not to write more uncovered puts than your financial situation allows. This is especially true if you are trading with borrowed money from your broker (margin). Please reread the warning in Chapter 11.

QUICK REVIEW

Consider two positions:

1. Covered call

   Buy 200 shares of MDY at $118.
   Write 2 Dec 118 calls at $2.00.

2. Naked put

   Write 2 Dec 118 MDY puts at $2.00.

Table 16.1 lists the risks and rewards of owning each position. Notice the risk profiles are identical. The maximum potential profit and the downside break-even point are the same. Neither position is riskier than the

TABLE 16.1 Compare Covered Call with Uncovered Put

	Covered Call	Uncovered Put
Long Position	100 MDY @ 118	None
Short Position	1 MDY Dec 118 call @ 2	1 MDY Dec 118 put @ 2
Max Profit	$200	$200
Max Loss	$11,600	$11,600
Max Profit	MDY above 118	MDY above 118
Extra Gain if above 118	$0.00	$0.00
Downside B/E	116	116
Loss if below B/E	$100 per point	$100 per point

B/E: Break-even point

other, regardless of well-meaning investment advisors who tell you that writing naked options is dangerous.

Let's take a closer look at a hypothetical three-month trading period. The purpose is to illustrate the thoughts that occur to the investor/trader and how potential problems are resolved.

JUNE EXPIRATION

I have $100,000 to invest. After careful consideration, I'm going ahead with the naked put writing program. I'm going to concentrate on the American stock market. Yet with thousands of stocks, I feel sufficiently diversified. I've had success investing in small-capitalization stocks over the years, so I am going to emphasize those in my portfolio. I'm also investing a small amount in high-technology stocks. I've decided to take positions in these ETFs:

- IWV (Russell 3000 index consists of the 3,000 largest capitalized stocks)
- IWM (Russell 2000 Index consists of the smallest 2,000 stocks in the 3000 index)
- QQQ (Nasdaq 100 index)

My plan is to be virtually 100 percent cash backed, but I'm not going to be concerned if I fall a few dollars short.[5] There are currently five weeks until the June expiration.

I found it simple to make my trades, and the positions are listed in Table 16.2A. I'm writing put options that are slightly out of the money, positions that are equivalent to covered call positions that are slightly in the money.

TABLE 16.2A June Expiration Trades

B/S/W	Qty	SYM	Price	Put	Prem	Comm	Net Credit	Cash Backing
W	4	IWV	65.10	Jun 65	$0.90	16.00	$344.00	$26,000.00
W	4	IWM	118.00	Jun 118	$3.00	16.00	$1,184.00	$47,200.00
W	7	QQQ	38.22	Jun 38	$0.85	20.50	$574.50	$26,600.00
		Collected					**$2,102.50**	
		Required						**$99,800.00**
		Cash Start					$100,000.00	
		Cash Now					**$102,102.50**	
		Excess Cash					$2,302.50	

Net Credit: Cash collected from writing put options
Cash Backing: Cash required to maintain each position, if not using margin
Required: Total cash required to maintain all positions, if not using margin
Excess Cash: Cash above requirement

Methodology

If the put expires worthless, then I'll achieve the same result I would have achieved with a covered call position. That means I'll have the same profit (in reality, a slightly higher profit due to reduced commissions) and no residual position. I'll have to reinvest in a new position after expiration.

If the put finishes in the money, I'll be assigned on my position and own the ETF shares, paying the strike price. This is the identical result as the covered call writer has when the call options expire out of the money (and worthless), leaving that investor owning the ETF shares. Just as the covered call writer writes new calls after expiration, I plan to do exactly the same.

If those covered call options expire worthless, I'll continue to write new calls the following month. If I am assigned and forced to sell my ETF shares, I'll continue with my investment strategy by initiating a new position—writing naked puts for the following expiration period.

Thus, if my puts expire worthless, I'll continue with my plan to write new puts. But if I'm assigned and own the shares, I'll revert to the covered call writing program. This method is flexible.

Note: When writing naked puts, the profit potential equals the premium collected from those sales.

The positions and the profit potential for each position are listed in Table 16.2B.

June (this is not the same year as used for the covered call writing examples) is a mixed bag for the market. The S&P 500 is unchanged, but technology stocks take a beating and I am assigned on my QQQ puts. However, the good news is that my other puts expire worthless. Overall my first month writing naked puts is profitable. The results are listed in Table 16.2C.

JULY EXPIRATION

I own shares of QQQ so am writing call options against them. I'm also initiating new positions in IMV and IMW put options.

The market opens almost unchanged from last Friday's close, and I quickly open my new positions. The trades are listed in Table 16.3A. The July expiration is only four weeks away, so option premiums are lower than last month.

There was enough excess cash to allow me to buy an extra 100 shares of QQQ and write eight calls, instead of seven. I chose not to make this trade, even though I want to remain as fully invested as possible. Here's why: I feel I already have enough invested in the technology index and pre-

TABLE 16.2B June Expiration Positions

ETF	Qty	Price	Put	Put Sale	Cash Backing	Break-Even	Profit Potential	Down Protect	% P/L
IWV	4	65.10	Jun 65	$344.00	$26,000.00	$64.19	$344.00	1.40%	1.32%
IWM	4	118.00	Jun 118	$1,184.00	$47,200.00	$115.09	$1,184.00	2.47%	2.51%
QQQ	7	38.22	Jun 38	$574.50	$26,600.00	$37.21	$574.50	2.65%	2.16%
		Collected		$2,102.50			$2,102.50		2.11%
		Required			$99,800.00				
		Account Value		$100,000.00					
		Cash		$102,102.50					
		MAX Value		$102,102.50					

Cash Backing: Cash required to buy ETF shares, if assigned on puts.

Break-Even: Downside break-even price. Includes payment of $20 assignment fee.

% P/L: Profit divided by cash backing requirement. *Note:* This is the conservative calculation. If using margin, potential returns are significantly higher.

MAX Value: Value of account, if all puts expire worthless.

199

TABLE 16.2C June Expiration Results

ETF	Opening Price	Ending Price	Assigned	Current Position	Cost	Current Value	P/L	% P/L
IWV	65.10	65.05	No	0			344.00	1.32%
IWM	118.00	118.04	No	0			1,184.00	2.51%
QQQ	38.22	36.67	Yes	700	$26,045.50	$25,669.00	(376.50)	-1.45%
		Total			**$26,045.50**	**$25,669.00**	**1,151.50**	**1.15%**
		Cash Start			**$102,102.50**			
		Cash End			**$75,482.50**			
		Beginning Account Value			**$100,000.00**			
		Ending Account Value			**$101,151.50**			

Current Position: Number of shares owned, if assigned

Cost: # Shares × Strike Price + $20 (assignment fee) – put premium collected

%P/L: Profit (Loss) / (Cash Backing Requirement)

Cash End: Starting cash less ETF cost

TABLE 16.3A July Expiration Trades

B/S/W	Qty	SYM	Price	Option	Prem	Net Comm	Cash Credit	Backing
W	4	**IWV**	65.02	Jul 65 **Put**	$0.85	16.00	$324.00	$26,000.00
W	4	**IWM**	118.06	Jul 118 **Put**	$2.95	16.00	$1,164.00	$47,200.00
W	7	**QQQ**	36.70	Jul 37 **Call**	$0.75	20.50	$504.50	
			Collected				**$1,992.50**	
			Required				**$73,200.00**	
			Cash	Start			$75,482.50	
			Cash	**Now**			**$77,475.00**	
			Excess	Cash			$4,275.00	

Option: Call or put
Cash Backing: Cash required to maintain each uncovered *put* position

fer to put my money to work by buying additional shares of the Russell 2000 index. I'll use idle cash to buy 100 shares of IWM at my first opportunity. My current positions are listed in Table 16.3B.

July is a losing month for the market. The decline starts slowly and picks up momentum as the days pass. Within two weeks the S&P 500 index has declined almost 3 percent. My positions are still reasonable, as two of the three ETFs I own are trading near my break-even prices. I don't want to roll the positions but will do so in the interests of protecting the value of my portfolio. If I don't roll, I'll be betting the market will recover its recent losses. I don't want to find myself betting on the direction of the next market move. By owning a bullish portfolio, I'm already positioned to profit when the market rallies, so buying additional protection against loss is a prudent investment choice.

Notice my downside protection for IWV is only about half that for the other ETFs (Table 16.3B). Here's why: The Russell 3000 index is not very volatile, and the implied volatility of the options is fairly low. As a result, the premium I collect when writing new IWV options is less than the premium I receive from writing options on my other ETFs. Lower option premium means less downside protection as well as lower potential profit.

One of the reasons I prefer to own shares of IWV is because of its reduced volatility. It is safer to own IWV shares than it is to be an investor in some of the other ETFs. In return for that extra safety, I must accept lower option prices (less risk = less reward). This is one of those areas in which each investor's individual tolerance for risk enters the picture. If you prefer to seek higher returns and are willing to own a more volatile investment,

TABLE 16.3B July Expiration Positions

ETF	Qty	Price	Option	Cash Backing	Invested	Break-Even	Profit Potential	Down Protect	% P/L
IWV	4	65.02	Jul 65 Put	$26,000.00		$64.24	$324.00	1.20%	1.25%
IWM	4	118.06	Jul 118 Put	$47,200.00		$115.14	$1,164.00	2.47%	2.47%
QQQ	700	36.70			$25,185.50				
QQQ	7		Jul 37 Call		$25,185.50	$35.98	$694.50	2.81%	2.76%
			Required	**$73,200.00**	**$25,185.50**		**$2,182.50**		**2.22%**
			Account **Value**		$101,150.50				
			Cash **Value**		$77,475.00				
			MAX **Value**		$103,333.00				

then the mix of ETFs in your portfolio can be shifted to reflect those wishes. For example, if I were interested in trying to earn a higher return, I would own fewer shares of IWV and more shares of IWM.

Note: Indexes are composed of many stocks and are less volatile than most individual stocks. One reason: When some stocks in the index decrease in value, others increase. These price changes offset each other, making the overall index less volatile. Thus, if you are seeking even higher returns from writing covered calls or writing uncovered puts, then you can include some individual stocks in your portfolio mix. Just be aware that doing so significantly increases overall risk. Here's why: Any individual stock can have a surprise announcement at any time, and that announcement can have a large influence on the stock price. It is far less likely that the price of an index will undergo a rapid price change; such a change requires a news event that affects the whole stock market. This is more of the same old story—seek a higher return on your investment if you choose to do so, but you must accept a higher risk in an attempt to earn that return.

Having decided to roll my positions, the trades are listed in Table 16.3C. My positions and optimal results are listed in Table 16.3D.

The IWV numbers represent one of the potential unhappy outcomes when forced (for safety considerations) to roll a position. The potential profit is negative. Thus, if the best possible result is obtained—the put expires worthless—the position still loses money for the month. This occurs because it cost more cash to roll the position than I received when writing the puts in the first place. Thus, I have a net debit,[6] and there is no way to recover that cash from the current position.

The market continues to drift lower and then rallies. Expiration arrives with the major market indexes lower by about 3 percent for the month. The QQQ calls expired worthless, and I was assigned on my short IWV put options.

But something unusual happened with my IWM position. Two puts expired worthless, and I was assigned on the other two. This situation doesn't occur often, but whenever the option is within a few pennies of the strike price, it's possible for options to expire worthless, even if they are in the money.

There are several reasons why slightly ITM options can expire worthless:

- When options cease trading a few minutes after the market closes on expiration Friday, there is usually no bid higher than zero for these options.[7] Thus an investor who still owns these options is unable to sell.
- If the option owner decides to exercise the option, there are expenses and risks involved.
  - The option owner must pay a commission to exercise the options

TABLE 16.3C July Expiration: Trades To Roll Position

ETF	Qty	Current Price	Bought Option	Buy Price	Sold Option	Sell Price	Spread Cash	Comm	Net Cash
IWV	4	63.08	Jul 65 Put	$2.05	Aug 63 Put	$1.00	($1.05)	$32.00	($452.00)
IWM	4	114.50	Jul 118 Put	$4.10	Aug 115 Put	$3.40	($0.70)	$32.00	($312.00)
QQQ	7	35.48	Jul 37 Call	$0.15	Aug 36 Call	$0.80	$0.65	$41.00	$414.00
					Cost to Roll				($350.00)
					Old Cash				$77,475.00
					New Cash				$77,125.00

Net Cash: Difference between buy and sell prices.
Negative value: net debit paid; positive value: net credit collected.

TABLE 16.3D July Expiration: Positions after Rolling

ETF	Qty	Current Price	New Option	Put Sale Proceeds	Invested	Cash Backing	Break-Even	Profit Potential	Down Protect	Return
IWV	4	63.08	Aug 63 Put	($128.00)		$25,200.00	None	($128.00)	None	−0.51%
IWM	4	114.50	Aug 115 Put	$852.00		$46,000.00	112.87	$852.00	1.42%	1.85%
QQQ	700	35.48			($24,771.50)					
QQQ	7		Aug 36 Call				35.39	$408.50	0.26%	1.65%
					($24,771.50)	$71,200.00		$1,132.50		1.12%
			Cash		$77,125.00					
			Beginning Value		$101,150.50					
			New MAX Value		$102,283.00					

Qty: Number of options or ETF shares

Put Sale Proceeds: Total for month: original put sale plus cost to roll

Break-Even: "None" means position cannot return a profit this month

Down Protect: "None" means there is no price at which position is profitable this month

- The option exerciser incurs the risk of owning a position—long if the option is a call and short if the option is a put—in the underlying asset until the market opens next Monday. The market can easily move in the wrong direction, resulting in a significant loss.
- The option exerciser must pay another commission to close the position.
- Two commissions plus market risk make it easy for the investor who owns the option simply to allow it to expire worthless. There is too much expense and risk involved in attempting to capture the few pennies of intrinsic value in the option.

Results for July are listed in Table 16.3E.

July was an interesting month. Not only did I earn a small profit when the market was lower, but I also discovered for myself that I cannot make any assumptions regarding assignments. I now know it's important to check with my broker *before* making any trades on the Monday following expiration to verify which options expired worthless and which were assigned.[8]

AUGUST EXPIRATION

I am still long my QQQ shares and am writing new call options against them.

I now own 200 IWM shares, so I have two call options to write. Because I want a position representing 400 shares and because I prefer to write put options, I'll also write two new put options. Thus I'll have two separate positions in IWM: two covered calls and two uncovered puts. That's equivalent to two covered straddles.[9]

I was assigned on my IWV shares, and I am writing calls to hedge the position. But after writing new options this month, I'll have enough excess cash to increase my investment in IWV. I plan to purchase 100 additional shares of IWV and write an additional call. There are two points of interest here.

1. I prefer writing a put option, but because I already own 400 shares and am writing four call options, it's easier (and saves money in commissions) to add to my covered call position than to write a new uncovered put position. If I were buying more than 100 shares, then I would probably choose to write put options.

2. To ensure that I have enough cash to make this new trade and to minimize commissions, I plan to make this transaction last. First, I'll sell all the options I'm selling this month. (This generates some of the cash I

TABLE 16.3E July Expiration Results

ETF	Opening Price	Ending Price	Assigned	Current Position	Position Cost	Current Value	P/L	% P/L
IWV	65.02	62.90	Yes	400	($25,348.00)	$25,160.00	(188.00)	−0.72%
IWM	118.06	114.96	Yes	200	($22,594.00)	$22,992.00	398.00	1.69%
IWM	118.06	114.96	No	0			426.00	1.81%
QQQ	36.70	35.20	No	700	($24,772.00)	$24,640.00	(132.00)	−0.52%
		Total			($72,714.00)	$72,792.00	504.00	0.50%
	After Roll:	Account	Cash		$77,125.00			
		Ending	Cash		$28,885.00			
		Beginning	Account	Value	$101,150.50			
		Ending	Account	Value	$101,654.50			

IWM: Assigned on two put options; the other two expired worthless need to make the trade.[10]) Then I'll buy 100 IWV. Then I'll write five call options. If I write four options initially, buy 100 shares, and then write another call option, most brokers charge an additional $10 commission because there is a $10 fee per order.

The market is still drifting as I make my trades for the August expiration period (see Table 16.4A).

My positions and the potential profits are listed in Table 16.4B.

August is an ideal month for uncovered put writers. The market drifts higher, then lower, never moving significantly in either direction. Expiration arrives with the S&P 500 index up less than 0.25 percent. It appears that I am going to be assigned on all my short calls and my puts are going to expire worthless. My account has no remaining positions, only cash. The results are listed in Table 16.4C.

I'm ahead by over 3.6 percent for the three months, when the market has declined in value. I'm pleased with my performance. I plan to continue writing uncovered put options and switching to covered call writing if and when I am assigned on any puts.

Because my account contains only cash, next month I'll continue my investment program by writing puts on each of my three ETFs.

TABLE 16.4A August Expiration Trades

B/S/W	Qty	SYM	Price	Option	Prem	Comm	Net Cash	Cash Backing
B	100	**IWV**	62.85			10.00	($6,295.00)	
W	5	**IWV**		Aug 63 Call	$0.85	17.50	$407.50	
W	2	**IWM**	114.98	Aug 115 **Call**	$2.75	13.00	$537.00	
W	2	**IWM**		Aug 115 **Put**	$2.60	13.00	$507.00	$23,000.00
W	7	**QQQ**	35.20	Aug 35 Call	$0.95	20.50	$644.50	
							($4,199.00)	**$23,000.00**
			Collected				**($4,199.00)**	
			Required				**$23,000.00**	
			Cash	Start			$28,885.00	
			Cash	**Now**			**$24,686.00**	
			Excess	Cash			$1,686.00	

TABLE 16.4B August Expiration Positions

ETF	Qty	Price	Option	Option Proceeds	Cash Backing	Invested	Break-Even	Profit Potential	Down Protect	% P/L
IWV	500	62.85				($31,017.50)				
IWV	5		Aug 63 Call	$407.50			$62.04	$462.50	1.30%	1.49%
IWM	200	114.98				($22,459.00)				
IWM	2		Aug 115 Call	$537.00			$112.30	$521.00	2.34%	2.32%
IWM	2		Aug 115 Put	$507.00	$23,000.00		$112.57	$507.00	2.10%	2.20%
QQQ	700	35.20				($23,995.50)				
QQQ	7		Aug 35 Call	$644.50			$34.28	$484.50	2.62%	2.02%
						($77,472.00)		$1,975.00		1.97%
			Collected	$2,096.00						
			Required		$23,000.00					
		Account	Value		$101,654.50					
		Cash			$24,686.00					
		MAX	Value		$103,629.50					

TABLE 16.4C August Expiration Results

ETF	Opening Price	Ending Price	Assigned	Current Position	Cost	Cash Proceeds	P/L	% P/L
IWV	62.85	63.10	Yes	0	($31,017.50)	$31,480.00	$462.50	1.49%
IWM	114.98	115.21	Yes (Calls)	0	($22,459.00)	$22,980.00	$521.00	2.32%
IWM	114.98	115.21	No (Puts)	0	$507.00		$507.00	2.20%
QQQ	35.30	35.24	Yes	0	($23,995.50)	$24,480.00	$484.50	2.02%
		Total			**$101,654.50**	**$78,940.00**	**$1,975.00**	**1.97%**
		Beginning Account Value			**$101,654.50**			
		Beginning Cash			**$24,686.00**			
		Ending Account Value			**$103,629.50**			

SUMMARY

Cash-secured put writing is a conservative options strategy that provides a method of accumulating investments (stocks of ETFs) at below-market prices. If the market does not decline, and if you are unable to buy your ETFs at the discounted price, this strategy provides a constant income stream. Coupled with covered call writing, this strategy allows you to operate your own hedge fund—providing you with reduced risk and an increased chance of beating the market.

CHAPTER 17

Odds and Ends and Conclusion

In Chapter 15 we discussed rolling a position either to prevent losses or to reduce the likelihood of incurring a loss. We also looked at rolling a position in an effort to achieve additional profits. Rolling a position may be appropriate in two other situations.

ROLLING A POSITION TYPE III.
ROLLING TO PREVENT AN ASSIGNMENT

When the call option you wrote is in the money and expiration is approaching, you know there is a strong chance the option is going to finish in the money and that its owner is going to exercise. Sometimes you may prefer not to sell your exchange traded fund (ETF). To prevent being assigned, buy back the option you sold and immediately sell another option to replace it, choosing an appropriate strike price and expiration date.

This temporary solution prevents being assigned immediately, but the same problem may arise next month.

The question arises as to why you may not want to be assigned an exercise notice. One answer is that selling the security may place you in an undesirable tax situation. If you prefer to collect a capital gain next year rather than this year, one solution is to roll the call you write so it expires in the following year.

ROLLING A POSITION TYPE IV. ROLLING TO COLLECT AN ATTRACTIVE PREMIUM

Let's consider an example:
Suppose you own a covered call position on an ETF, ETFQ. Assume you hope to earn a time premium of approximately $200 each month when you write a call option. Assume there is still one week remaining before the current option expires (June) and these prices obtain:

ETFQ is $40.36.

ETF Jun 40 call can be purchased for $0.65.

ETF Jul 40 call can be sold for $3.00.

You have two choices:

1. Wait for expiration and hope the July call maintains a high premium.

2. Take advantage now by buying back the June call for $65 per contract and simultaneously writing the July call, collecting $300 per contract. The result is you receive $235 (before costs), when you would have been pleased to receive $200.

What can go wrong if you choose to wait for expiration instead of rolling?

• If the ETF drops in price before expiration, the Jul 40 call may be much lower than $2.00 when it is time to sell it.
• If the ETF makes a substantial increase in price before expiration, you may not be able to collect a time premium of $2.00 when you write the Jul 40 call.[1]

Thus, if you find the spread between the option you are short and the option you plan to sell is attractive, you can elect to collect that spread difference early, rather than waiting for expiration to arrive.

TOO BUSY?

Taking care of finances is a very important consideration for everyone. Unfortunately, people many don't recognize that fact until much later in life. The earlier you get started, the better your future financial condition is going to be.

If you like the ideas presented in this book—attempting to beat the market by collecting option premium on a portfolio of exchange traded funds—but are far too busy to devote the necessary time to this project, there is still a way for you to participate. Work with your financial planner or stockbroker. This must be someone you trust—someone who has integrity, the ability to understand this investment methodology, and who can devote the time necessary to making intelligent decisions for you. Work with that person to build a suitable portfolio of ETFs. But insist on these points. (After all, your advisor is merely that—an advisor. Make the final decisions yourself.)

- Buy ETFs only in round lots (increments of 100 shares).
- Buy *only* optionable ETFs (see the lists in Tables 13.1 and 13.2).
- Be certain your advisor understands:
  - Your desire to write covered call options on every ETF you own.
  - Your desire to write new calls immediately (early Monday morning after expiration).
  - Your desire to write new options EVERY month. There is to be no attempt to time the market.
  - Your preference to write options expiring in the front month (or two).
  - Your preference for choosing the strike price of the options to be sold—at the money (ATM), out of the money (OTM), or in the money (ITM).
  - To discuss it with you before rolling a position. You must be certain your advisor understands the process well and is not rolling merely to generate additional commissions. Be aware—when using a broker, commissions are going to be expensive.

If you prefer to do the work yourself, but feel it is too time consuming, there is a compromise choice. By choosing options that expire in three months or six months, there is much less work to do, as it is necessary to make investment decisions less often. Note, though, that it's still important to check your portfolio once in a while—perhaps every week or two—just to be certain no major adjustments are necessary.

INVESTMENT CLUBS

Investment clubs are composed of individual investors, often beginning investors who want to learn about the stock market. The goal is education. You can form a more sophisticated group composed of people who already understand the workings of the market. If you find like-minded investors who want to adopt covered call writing (lend colleagues a copy of this book, or better yet, buy them their own copy) and if you want company when getting started, forming an investment club is the perfect way to proceed.

Each member invests money each month. The group opens an account with a broker, meets (suggestion: meet over the weekend following options expiration) to select investment choices, and invests the money. Your club can write cash-secured uncovered puts or covered calls. Of course it's OK to buy individual stocks, but I hope the advantages associated with choosing to invest in exchange traded funds convinces your group to build a portfolio consisting of ETFs.

Remember the purpose of the investment club is to educate your members. But being profitable is also a goal. The methods described in this book take some of the risk out of investing and significantly increase your chances of beating the market.

If you do form such a club, I'd love to hear about it (mark@ mdwoptions.com).

CONCLUSION

Making the decision to write covered call options against a portfolio you already own leads you on a path of reduced volatility, as the value of your account fluctuates less. It's also one road to enhanced earnings, despite the fact that you will, on occasion, have to settle for reduced profits if and when one of your holdings explodes in value. However, this investment methodology enhances your stock market performance over the years, helping you achieve financial goals. Your portfolio outperforms the market averages under the majority of stock market conditions, comparing unfavorably only when the market surges.

Writing uncovered put options is an equivalent strategy that provides the same reduction in portfolio volatility and the same enhancement of returns as covered call writing. The risk profile is identical with that of covered call writing, if positions are cash backed.

Using options in the relatively conservative manner outlined in this volume along with adopting the teachings of modern portfolio theory (MPT) should enable you to outperform the market averages in the years ahead. If you recognize that it's extremely unlikely that you can beat the market averages by selecting your own stocks, and if you accept the conclusion of MPT that indexing provides the best opportunity for your investments to prosper, then the recommended investment strategy provides an excellent path to earning market-beating returns on a consistent basis. Thus:

- Index your investments using ETFs, the best low-cost, modern method of indexing.
- Adopt option-writing strategies to hedge your investments and enhance returns.

Welcome to the twenty-first century of investing. Operating your own hedge fund can be both fun and profitable.

Notes

Chapter 1

1. Morningstar, Inc. is a global investment research firm, providing information, data, and analysis of stocks, mutual funds, and exchange traded funds.

2. Sadly, recent disclosures show that some stockbrokers put their own interests ahead of those of the investor and recommend funds which provide the highest sales commission for the broker regardless of the fund's ability to earn profits for the investor.

3. From 1926 through 2000, investing in the Standard & Poor's 500 index returned an average of 11.0 percent annually.

4. The risk-free rate is generally defined as the interest rate available from U.S. Treasury securities for the time period under consideration. These Treasury securities are (currently) as risk-free as an investment can be. There is no guarantee this will always be true.

5. Harry M. Markowitz, "Portfolio Selection," *Journal of Finance* 7, no. 1 (March 1952): 77–91.

6. The original work is summarized and expanded in Markowitz, *Portfolio Selection.*

7. William F. Sharpe, *Portfolio Theory and Capital Markets* (New York: McGraw-Hill, 1970); William F. Sharpe, *Investments* (Englewood Cliffs, NJ: Prentice-Hall, 1978); Cootner, ed., *The Random Character of Stock Market Prices*; and Fama, "The Behavior of Stock Market Prices."

8. Andrew Rudd and Henry K. Clasing, Jr., *Modern Portfolio Theory: The Principals of Investment Management* (New York: Dow Jones-Irwin, 1982).

9. Merton Miller also shared the prize, but his contribution was in the field of corporate finance.

10. See, for example: Harry M. Markowitz., *Portfolio Selection: Efficient Diversification of Investment* (New York: John Wiley & Sons, 1959); Paul Cootner, ed., *Random Character of Stock Market Prices* (Cambridge, MA: MIT Press, 1964); or Eugene F. Fama, "The Behavior of Stock Market Prices," *Journal of Business* 20 (1965): 34–105.

11. The prudent man rule consists of guidelines ensuring that a fiduciary invests a client's money as other prudent investors, with similar investment goals, invest.

12. One such book is: Roger C. Gibson, *Asset Allocation: Balancing Financial Risk* (New York: McGraw-Hill, 2000). Another is: John J. Brown, Jr., Carl H. Reinhardt, and Alan B. Werba, *The Prudent Investor's Guide to Beating the Market* (Chicago: Irwin Professional Publishing, 1996).

13. *Restatement of the Law/Trusts/Prudent Investor Rule* (St. Paul, MN: American Law Institute Publishers, 1992): ix.

14. As of July 2003, over 53.3 million American households own mutual funds, according to the Investment Company Institute (ICI), www.ici.org/shareholders/us/index.html.

Chapter 2

1. Timing the market refers to attempting to buy before rallies and/or sell before declines.

2. From John C. Bogle, foreword in W. Scott Simon, *Index Mutual Funds: Profiting from an Investment Revolution* (Carnarillo, CA: Namborn Publishing, 1998).

3. Efficient market theory was introduced by Eugene F. Fama, "The Behavior of Stock Market Prices," *Journal of Business* 20 (1965): 34–105.

4. The expectation is that owning ETFs provides a performance that matches the market. Adopting an options strategy (covered call writing) makes it likely you will perform even better, based on statistical evidence of the past 16 years. Chapter 12 presents that evidence.

5. Data supporting this statement can be found in Baer and Gensler, *The Great Mutual Fund Trap*.

6. The performance of the S&P 500 has a greater than 99 percent correlation with the results of the entire market.

7. For example, the largest index fund of them all, the Vanguard S&P 500 Index Fund, grew by 37, 23, 33, 29, and 21 percent from 1995 through 1999 respectively.

8. For example, assume the fund managers must purchase 800 shares, but only 200 shares are offered at the asking price. The price they must pay to buy those additional 600 shares could be significantly higher than the current price because there may be few, if any, shares offered for sale at any given time. That means paying too much for the shares. The same situation could occur when selling shares. That is not efficient, and index fund managers must trade stocks efficiently to produce satisfactory performance.

9. For example, three stocks were added, and three removed, from the DJIA in April 2004.

10. Larry E. Swedroe, *The Successful Investor Today: 14 Simple Truths You Must Know When You Invest* (New York: St. Martin's Press, 2003).

11. For example, see: Baer and Gensler, *The Great Mutual Fund Trap*, or Burton G. Malkiel, *Random Walk Down Wall Street* (New York: W. W. Norton, 2000).

12. Source: Investment Company Institute, www.ici.org.

13. Ken Gregory and Steve Savage, "When Funds Behave Badly," *Kiplinger's Personal Finance* (November 2003): 53–4.

14. They are careful to tell investors that past performance is not an indicator of future performance. But the very fact that they promote past performance shows they want to convince investors that past performance is indeed such an indicator.

15. Brad Barber and Terrance Odean, "Too Many Cooks Spoil the Profits: The Performance of Investment Clubs," *Financial Analyst Journal* (January–February 2000): 17–25.

16. Brad M. Barber and Terrance Odean, "Trading Is Hazardous to Your Wealth: The Common Stock Investment Performance of Individual Investors," *Journal of Finance* 55, no. 2 (April 2000): 773–806.

17. Frank A. Armstrong, *The Informed Investor: A Hype-Free Guide to Constructing a Sound Financial Portfolio* (New York: Amacom, 2002): 78.

Chapter 3

1. Source: Hedge Fund Research.

2. Neil Weinberg and Bernard Condon, "The Sleaziest Show on Earth," *Forbes* (May 24, 2004): 110–118.

3. See www.better-investing.org.

4. http://www.bivio.com.

Chapter 4

1. The Templeton Emerging Markets Fund once traded with a 20 percent premium. The presence of a "hot" fund manager coupled with owning stocks in the "hot" emerging market arena convinced some investors that it was a good idea to pay $1.20 for stocks worth $1.00. Source: David Lerman, *Exchanged Traded Funds and e-Mini Stock Index Futures* (New York: John Wiley & Sons, 2001): 65.

2. Cited in Joseph Nocera, "The Age of Indexing," *Money Magazine* (April 1999): 103–112.

3. Jason Zweig, "The 75 Year History of Mutual Funds," *Money Magazine* (April 1999): 94–101.

Chapter 5

1. The rules stipulate that no one can buy or redeem shares after the market closes for business on a given day. When very bullish news appears after the close of trading, unscrupulous traders who can purchase shares of a fund after the market has closed and pay the closing price established earlier have a huge advantage, as the fund is very likely to trade higher the next day (because of that bullish news). The privileged buyer then sells the shares to lock in an undeserved profit. The other shareholders are left holding the bag for the expenses of the trade.

2. Mutual funds have admitted allowing privileged clients to use market timing to buy and redeem shares whenever they pleased. Public customers either were not allowed to redeem shares soon after purchase or were charged a stiff fee for doing so. Today, forced by public opinion, more and more funds are leveling the

playing field by imposing the same fee on everyone who makes an early redemption.

3. A one percent management fee (and most fees are higher) on $200 billion of managed assets provides income of $2 billion per year. That's real money.

4. These examples are taken from Ken Gregory and Steve Savage, "When Funds Behave Badly," *Kiplinger's Personal Finance* (December 2003): 53.

5. An eye-opening book that provides evidence supporting the statement that professional money managers fail to beat the market: Gregory Baer and Gary Gensler, *The Great Mutual Fund Trap* (New York: Broadway Books, 2002).

6. Baer and Gensler, ibid. p. 70.

7. John C Bogle, foreword, in W. Scott Simon, *Index Mutual Funds: Profiting from an Investment Revolution* (Carnarillo, CA: Namborn Publishing, 1998).

8. Prem C. Jaji and Joanna Shuang Wu, "Truth in Mutual Fund Advertising: Evidence on Future Performance and Fund Flows," *Journal of Finance* 15 (April 2000): 937.

9. Alfred Cowles III constructed the precursor to the S&P 500 index. He also discovered that the best market forecasting methods did no better than an equal number of random selections would have done.

10. Quote taken from: Peter Bernstein, *Capital Ideas* (New York: Free Press, 1992), pp. 35–6.

11. Jim Rogers *SFO Magazine*, "Back From the Global Highways, The Adventure Capitalist Speaks Out" 2 (October 2003): 22–31.

12. The institute evaluated fee trends using a comprehensive measure that represents the cost an investor incurs when buying and holding mutual fund shares.

Chapter 6

1. Some funds allow trading at specified times during the day, but that is the exception.

2. A front-end load is paid when you buy the shares. Some funds use a back-end load instead, where you pay the sales charge when redeeming your shares. Usually the longer you own the fund, the lower the back-end load.

3. Even though the fund may be losing value, whenever the fund managers sell a stock bought at a lower price, they earn a taxable profit. That profit represents a capital gain and is distributed to the shareholders.

4. It's possible to buy 100 shares of an ETF and pay a commission as low as $1. Other discount brokers charge only $5 to $8 to purchase any number of shares between 100 and 5,000. Full-service brokers charge much higher commissions.

5. Comparing fees for traditional mutual funds and ETFs, "The average index fund is at least 100 basis points (1% per year) cheaper, and the average exchange traded fund (ETF) is cheaper still." David Lerman, *Exchange Traded Funds and e-Mini Stock Index Futures* (New York: John Wiley & Sons, 2001): 8.

6. OPALS (optimized portfolios as listed securities) trade on the Luxembourg Exchange and are available for many indexes and single country indexes. American investors are *not* allowed to trade OPALS.

7. Morgan Stanley Capital International (MSCI) developed the EAFE as an equity benchmark for international stock performance. The index includes stocks from Europe, Australasia, and the Far East. The S&P 100 Global index consists of large-capitalization transnational companies from around the world. American companies are well represented in this index. General Electric and Exxon Mobil are currently the two largest holdings.

8. The price-to-book ratio is the stock price divided by the book value per share. Half of the stocks (with the highest ratio) are considered to be in the growth category and half are considered to be value companies.

9. The market capitalization of each stock in the index is calculated by multiplying the total number of shares outstanding (for each stock) by its market price. The individual market caps are totaled. The percentage of that total for each stock represents the percentage of shares of each stock in the index.

10. New ETFs are constantly being listed. See www.amex.com for a current listing.

11. For the most up-to-date listing of iShares, visit www.ishares.com.

12. The first HOLDR was TBH, a compilation of 12 "baby bras." These 12 companies were the result of the breakup of the Brazilian telecommunications company Telebras. Merrill Lynch decided to "reassemble" Telebras into one trading vehicle. It was a big success. Merrill followed by introducing other HOLDRs in September 1999.

Chapter 7

1. For beginners, I recommend my recent book: Mark D. Wolfinger, *The Short Book on Options: A Conservative Strategy for the Buy and Hold Investor* (Bloomington, IN: 1stBooks Library, 2002). A more thorough text is: Lawrence G. McMillan, *Options as a Strategic Investment*, 4th ed. (Englewood Cliffs, NJ: Prentice-Hall, 2001). I encourage you to spend some time in your local library or bookstore for other appropriate titles.

2. Selling short means selling a security that is not owned. The shares are borrowed from the broker and delivered to the buyer. The seller is obliged to repurchase those shares at some (unspecified) time in the future.

3. The description of every option includes the month of expiration. Example: IBM Apr 95 Call. This option represents the right to buy 100 shares of IBM at the strike price of $95 per share any time before the option expires in April. Chapter 8 presents a more detailed explanation of the description of an option.

Chapter 8

1. The U.S. options exchanges are the Chicago Board Options Exchange, American Stock Exchange, Philadelphia Stock Exchange, Pacific Coast Stock Exchange, International Securities Exchange, and Boston Options Exchange.

2. The current list includes: Advanced Micro Devices (AMD), AMR Corporation (AMR), Applied Materials (AMAT), AT&T Wireless Services (AWE), Brocade Communications Systems (BRCD), First Data Corporation (FDC), Calpine Corporation (CPN), EMC Corporation (EMC), El Paso Corporation (EP), E*Trade Financial Corporation (ET), Juniper Networks (JNPR), Liberty Media Corpora-

tion (L), Lucent Technologies (LU), Motorola (MOT), Micron Technology (MU), Nortel Networks Holding Corporation (NT), Oracle Corporation (ORCL), Sun Microsystems (SUNW), Tenet Healthcare Corporation (THC), Time Warner (TWX), Tyco International (TYC), JDS Uniphase Corporation (JDSU), and Xerox (XRX).

3. For example, a trader with a short position in the underlying stock might exercise a call option that is exactly at the money in order to buy stock at the strike, thereby eliminating the short position. Similarly, a trader who owns a stock position might exercise an at-the-money put to eliminate the long position.

4. If exchange members or public customers request that the short-term option be listed, the exchanges usually comply, even if there are fewer than 30 days before expiration.

5. If the stock moves as hoped, the option owner often decides to sell and collect a profit. If it does not move as hoped or if it does not move at all, the option loses value. When the stock does not move as anticipated, the option owner can cut losses by selling the option to recover part of the purchase price. Knowing when to cut losses is a trading skill that traders who are new to options lack. Many option buyers continue to hold the option, hoping the stock finally will make a move in the right direction. Thus, too many newcomers to options hold their positions until options expire worthless.

Chapter 9

1. If the option is in the money, the entire investment is not lost—only the time value of the option is lost. Don't be concerned with this detail at this point in your options education.

2. Selling the option before expiration could have salvaged part of the investment. However, it is not an easy decision to sell a call option (especially at a loss) as the stock is rallying.

3. A short position occurs when investors sell stock (or other assets) they *do not own* in anticipation of buying that asset at a later date and at a lower price. Selling stock short can be transacted only in a margin account, and prior approval by the broker is required.

4. In theory, the price of a stock can rise forever. The naked call writer may eventually be forced to repurchase the call option or buy stock. The higher the repurchase price, the greater the loss.

5. The stock price can only fall to zero. Thus, the maximum loss per share is the strike price minus the option premium. When selling naked calls, there is no limit to the loss.

Chapter 10

1. Commissions are *very* important when trading options. If you are able to make your own investment decisions, seriously consider trading online using a deep-discount broker. However, using a full-service broker may be appropriate for some investors as low commissions are not the only consideration.

2. Unless you are assigned an exercise notice before the stock goes ex-dividend. Remember, the option owner has the right to exercise the option *any time* before it expires.

3. Some online brokers make this information available on Sunday. All brokers *must* provide this information before the market opens on Monday. Don't take any chances. Don't make any assumptions. If you cannot find out online whether you have been assigned an exercise notice, call your broker and ask.

4. The OCC is a clearinghouse for information about who owns, and who has sold, every outstanding option contract. The OCC verifies that the exerciser owns the option and has the right to exercise it. Next it selects, at random, one of the accounts that currently has a short position in the identical option. That account owner is assigned an exercise notice, and must fulfill the conditions of the contract.

5. In-the-money options are more expensive than other options, and the extra cash reduces the break-even point, thereby increasing the amount the stock can drop before a loss in incurred.

6. Profit is $400 ($0.80 per share; 500 shares). Investment is $14,600 ($32.50 minus $3.30 for each of the 500 shares). Return = 2.74 percent. In this discussion, annualized returns are not compounded. Thus, the annualized return is 12 times the monthly return.

7. As discussed earlier, the time premium in the price of the option represents the most you can earn when selling that option. Options close to the strike price have the highest time premium.

8. Stock price, strike price, option type (put or call), volatility of underlying stock, interest rates, and size of dividend all are factors in determining the price of an option. The most important factor of all is supply and demand. When there is a preponderance of option buyers, prices rise. When sellers outnumber buyers, option prices decline.

9. Your broker should provide this data, but 20-minute delayed option quotes are readily available. One site offering the data is the CBOE: http://www.cboe.com/delayedQuote/QuoteTable.aspx.

10. If you are extremely bearish, it's not advisable to be fully invested in bullish positions. (Covered call writing is a bullish strategy.) Covered call writing significantly reduces losses during down markets, but if you are able to predict a bear market, you'd be best advised to own few, if any, bullish positions when the market is declining. Those of us who are unable to predict market direction should remain fully invested.

11. Traders with a short time horizon must first buy stock and write a call. To close the position, they must then buy the option and sell the stock. Thus, they make four trades, incurring trading expenses. On top of that, often they must buy at the offer price and sell at the bid price, again increasing expenses. These added trading costs often make this strategy unprofitable for the short-term trader. The trader who holds a position for a short period does not hold long enough to benefit from the passage of time, as does the investor.

Chapter 11

1. As with covered call writing, you can expect to earn a better return than that provided by the market averages, except when the market surges. Even then you do well, but usually less well.

2. Reminder: The volatility of a stock is one of the factors used to determine the price of an option. The options of more volatile stocks are more attractive to own than options of non-volatile stocks, and buyers willingly pay higher prices to obtain them.

3. It's possible to lose money if the stock keeps declining in price while you own it. But this loss is less than any other stockholder incurs, since that stockholder does not collect premium by writing covered call options.

4. A margin call is a demand for cash or marketable securities to be deposited into your account. If you fail to meet a margin call, your broker will liquidate some positions (you have nothing to say about which positions) to raise cash to meet the obligation. For most investors this is a very bad situation and can be very costly. Avoid margin calls.

Chapter 12

1. Options on the SPX differ from options on individual stocks because they expire at the opening of the market on the third Friday of the month rather than at the close.

2. For the most recent data, visit the CBOE site: www.cboe.com/micro/bxm/index.asp.

3. It is not in every investor's best interest to adopt this slightly bullish strategy of writing out-of-the-money calls. For some investors, the safety that comes with a reduced potential profit potential coupled with additional downside protection is more important. As discussed in Chapter 10 those investors would do better to write at-the-money or slightly in-the-money call options.

4. See www.croftgroup.com. The data are available at the site of the Montreal Stock Exchange: www.me.org/produits_en/produits_indices_mcwx_en.php.

5. Richard Croft's Option Commentary, September 2003. The variance in returns is reduced by 25 percent. Option Commentary is available through E*Trade Canada.

6. See www.cboe.com/LearnCenter/pdf/bxmqrg.pdf.

7. When only eight days remain until expiration, the soon-to-expire options are no longer used and the VIX value is calculated using data from the second and third months.

8. See www.cboe.com/micro/vix/vixwhite.pdf.

Chapter 13

1. If you buy 435 shares, for example, you will be able to write only four call options, leaving 35 shares unhedged.

2. The worth of the company's common stock as it appears on a balance sheet. It's equal to total assets less all liabilities, including preferred stock and goodwill. If the company were to go out of business today, the book value represents the value of anything remaining.

Chapter 14

1. Because several holidays are celebrated on Monday, if the exchange is closed, Tuesday morning is the appropriate time to initiate new covered call positions.

It's OK to wait a few days, but if you are following the precepts of MPT, you always want to be fully invested.

Chapter 15

1. The fee is charged every time you receive an assignment notice. Thus, if you are assigned on 10 MDY calls, the commission is $20. If you are assigned on 3 MDY and 5 VTI, the commission is $40.

2. Reminder: Time value for an option increases as the stock price gets nearer the strike price.

3. The amount of downside protection (in this specific example) equals the maximum percentage return.

4. If you're the type of investor who doesn't watch the market closely, but pays attention only when a statement from your broker or mutual fund manager arrives in the mail, checking in once per month (expiration Friday and the following Monday) may work for you here—but try to watch more frequently.

5. I received an assignment notice and sold my EFA shares at $134. I also paid an assignment fee (commission) of $20.

6. Calls increase in value as the price of the underlying increases and decrease in value as the underlying declines.

7. If the market heads higher and I can write the (currently) OTM option when it becomes at the money, I'll get a higher selling price and make additional profits. On the other hand, if the ETF declines in price, I'll be forced to sell the option that is currently in the money when it becomes at the money. If that happens, I'll be forced to accept a lower price when selling compared with the price I can get now. I'm not going to take that chance because I don't believe in attempting to time the market.

8. It may be trivial to mention, but each quarter of the year is 13 weeks long. Thus, two of every three expirations are four weeks long, and the other is five weeks.

9. If the broker is unable to execute *both* the buy and sell at prices that allow my conditions (credit of $2.75 or better) to be satisfied, then the order will not be filled and I will continue to own my current position.

10. Limit orders are not always filled because you cannot receive a price worse than you stipulate. Entering a market order guarantees the order is filled at the "best available prices," but you run the risk of getting very poor prices.

11. Remember, the more time remaining until expiration, the more an option is worth and the more you receive when selling.

12. Why don't call prices get crushed when the market heads lower? Call prices do decline, but not nearly as rapidly as one would expect. Arbitrageurs buy calls, sell puts, and sell stock short, creating a position with almost zero risk. When put prices increase, they are willing to pay higher prices for calls. This call buying decreases the rate at which call prices decline. If put prices go high enough, then call prices can rise as stocks fall. This occurred to an incredible degree when the market crashed in October 1987.

13. Implied volatility is an estimate of how volatile stocks will be from the current moment until options expire. Higher implied volatility produces higher option prices.

14. At expiration, all options have zero remaining time premium. They are worth the intrinsic value only.

15. See, for example, www.mdwoptions.com/OptionCalculator.html or www.cboe.com/TradTool/OptionCalculator.aspx.

16. Many options traders went out of business overnight in 1987 because they were short too many options and were unable to cover at reasonable prices. There was a great shortage of options for sale. But there was no shortage of option buyers. This imbalance, coupled with fear of the future, raised option prices to unbelievable levels.

17. Rolling options one point in either direction does not pay because commissions represent a significant portion of the potential benefit, and there is too little cash available from rolling.

18. Traders are whipsawed when they take a position, then quickly have to reverse that position, locking in a loss. Often the market moves in the original direction again, and the second trade must be reversed, locking in another loss.

Chapter 16

1. Legging refers to the process of making a trade for one portion (a leg) of a hedged position (e.g., buy 200 ETF shares) and then entering an order (e.g., write two calls) for the second part of the position. When legging, there is always the risk that the price of the leg you already traded will make a move against you before the trade for the second leg of the position can be executed.

2. But the risk is *reduced* because you received cash for writing a put option.

3. The same risk as any shareholder. I repeat this statement for emphasis, as many believe writing uncovered puts is very risky. In fact, it is not any riskier than owning stocks.

4. Your broker requires an initial margin deposit to open an uncovered put position. Margin requirements vary over time, but currently the amount is approximately 20 percent of the strike price (with some other factors involved), with a minimum of $250 per option.

5. This increases risk by an almost insignificant amount. *Note:* you must be 100 percent cash backed in a retirement account.

6. Carrying this position requires the payment of cash. A position with a net credit occurs when cash is collected.

7. Anyone who buys this option must hold it and hope for a profit the following week. This is risky. Thus, the only potential buyers of this option are those who have a short position and are willing to pay the minimum bid of $0.05 ($5 per contract) to buy-in their short option and eliminate all risk.

8. Some brokers provide this information to their online customers on Sunday.

9. A straddle is one call and one put on the same underlying equity with the same expiration date and strike price. The investor is long the straddle when both the put and call are bought; and the investor is short the straddle when both are sold. This straddle is "covered" when the investor has a long stock position to cover the short calls.

10. Unless I choose to use a margin account and borrow money from my broker. For simplicity, I assume I'm *not* borrowing any such money. Retirement accounts are not allowed to borrow, and by adhering to that rule, every recommendation in this book is appropriate for investors to apply to their retirement accounts. Warning: Some brokers do not allow uncovered put writing in retirement accounts, even though it is perfectly acceptable to the Securities and Exchange Commission.

Chapter 17

1. The time premium in an option shrinks as the underlying moves away from the strike price. If ETFQ rises to 43, it's reasonable for the Jul 40 call to be trading near $4.40. That $4.40 is $3.00 in intrinsic value, but only $1.40 in time value, or much less than the $2.35 in time premium that's available to you today. Rolling early (in the example situation) allows you to take the $2.35 and not gamble on future option prices.

Glossary

Assigned (an exercise notice) Notification that the option owner has exercised rights, making the recipient obligated to fulfill the terms of the option contract.

Assignment The process by which option writers fulfill their obligation. The call writer sells, or the put writer buys, the underlying at the strike price.

At the money (ATM) An option whose strike price is identical (or nearly identical) to the price of the underlying asset.

Break-even point The stock price at which the profit earned from a position using options equals the profit earned from a stock position without options (upside break-even) OR, the stock price at which a position using options is no longer profitable (downside break-even).

Buy-write transaction The simultaneous purchase of 100 shares stock and the selling of one call option.

Call A type of option that grants its owner the right to buy (before expiration) a specified asset at the strike price.

Cash backed The situation in which your brokerage account contains enough cash to completely pay the cost of stock, if you are assigned an exercise notice on put options you sold.

Cash settled An expiration process in which cash, not shares of the underlying, is transferred from the option writer's account to the account of the option owner.

Covered A position in which a put or call option is backed by the shares underlying the option contract.

Credit Cash received when making a trade.

Debit Cash paid when making a trade.

Deep in the money A term applied to an option that is so far in the money (ITM) that it's unlikely to move out of the money before it expires.

Downside break-even point The stock price below which the covered call writer begins to lose money.

Exercise The process by which the option owner chooses to do what the contract allows: The call owner buys, or the put owner sells, the underlying asset at the strike price.

Exercise notice Formal notification to the option seller that the option owner has chosen to buy (call) or sell (put) the underlying at the strike price. The option seller is now obligated to honor the conditions of the contract.

Expiration   The last day an option is a valid contract.

Expiration day   For listed stock options, the third Friday of the specified month.

Expire worthless   What happens to an option when expiration arrives and the option is out of the money and the owner elects *not* to exercise.

Far out of the money   A term applied to an option that is so far out of the money (OTM) that it's unlikely to move in the money before it expires.

Front month   The month with the nearest expiration date.

Fungible   An item that is completely interchangeable with another in satisfying an obligation. Any call or put option with the same underlying, expiration, and strike price is fungible.

Hedge   An investment that reduces the risk of another investment by partially offsetting the risk of owning the original investment.

Implied volatility   An estimate of the volatility of the underlying asset between now and the expiration of an option. It's the volatility estimate used in option pricing models to make the actual market price of an option equal its theoretical value.

In the money (ITM)   An option with intrinsic value.

Intrinsic value   The amount by which the price of the underlying asset is above the strike price of a call option (or below the strike price of a put option).

LEAPS   Acronym for *l*ong *t*erm *e*quity *a*nticipation *s*eries. Call or put options with longer expirations (nine months to three years), expiring in January.

Leverage   Using borrowed money (buying on margin), or using derivatives such as options, to enhance returns without increasing the size of an investment. Leveraged investing is risky because you can lose more than your entire investment.

Naked   *See* uncovered.

Obligations   The requirements imposed on the seller of an option contract if an option owner exercises rights.

Option   A contract that gives its owner the right, but not the obligation, to buy (call) or sell (put) the specified asset at a specified price (strike price) for a specified time.

Out of the money (OTM)   An option with no intrinsic value. For a call option, the strike price is higher than the price of the underlying; for a put option, the strike price is lower than the price of the underlying asset.

Premium   The price of an option.

Put   A type of option that grants its owner the right to sell (before expiration) a specified asset at the strike price.

Rights   Privileges granted to the owner of an option contract.

Rolling (a position)   The process of buying an option sold earlier and selling an option with a more distant expiration date

Sell short   The sale of an asset (stock or option) not owned. There is an obligation to repurchase in the future. *Note:* If the option eventually expires worthless, the obligation to repurchase is nullified.

Strike price   The price at which the asset underlying an option can be bought (call) or sold (put).

Spread   The simultaneous sale or purchase of two or more option contracts. A spread usually establishes a hedged position.

Strike price   The price at which an option owner has the right to either buy (call) or sell (put) the underlying.

Standardization of options   Establishing consistent and predictable expiration dates and strike prices for options. Options became standardized when the Chicago Board Options Exchange (CBOE) first listed options for trading (April 1973).

Straddle   One call and one put with the same underlying, strike price, and expiration date.

Theoretical value   The worth of an option as calculated with an option-pricing model.

Time value   The portion of the option premium above the intrinsic value.

Wasting asset   An item with a limited lifetime that decreases in value as time passes.

Upside break-even point   The price above which the covered call writer does not earn any additional profit.

Uncovered   A short option position that is *not* backed by shares of the underlying. Also called a *naked* position.

Underlying   The security that an option contract gives its owner—the right to buy or sell. It's the asset from which an option derives its value.

Volatility   The relative rate at which the price of a security undergoes daily changes.

Write   Sell (an option).

Index

Printed and bound by CPI Group (UK) Ltd, Croydon, CR0 4YY

16/04/2025

14658454-0003